THE PRISON DIARY OF A.C. BARRINGTON

The Prison Diary of A.C. Barrington

DISSENT AND CONFORMITY IN
WARTIME NEW ZEALAND

JOHN PRATT

With an introduction by John Barrington

OTAGO
UNIVERSITY PRESS

Published by Otago University Press
Level 1, 398 Cumberland Street
Dunedin, New Zealand
university.press@otago.ac.nz
www.otago.ac.nz/press

First published 2016

Published with the assistance of Creative New Zealand

ISBN 978-1-927322-31-4

Editor: Imogen Coxhead
Design and layout: Fiona Moffat
Index: Diane Lowther

Printed in New Zealand by Printing.com, Wellington

Contents

Acknowledgements

Writing this book would not have been possible without the following vital contributions: Archie Barrington himself, able to rise above the bleak surroundings of Mount Crawford and keep such a meticulously detailed diary of all going on around him in the prison; Mr Flipp, the prison butcher and friend of the Barrington family who smuggled the various volumes out of the prison; John Barrington who, many years later, found the diary and painstakingly reconstructed it; his sister Janet Jackson who helped to type up the manuscript; David Grant for his pioneering work on pacifism in New Zealand; Swati Bhim, Lara Teesdale and Anne Holland who all worked as research assistants for me while the book manuscript was being developed; the manuscript librarians at the Alexander Turnbull Library, Wellington, and also staff at the Nelson Provincial Museum; Emeritus Professor David Brown, University of New South Wales, Professor Mark Finnane, Griffith University, and readers for Otago University Press who provided such insightful, helpful comments on an earlier draft of the manuscript; and Rachel Scott and Imogen Coxhead at Otago University Press for their encouragement and guidance.

Introduction

JOHN BARRINGTON

In May 1941 A.C. Barrington (known to friends and family as Archie or Barry) sat in his solitary cell at Wellington's Mount Crawford Prison and began to write an illicit diary of about 800 words a day. I was his son, aged five and in my first year at Lyall Bay School, and for the next eight months my mother, brother, sister and I regularly visited him there. His diary records, 'Today brought first letter to "Dad" from John Michael with some assistance from mother.' He notes that my mother tells him that my sister, who had just turned two, misses him most because the boys are able to understand: 'she asks for me, and even pushed a letter under my den door the other morning' (24 May 1941).

Why was he there? A leading Methodist layman with strong Christian pacifist beliefs, he had been convicted of 'publishing a subversive statement' (a cyclostyled advertisement for a meeting entitled *Defend Peace and Freedom at Home*) and 'attempting to hold a meeting prohibited by the Superintendent of Police'.[1] He was sentenced to 12 months hard labour under the Public Safety Emergency Regulations 1940. National Party leader Adam Hamilton had expressed concern about the extent of the powers given under the regulations, suggesting in parliament that 'in times of grim defence of our cherished heritage of liberty, freedom and justice we interfere with the things we hold most dear'. He warned that the government, as the people's representative, must protect their rights for the duration of the conflict. But as Grant points out, 'he was a lone voice in Parliament'.[2]

Summarising the prosecution's case against my father, Detective Browne told the court that 'apart from his activities in connection with the Christian Pacifist Society', of which he was New Zealand secretary, Barrington was a 'desirable citizen'.[3] Reporting on 'Cause of Criminality' to the Prisons and Parole Board, Browne wrote that Barrington 'believes he is bound to preach pacifism even though it conflicts with law of the state'.[4] Somewhat ironically, his imprisonment occurred under a government whose prime minister, Peter Fraser, and several senior ministers, including Bob Semple,

Tim Armstrong, Jim O'Brien and Paddy Webb, had themselves been imprisoned for opposing conscription during World War I.[5] His loyal wife, my mother Janet (also referred to in the diary as 'Jan' or 'Jane') commented in her own diary that when defending his case in the Supreme Court he had 'made statements that will surely live in the history of pacifism – and must have impressed all who heard them' (J. Barrington, 6 May 1941).

Finding the diary

Going through my father's papers at Wellington's Alexander Turnbull Library, I came across a book titled *Pennsylvania 1681–1756: The state without an army.*[6] I could easily have ignored it, but knowing this title would have interested him I opened it and was amazed to find the diary written around its margins.

Then I found another book, *Jesus of Galilee,*[7] which continued the diary. It began on 12 May 1941 and the last entry was dated 13 August 1941, although he was not released from Mount Crawford until 24 December 1941. While it seems unlikely that he would have discontinued a diary, despite considerable efforts I was unable to locate another covering the latter period and can only speculate on the reasons for this.

My sister recalled our father showing the diary to her and explaining how he had smuggled it out of the prison with Frank Flipp,[8] the family butcher in Kilbirnie who also supplied the prison with meat, who then passed it on to our mother. As a life-long lover of books, my father had accumulated a large collection. Following my father's death, a librarian from New Zealand's National Library visited our family home to decide which of his books and papers should be kept in the Alexander Turnbull Library. By great good fortune, the two books containing the diary were among the small number of volumes she selected.

It seemed miraculous that the diary had survived and been found, quite by accident. I sensed it was a fascinating document, not only for family history but also because of the rare insight it gave into life in prison at that time. Given the circumstances of its composition my father's writing seemed fresh and vivid, enhanced by his intelligence and observational powers.

Nowhere does he explain why he kept a diary. He was a persistent keeper of other records of his life so perhaps it was just an extension of that habit. Or perhaps he thought that a diary might become significant in the context of the cause for which he was imprisoned, or that it provided a unique opportunity for an 'insider' account of prison life. It is only possible to speculate.

In considering publication, one possibility was to publish the diary as a whole with annotations, allowing my father 'to speak for himself'. A problem with that, however, was the unavoidably repetitious nature of the entries, revolving as they do around food, work, warders, fellow prisoners and so on. Another possibility was to place the diary within the history of the conscientious objectors (COs) in World War II – but that had already been well covered by David Grant.[9] A third possibility, as I did not wish to undertake the work entirely myself, was to approach John Pratt, Professor of Criminology at Victoria University, to see if he might be interested in working with me. He responded that the diary 'sounded like a real treasure trove'.

Although there are many prison memoirs and biographies – particularly British ones from 1860 to 1960 – there is very little New Zealand material of this kind; Greg Newbold's autobiography *The Big Huey*[10] is the best known. My father's work appeared special because it was in the form of a daily diary, whereas most memoirs, whether from New Zealand or elsewhere, have been reconstructed after release, from memory, notes, letters and the like. Pratt and I agreed to collaborate. With the assistance of my sister Janet, I would type up the diary and write an introductory chapter. He would then analyse the diary within a penological context.

The historical background

Anti-war sentiment remained strong among some New Zealanders following the bloodshed of World War I. The Methodist Church declared at its 1935 conference that war was contrary to Christ's teaching and a crime against humanity.[11] In 1936 my father and the Rev Ormond Burton, both Methodists, formed the New Zealand Christian Pacifist Society (CPS), aimed at uniting all Christians in work for peace. Among several hundred who signed the CPS covenant were 40 Methodist ministers and home missionaries. My father remained national secretary or president of the CPS for the next 25 years.

Born in 1906, like many of his generation he finished schooling at the age of 12. Bright and energetic, he then entered full-time employment as a junior clerk with a Marton law firm, transferring after nine years to an amalgamation of the same firm in Wellington. Passing professional examinations, as well as subjects for an accountancy degree at the University of New Zealand, he became the firm's accountant, secretary to several private and public companies and, in 1932, was made a Fellow of the Chartered Institute of Secretaries (UK). In 1935 he married Janet Elizabeth Galpin from a Rangitikei farming family. From 1932–36 he was national secretary and in 1937 treasurer of the Methodist Young Men's Bible Class Movement, which had a membership of approximately 3000. He also held executive positions on hockey and tennis clubs.[12] In October 1937 in her own diary, my mother recorded him 'talking of war and how it must affect us – which is sad when it makes me think of the children being without him' (J. Barrington 1941). By now he had come to feel that working 'at the heart of the legal, commercial, financial' world in a law firm conflicted with his personal beliefs, and sought more compatible employment. He applied, unsuccessfully, for the position of assistant secretary of the Wellington Education Board. But in 1936, giving notice to his employer of 18 years, he took a part-time position as secretary of the Wellington Workers' Education Association (WEA). After about a year this was expanded into a full-time position as the WEA's national secretary, with the addition of a Victoria University appointment as librarian.

Ormond Burton had won a reputation for bravery in World War I, initially as a medical orderly and then as an active soldier. Wounded three times, he was awarded both the Military Medal and the *Medaille d'honneur*, one of France's highest military awards. At war's end he was asked by Major General Sir Andrew Russell to write a brief account of the New Zealand Division, a copy of which was given to every serviceman. Burton was then asked to write the history of the Auckland Infantry Regiment, based largely on interviews with soldiers he had fought alongside. In 1935 he wrote the last of his war books, *The Silent Division*, a vividly realistic account of the life of the ordinary soldier. But by this time, having fought the war to defeat Prussian militarism, he had become 'horrified and disillusioned with the terms of the Treaty of Versailles' and 'became a resolute convert to Christian pacifism'.[13] After training as a Methodist minister Burton was appointed to Webb Street Methodist Church, located in one of Wellington's most deprived areas.

The CPS's first public activity was a protest meeting at a military display held at Rongotai Airport (Wellington) in June 1938, during King's Birthday weekend. Burton spoke and anti-war leaflets were handed out. At a military parade through the city on the following Monday, my father and several others carrying sandwich boards with pacifist slogans marched alongside soldiers. These poster-parades subsequently became regular events, as did open-air meetings.

My father's activities included making written representations to the Minister of Immigration, Walter Nash, in an effort to persuade the government to permit a number of Czechoslovakian Jewish families to enter New Zealand.[14] But despite offering a full guarantee against any claims on the government, he was 'fobbed off' with the suggestion that New Zealand might suffer if the number of inassimilable immigrants was increased. I was ashamed of my country.'[15]

Keen to broaden his experience in adult education, in 1939 he applied (unsuccessfully) for the travelling fellowship offered by the Imperial Relations Trust (UK). In a supporting testimonial, A.E. Campbell, who had come to know him through his involvement with the WEA and was now director of the New Zealand Council for Educational Research (later New Zealand's director-general of education), wrote:

Mr Barrington is a conscientious and efficient secretary and accountant, and a good organiser who gets on well with all kinds of people. He is also a man of wide intellectual interests, whose knowledge of contemporary affairs is much broader and deeper than that of many university graduates. He is a practised and effective public speaker and has considerable ability as a writer. Mr Barrington's most striking qualities, however, are moral courage and a determination to devote himself to work of genuine social value. It is typical of him that he threw up a well-paid position in the commercial world, with excellent prospects of advancement, for his present work, which is very modestly remunerated and not conspicuously secure. There is no other worker in the field of adult education of whom it is truer to say that he is in it because he believes in it, and for no other reason.

Mr Barrington therefore appears to me to be very well qualified for the fellowship for which he is applying. He is already playing an important part in adult education in New Zealand, and can be counted upon to make the most of any opportunities he has for overseas study.[16]

After war was declared, my father, Burton and others went to Parliament Buildings and started a meeting. Burton and another man were taken away by police and held in Mount Crawford Prison but then released, subject to being called up for sentence within six months. They had been returned to the Wellington Central Police Station after a call from Prime Minister Peter Fraser, who had known Burton from earlier days in the Labour movement. Fraser took the extraordinary step of visiting the station where, Burton said, he 'pleaded with me to go on with my "good work" and allow him to go on peacefully with the war. I told him I was unable to give him any promises.'[17] Two days later Burton was back speaking at the CPS's regular Allen Street meeting. Arrested for 'obstructing a constable', he described being taken to Wellington Police Station:

> We were searched and charged. The room was crowded with police who had just come in from the meeting. A young man at the charge desk who was taking particulars was something of a smart alec and also a bully and certainly, I should imagine no churchman. 'Any marks on your body?' I'm afraid this stirred what HJD Mahon used to call my perverted sense of humour. 'Gunshot wound left chest.' The buzz of conversation behind me seemed to moderate. 'Bayonet wound left knee.' The office was quiet now. 'Shrapnel wounds right leg.' A very considerable stillness. 'Gunshot wound left arm.' Absolute stillness and not much more coming from the bright young man.[18]

It had been agreed that my father would not speak at the Parliament Buildings meeting but would go home and write a report to CPS members. This was the start of the *Bulletin*, the cyclostyled newsletter that became the object of confiscation in the post, searches of the homes and offices of my father and others and, later, Supreme Court trials.

Burton's fine for 'obstructing a constable' led Wellington City Council to ban public meetings in streets, public places and reserves and to withdraw permission for the CPS to carry sandwich boards advertising pacifist beliefs when marching against the war. But these measures had little effect: meetings in Allen Street continued and a second one was started in Swan Lane. Even the poster ban was ignored, with 20 delegates to the CPS national conference parading through the city. In one attempt to drown out the pacifist speakers, the army positioned a recruiting van and uniformed speakers with loud hailers at the entrance to Swan Lane. It is probable, ironically, that my father's brother Ben organised this. An inspector with the National Insurance Company before the war, he maintained his connection with the Territorials and rose to the rank of major. In 1939 he was appointed army recruiting officer for Wellington and Taranaki, and at the outbreak of war he was posted to army headquarters as staff officer to the director of mobilisation. He subsequently had a distinguished military career, rising to the rank of brigadier.[19]

As a result of concerns about crowds blocking Cuba Street, the pacifists moved their meetings to a large grassy reserve between Manners and Dixon streets (Pigeon Park). In her autobiography *Bread and Roses*, the Labour MP Sonja Davies described going to the park at the age of 17 to hear my father and Burton speak against war and for peace:

> *Standing in the chill Friday evening air, a knot of supporters around them and an angry crowd of anti-pacifists at the edges trying to shout the speakers down, I was impressed by the courage of these two men. Their convictions were so strong that in the midst of patriotic fervour they felt they had to speak out. It was the most significant meeting of my early adolescence. I was aware that I was going to have to think very hard and make some choices. I went home full of what I had heard. Mother was doubtful, Dad genuinely angry. As far as he was concerned, all pacifists should be lined up against a wall and shot. Would he come to a meeting and listen and judge for himself? Certainly not, he would not be seen dead in the vicinity.* [20]

Prior to a Wellington meeting on 9 February 1941, Wellington's mayor, T.C.A. (Tommy) Hislop described all war dissenters as 'shirkers' and declared he would do everything in his power to prevent them having a meeting, informing the press that 'if they want a fight they can have it'. A tightly packed crowd estimated at close to 6000, no doubt stirred by the advance publicity it had received, attended Pigeon Park.[21] Burton later wrote of the occasion, 'I barely managed to say "Ladies and Gentlemen" when the blue wave broke over me. I went down with a mass of them on top of me. It has quite the same homely feeling that a half-back has when he goes down under the feet of half a dozen big forwards.'[22] For what was surely one of the shortest speeches on record, Burton was sentenced to one month's hard labour at Mount Crawford; because of an oversight on the charge sheet, my father, who had also been charged, was released.

Burton was working in the prison garden with a view of Wellington Harbour when ships carrying the 2nd Echelon left for the war. The former soldier wrote:

The great ships passed immediately below the prison garden. Some twenty-five years before I had been with the cheering transports that swung out from Mudros to the beaches of Gallipoli where the gallant companies were torn to bloody shreds by the bursting shrapnel and the hail of machine-gun fire. In my mind's eye I could see the battles that were to come and how the strong and exultant young men who crowded these decks would be broken under the barrages. I found it very moving, as one always must when one senses the willingness of men to suffer and die for a cause that seems to them so right. So, standing in the garden in my prison dress of field grey, I gave the general salute with my long-handled shovel – very reverently.[23]

In February 1941 my father toured the North Island holding open-air meetings. He was arrested at Whanganui, Auckland and Gisborne, was 'marched out' of Stratford, Te Kuiti and Tauranga by World War I returned soldiers, and had his 'soap-box' kicked to pieces by an angry policeman at Hawera. In Auckland following newspaper reports of incidents along the way, including arrests, posters advertising the weekly newspaper *Truth* screamed: 'We'll throw you in the river!' He described receiving a telegram from my mother who, at home with three small children, undoubtedly felt apprehensive. The telegram read, 'Stout fella. Carry on. Love Jan.'[24]

His refusal to pay one of the fines for this activity led to his first prison term. This was for six days and he described it as 'quite an experience'. He was released early, however, when Dr F.W. Dry of Massey University College, a Quaker, paid the balance of the fine.[25] My father later described a playmate of mine who lived next door saying, 'My daddy's gone to work. Where does your daddy work, John?' According to my father, I puffed out my five-year-old chest and replied, 'Oh, he goes to meetings. My father stops wars.'

Despite these activities my parents continued to be treated as part of respectable Wellington society. This included receiving official invitations to attend Government House in January 1940 (somewhat ironically) for the official farewell to members of the 2nd New Zealand Expeditionary Force Central Military District and, in February 1941, to attend the swearing-in of the governor-general. My father's employment with the WEA also continued, including organising the association's annual summer schools. On 8 April 1941, however, he wrote to its national council to inform them that at the Supreme Court session on 5 May it was 'practically certain that

I will be sentenced to imprisonment, probably for not less than one year', and offered his resignation.[26] But neither the council nor Wellington WEA agreed to accept this, deciding instead to grant him leave of absence if he were imprisoned.[27] That decision led to the Wellington WEA losing all its local body grants, including those from the Wellington City Council, Wellington Harbour Board, Lower Hutt City Council and the McCarthy Trust, because it continued to employ what the mayor of Wellington called 'a leading peace-monger.'[28] WEA annual reports for 1942–43 point out that while 'the sudden cancellation of these substantial and long-standing grants, through obvious and unjustified prejudice' was one factor contributing to 'an unprecedented financial crisis', it also caused 'a remarkable, spontaneous and general rallying of sympathisers without and within the WEA, so that it emerged in a healthier position than ever.'[29]

The Methodist Church had gradually moved away from its earlier opposition to war and at its 1940 conference disassociated itself from its pacifist members, particularly Burton, who was already in prison. 'It no longer repudiated war, declared loyalty to the Crown and held that New Zealand was at war because there was no other honourable alternative. Conscientious objectors (COs) should be respected but all objectors should render alternative service. It accepted the State's ban on subversive utterances and opposed recruiting or pacifism from pulpits.'[30] Here was one reminder that, particularly after war began, the uncompromising anti-war attitude of people like my father and Burton was 'a passion for a very few New Zealanders'; their views were limited to a very small proportion of the population.[31] Attitudes towards them at public meetings ranged from respect for their right to freedom of speech to amused tolerance and outright hostility. At least one High Court judge they appeared before, himself a Jew, regarded them as fanatical cranks, particularly as reports of Nazi barbarism became a staple diet in newspapers.

In these circumstances, family members sometimes had to choose sides. Prior to embarking for overseas my father's brother Ben wrote to him from army headquarters:

Although your ideas and my ideas of duty are vastly different I just want to say au revoir and hope that it will not be long before I return. I trust that the job I am setting out to do will result in the overthrowing of ideals which I am not prepared to accept, and as you are prepared to make a sacrifice in the interests of conscience so am I. Kind regards to Jan, the family and yourself, and thanking you for the assistance you have often rendered.[32]

Alison Parr's[33] interviews with women whose husbands were pacifists illustrate how adopting a pacifist position during wartime sometimes led to divisions within families and church congregations. Taylor[34] discusses the difficulties pacifist parents' beliefs sometimes created for their children, including being taunted at school. I cannot recall this happening to me during the war years, but it may have affected me indirectly. When Parr interviewed me I told her, 'I had to play football very hard'; a high-school teacher told my father, 'Your son won't be a pacifist, Archie, he's too good at rugby.' I admired many of my father's qualities, but often argued with him over his absolutist pacifist position.

In spite of the attitudes of the wider public, my father's prison diary records that close neighbours remained friendly and helpful, even after he was imprisoned: 'Mr Trail has offered to look after garden'; 'Mr Hollis (big burly man down the road) offered to do anything at all for her [Jan]' (13 May 1941); my mother and my father's sister were 'brought out here [to the prison] by Mr Ruddick borough foreman who lives up the road. Mrs Hollis down the road sent up fish the other day' (23 May 1941). My mother commented in her own diary that despite a leading article in the *Evening Post* dealing with pacifist activity, including arrests and sentences, 'people seem to have a very nice attitude to us and are very friendly' (J. Barrington, 9 May 1941).

Support also came from colleagues and friends. My mother recorded receiving a donation of £5 from Archibald Baxter, a conscientious objector who was brutally treated during World War I, and small amounts from others (J. Barrington, 9 May 1941). My father wrote, 'Mr Ockendon is sending a dozen eggs weekly from Christchurch', and 'Mrs Maslen [WEA colleague] has sent 5/-!' (24 May 1941).

> Jan has received a mysterious cheque from J. Fanny and Co Land Agents, with a note just saying, 'I have been asked to send you £5 and enclose cheque for this amount, signed AA Weybourne. Weybourne belongs to Hutt Debating Club and I can account for it only in the possibility of their having made it as a donation. I spoke as their guest speaker last year at monthly forum of Wellington Union of Public Speaking Societies on pacifism, and though practically all disagreed with me we had an enjoyable time (31 May 1941).

Cheered-up letter from Jane with encouraging news of support and
sympathy from unexpected quarters. A hitherto unknown woman
at Ohakune learning of us through Hely of WEA wrote Jane most
encouragingly – asking her to bring family for a holiday (large house
and one child of 10) and a railway worker's wife sending 10/- ... Two
people from the Hutt knowing me through WEA also called and
brought a jar of cream and honey in the comb, having previously sent £1
(12 July 1941).

Christian pacifist Arthur Carman was also sentenced to 12 months hard
labour with my father in May 1941. He had been found guilty of attempting
to publish a 'seditious' document, *Defend Peace and Freedom at Home*,
which he had mailed out to his bookshop customers with their accounts.
Initially employed in the government audit office and a keen sportsman,
Carman developed an interest in cricket and rugby statistics and in 1924
was contracted by the *New Zealand Sportsman* to cover the All Blacks tour
of the British Isles.[35] By 1928 he owned a bookshop in Lambton Quay and
had begun a long career in local body politics, including election to the
Wellington Hospital Board for six years, the Johnsonville Town Board for
four and Tawa School committee for eight. In 1934 he and a colleague
started the well-regarded annual *Rugby Almanac of New Zealand*, of
which he remained the long-standing co-editor. In prison he stood as an
independent candidate for the Wellington City Council and received 2156
votes.

Other Christian pacifists gaoled in Mount Crawford around this time
included Basil Dowling, a Presbyterian minister and poet who, after
postgraduate study at Cambridge University from 1936–38, in 1939 had
been appointed chaplain at one of Wellington's foremost private schools,
Scots College. Others were Dave Silvester, Jack Hamerton, Ron Scarlett, Jim
Doherty, John Boal, John Woodley and Harold Bray. All had been among
the weekly roster of speakers at Wellington's Pigeon Park on Friday nights,
each in turn standing on a soap-box, attempting to speak, being arrested,
tried and imprisoned for periods ranging from three to 12 months. They
were joined in gaol by Sid Harrison, a communist and janitor at what was
then the University of New Zealand's (Victoria College) hall of residence,
Weir House, who had been found with three copies of the booklet *Peace
and Socialism* and six copies of *Tribune*. The judge said the maximum
12 months was light in the circumstances; he gave no recognition to a
declaration from the students that Harrison had never attempted to spread

subversive literature, and remarked to the jury that 'in most countries such an offender would be shot without trial, but in New Zealand the matter has to go before a jury'.[36] Also imprisoned was Connie Jones (later Summers), the only female CO gaoled during the war, who spent her time in the Point Halswell Reformatory, part of the Mount Crawford prison complex that also served as a women's borstal at that time.

The Christian pacifists at Mount Crawford were kept together as a group for work gangs and in the prison yard. Burton later commented that he was 'still not sure whether it was thought that we would corrupt the other prisoners or they us'.[37] He also recalled:

> *The first Sunday that we were turned out into the exercise yard the natural thing for us to do was to hold a service. Among other things we sang a hymn. Absolute consternation! A jangle of keys! The door flew open and the Chief Warder rushed in with the air of a man about to quell a dangerous insurrection. Nothing like this had ever happened before – a group of men coming together to worship God without official sanction ... I was hurriedly rushed in front of the Superintendent who fortunately took a reasonable view of the matter.*[38] *Post-release*

My father was released from Mount Crawford on 24 December 1941. Our mother made us miniature flags to celebrate his homecoming and we apparently marched along the footpath with them singing 'Our daddy's coming home from jail today!' Comments made in a publication in 1994 (after his death) suggest that the main charge for which he was gaoled should never have been laid. The author, the Rev Bob Mayson, pointed out that when teaching at the Methodist Wesley College he had agreed to

> *... take over the editing of the* CPS Bulletin, *a document subversive in the eyes of the law. I sent the [manuscript] to an address in Auckland, and from there it was sent to another place for duplication. I was not told who did the printing so that I could truthfully say I did not know if interviewed. Unfortunately the cover page was not altered to show the name of the new editor. Barry's [Archie Barrington] name was still there. Well, he was arrested and charged with sedition or some such offence. I knew nothing until I received a letter telling me that Barry had been arrested in my place. I immediately sent a registered letter to the Crown Prosecutor in Wellington, claiming full responsibility, and absolving Barry. I expected the Crown would dismiss the charge and*

arrest me. I waited. But they went on with the original charge, even though they knew him to be innocent. I was told that the letter had been passed onto the defending counsel. What happened to it, I was not told, nor shall I ever know.[39]

Armed forces appeal boards had been established to evaluate the sincerity of resisters to conscription, which was introduced in 1940. There was no right of appeal and 823 applicants were declined, meaning most usually spent a month in gaol followed by detention for 'the duration of the war'[40] – that is, for however many years the war lasted. Formerly, only 'habitual criminals' could receive such indeterminate sentences and every criminal had a right of appeal to a higher court against even quite small sentences. This right did not apply to those denied CO status, and they were sentenced to detention in camps that were designed to be 'less comfortable than the army but less punitive than jail'.[41]

Importantly, however, my father had been imprisoned not as a CO but for sedition: for proclaiming his pacifist views to all who would listen and, at the same time, encouraging others to join the cause. In 1942, however, he was given 'unconditional exemption from military service'. His sincerity was acknowledged by the board that examined him:

I expected a lively session as militant pacifists were not favoured. But after a preliminary skirmish the Crown Representative, who was a lawyer and had been president of the Wellington Returned Services Association (RSA), told the Tribunal that 'If there are two genuine COs in New Zealand they're Mr Burton and Mr Barrington and that's all there is to it as far as I'm concerned'.[42]

He resumed his employment as national secretary of the WEA. However, writing a page in the *Christian Pacifist Bulletin*[43] led to him again being prosecuted and involved in Magistrates and Supreme Court trials, where he defended himself. The first jury could not agree, but a fresh one with a new Crown prosecutor brought a verdict of guilty. Because the chief justice had recommended that certain points he had raised should be dealt with by a higher court, however, the case was referred to the Court of Appeal where two of the three judges agreed the conviction should be quashed.[44] In the 1943 general election, he stood as a candidate for Wellington East, the Labour stronghold of Robert Semple. His election address was delivered by householder post with the heading 'This man stands for peace.' He received 252 votes, eight of them from soldiers.[45]

He also engaged in issues relating to prison reform and rehabilitation, including challenging the views of retired judge Sir Hubert Ostler in a letter to the *Standard*, in which he concluded that, based on his personal experience, there was 'no educational or reformative element in the prison system as it obtains at Wellington prison; that there is no provision for recreation – games, musical expression, hobbies, crafts, and that the dominant consideration, if not the only consideration, is to get the prisoner from his starting date to the end of his term with as little trouble to the system as possible.'[46]

In 1947 our family moved to Riverside Community, eight kilometres from Motueka. 'When the decision [to move] was made,' he wrote, 'and I explained it to my friends in the WEA they protested – why bury yourself there; look at all the influence you have here with thousands of people through the WEA, in the universities, trade unions etc., I had to reply: but that "influence" is mainly talk and talk in the end without action becomes sterile.'[47] Riverside had been established in 1940 by orchardist Hubert Holdaway – who, like Burton, had returned from World War I a convinced Christian pacifist – with the idea of developing a community based on co-operative Christian pacifist ideals. Initially COs released from detention camps came and went but some stayed. Most were Methodists.

As my father's son, now aged 11, during my first few days at the Lower Moutere Primary School as a 'community kid' I faced hostility I had not experienced during the war. Ironically, some of it came from boys with German surnames – the Moutere valley had earlier been settled by Germans. I later realised they themselves had probably felt somewhat uncomfortable during the war and I was a convenient scapegoat. Not having adopted my father's pacifist beliefs I offered to fight them, but as I was tall and strong for my age there were no takers. This, and the realisation that I was a useful addition to the school's cricket and rugby teams, soon put a stop to the abuse. My father's beliefs made it impossible for me to enrol in high-school cadets, although I personally had nothing against doing so. On the first cadets' day I felt so embarrassed being the only boy on the bus not in uniform that for the next four years I biked the 18 km daily. The school, either unsympathetic to my situation or unaware of it, provided no alternative activity for me during cadet periods; I felt so conspicuous in the co-ed school that I spent every cadet period for the next two years sitting in the boys' lavatory to keep out of sight. On some days I felt unable to face school and went to the beach instead. At the start of my third year my mother, realising the situation, went to see the headmaster and it was arranged that I would spend cadet periods in the woodwork room. I received no hostility from other boys and expect that quickly making the school's first XV and first XI may have helped with that. I must have disappointed my father when, at the age of 18, I registered for compulsory military training.

Riverside Community achieved trust status under the Religious, Charitable and Educational Trusts Act 1908 and, with my father acting as its secretary/accountant, expanded and covered a total area of 208 hectares by 1991.[48] It developed one of the largest orchards in the district, a dairy herd of 180 cows, a sheep flock and woodlots. The community donated significant sums to such bodies as the Methodist Church, the South African Defence and Aid Fund and CORSO. As well, people in need of a fresh start were referred there by prison, child welfare and other authorities. The community maintained a nuclear family form of social organisation: members lived in their own houses but came together for daily work, meetings and worship. They also maintained strong links with the outside community, serving on church and school committees, and joining local sports teams and other organisations.[49]

My father and other members continued to be involved in social action, such as opposition to the plan to introduce compulsory military training in 1949. They were active in the 1959–60 'No Maoris No Tour' campaign, opposed the Vietnam war and supported the campaign for nuclear disarmament. My father wrote regular letters to newspaper editors on these and other matters. The chess he had begun playing in Mount Crawford remained a passionate hobby and he became a Nelson provincial representative, as well as playing numerous games by correspondence.

In 1949, after Mahatma Gandhi's assassination, he represented New Zealand as a guest of the Indian government at the Mahatma Gandhi Memorial Conference in India. This brought together individuals from many countries motivated by Gandhi's non-violent philosophy, to discuss post-war problems. As part of a small group that included Vera Brittain, author of the well-regarded *Testament of Youth*,[50] he toured the country observing economic and social developments. Brittain subsequently wrote about the Indian experience in *Search After Sunrise*[51] in which my father is frequently mentioned, and the two maintained a 20-year correspondence.

He continued to make a significant contribution to the Methodist Church, as treasurer and trustee of the Motueka Church, secretary-treasurer of the Motueka Council of Churches, district property secretary for the Nelson–Marlborough–West Coast districts of the church, and as executive member of the Nelson Action Committee on International Affairs. In 1973 he was elected vice-president of the church, its highest lay office. Although many in the church had often felt uncomfortable with his strongly held convictions, particularly during the war years, the election was recognition of the consistency and sincerity with which these had been held.

Archie Barrington died in Nelson Hospital on 4 March 1986; Jan Barrington died in 1999.

Chapter 1

Dissent, Imprisonment and the Barrington Diary

The Wellington *Evening Post* of 5 June 1941 carried a feature article under the headline: 'Flying Crosses: More New Zealanders. Awards to four pilots, two from Wellington.'[1] The article described the Distinguished Flying Cross, one of Britain's highest military awards presented to pilots for 'an act or acts of valour, courage or devotion to duty whilst flying in active operations against the enemy'. The article is a typical example of the way New Zealand's involvement in World War II is usually presented – and rightly so: it describes the heroics of the country's (mostly) young men, enduring great hardships, demonstrating remarkable courage and putting themselves at great risk – with the resultant deaths, serious injuries and incapacitation for many – and ultimately contributing to the downfall and total capitulation of Nazi Germany.

There is another, less well-known side to New Zealand's involvement in the war, however, that is captured in Archie Barrington's prison diary. On the same day the *Evening Post* carried the report from 'the front', Barrington wrote of his war experiences:

> Working with the pigs yesterday & day before my trousers, issued on Sat (and especially white & clean) are covered in mud & pigs sweat etc from knees down & some above and these trousers will last until Sat week. Fortunately my sense of smell is defective but it may be hard on visitors. Some of the others seized a late opportunity for a run in the yard, but though cold I was too comfortable & considered I was getting plenty of fresh air. It is bitter outside. Consequently I was within when distribution of pears took place. The quota was 3 but H must have given me at least 8. Then Mr M returning with the near empty case provides me with an extra one. I fare well and I've had the 3 [pears] with my dinner which was hot & good. Stew – meat, carrot, a little parsnip & traces of onion, gravy & potatoes. Crust & 'tea'.

He too, in common with his various pacifist and CO colleagues and, for that matter, most of the other inmates at Mount Crawford Prison, was experiencing hardships and difficulties. The working and living conditions were likely to put his health at risk even if, on this particular occasion, Barrington was able to supplement the evening meal with the extra pears that had been distributed.

Naturally, the hardships, difficulties and dangers these dissenters endured were of a lesser order altogether than those experienced by members of the armed forces. It is not the purpose here to argue that there was any kind of commensurability in the challenges the two groups faced. The point is, however, that one of the reasons the Allies fought the war was so that Barrington and his colleagues would be free to express opinions that were contrary to those of the government of the day, without fear of the persecution and prosecution that would inevitably have befallen them in Nazi Germany and its conquered territories.

Anti-war groups in World War II: Prosecution and punishment

A number of diverse groups opposed New Zealand's involvement in the war, some because of their religious beliefs – of whom Barrington and his fellow Christian pacifists were the most prominent; some for political reasons – primarily communists until 1941 when Russia joined the Allies and their opposition ceased; and others for a variety of personal reasons.

When conscription was introduced in 1940 regulations stated that all who held 'a genuine belief that it is wrong to engage in warfare in any circumstances shall be exempt from service in the armed forces'.[2] Those seeking exemption had to provide proof of their beliefs before an Armed Forces Appeal Board staffed by local dignitaries – mainly businessmen and farmers with 'little understanding of the part conscience has played in the lives of men'[3] – to which there was no right of appeal (unlike in Britain).

Those who succeeded in establishing their 'genuine belief' that warfare was wrong were granted CO status. Those who failed were then called up for action. If they did not obey this directive, and became 'defaulters', they were sent to detention camps. Some of these defaulters went further, refusing to obey instructions in the camps on the grounds that this represented a contribution to the war effort. These men were labelled 'absolutists' and faced further disciplinary action within the camps, and possible imprisonment.

However, even when CO status was granted, advertising pacifist beliefs to encourage others to take an anti-war stance was still prohibited.

Proving 'genuine belief' was virtually impossible for the communists and, as it turned out, was beyond the ability of most of the Christian pacifists. In the course of the war the authorities prosecuted about 800 men and one woman in New Zealand. Those sent to the 'defaulters' detention camps' were usually held for the duration of the war and sometimes beyond: an indefinite sentence, in effect. Lincoln Efford provided the following description of the camps:

> The largest ones are surrounded with high barbed-wire fences, with inner compounds of the same material, and some are floodlit at night to prevent escapes. The food and other physical conditions are better than in prison, and there is more freedom within the camps.[4]

Nonetheless, the camps had all the resonances of prison: there was rigid censorship of reading materials, and inmates' huts had to be 'stripped of unnecessary or superfluous articles and represent the disciplined tidiness of a barracks room, ship's quarter or prison cell'.[5] Letters in and out of the camps were more restricted than in prison, and visiting was difficult for many because of their geographical remoteness.

Most of the defaulters also spent two or three months in prison prior to being sent to a camp. Although this was initially for administrative convenience while the camps were being established, it also came to be something of a test of the strength of their convictions. As government minister Luxton put the matter, 'when the court finds that a person is a straight out slacker ... if he is betwixt and between he will go to prison for a shorter term and then be sent to a defaulters' camp. If he is just a poor misguided person with an inflexible idea, he will be sent straight to a defaulters' camp.'[6] Around 50 dissenters were imprisoned.

Unlike during World War I, when British dissenters had been subjected to ruthless and unforgiving treatment, Britain now recognised that political and religious beliefs might be 'conscientious' and prohibit the conscription of the individual concerned into military service. One of the reasons for the abandonment of Britain's merciless and punitive measures was that tolerance of dissenters demonstrated some of the important distinctions between democratic Britain and Nazi Germany. Churchill himself acknowledged this: '[T]he rights which have been granted in this war [to] the COs are well known and are a definite part of British policy. Anything in the nature of persecution, victimisation or man-hunting is odious to the British people.'[7] In so doing, the country could shine as a beacon of light against the darkness of Nazism. The acting leader of the House of Lords explained:

[T]here are, I hope and believe, those amongst us who would prefer to die rather than to do certain things; and to that extent we can at least understand the spirit of the [CO]. I hope ... that the time will never come when my nation will lack citizens who place their conception of right and duty above all other considerations – above derision, above penalties and above discomfort. I cannot help feeling that it is a good thing and helpful to all of us that there should be in our midst a moral witness against the fundamental evil of war.[8]

In Britain, then, those who opposed the war on religious or ethical grounds were not to be excluded from British society but were to have a rightful, legitimate place. It was important to have dissent, to hear alternative viewpoints, to be reminded that war was not glorious but evil (although for the vast majority of those who fought on the side of the Allies, it became a necessary evil). For these reasons, the British Broadcasting Corporation in 1941 lifted the ban it had imposed on broadcasts by dissenters, showing again that hostility to this group was tempered by the prevailing view that 'we can't have Hitlerism here'.[9] In Britain over the course of World War II, there were 10 times fewer prosecutions of those whose CO claims had been rejected than in the 1914–18 conflict. Furthermore, appeals were allowed against the decisions of the conscription authorities; in World War I there had been no such process. As Grant observes, 'Even during the gloomiest days of the Blitz, pacifist meetings were still held in Tower Hill and Hyde Park.'[10] The pacifist journal *Peace News* continued to be published in Britain throughout World War II.

When introducing Britain's conscription bill in 1939, Prime Minister Neville Chamberlain explained that the government had learnt from the previous policy:

[I]t often happens that those who hold the most extreme opinions hold them with the greatest tenacity. We learned something about this in the Great War and I think we found that it was both a useless and an exasperating waste of time and effort to attempt to force such people to act in a manner which was contrary to their principles.[11]

In practice, this meant that the anti-war activities of pacifists in Britain during World War II were largely ignored. Although 1891 men and 214 women were imprisoned for refusing to undertake military service after their application to be placed on the CO register had been rejected (about

1 in 10 of such decisions, compared to 1 in 3 in World War I), they were usually given only a three-month sentence.[12] The authorities paid much more attention to foreign nationals who might be enemy aliens, and to the British Union (of Fascists) led by Sir Oswald Mosley, with 750 of the latter interned by July 1940.

Australia, too, took a very tolerant approach to wartime dissent. Echoing Churchill, Prime Minister Sir Robert Menzies declared,

> We must remember that the greatest tragedy that could overcome a country would be for it to fight a successful war in defence of liberty and lose its own in the process ... I hope when the time comes for me to cease to exercise [wartime] powers I shall be able to say that they were exercised firmly, definitely and promptly, but with tolerance and with a due respect for the interests of minorities.[13]

Rather than facing prosecution, Australian objectors 'were directed into civilian work not connected with the war'.[14] As a consequence, only 98 Australians whose CO claims had been rejected were sent to prison for failing to undertake non-combative military service when ordered to do so.[15] Furthermore, in 1942 the Menzies government suspended all legal action on CO claimants until legislation had been adopted, which was similar to the approach taken in Great Britain. The Australian pacifist magazine *Peacemaker* continued to be published, apart from in June 1940 and early 1942.

The position was similar in Canada, where freedom of the press also remained in place.[16] In that country, where conscription for overseas service did not begin until 1944, only 300 of the 11,000 denied CO status were held in camps; the others worked in industry, fishing and farming.

It is clear, then, that New Zealand's treatment of wartime dissenters was much more punitive than that of its allies. In 1945 Efford calculated that 'if New Zealand standards were applied in Great Britain, 13,000 would be in indeterminate confinement there now, instead of eighty in temporary confinement. If British standards were applied in New Zealand, perhaps four would now be in confinement for a few months instead of 650 indefinitely'.[17] Unlike the emollient gestures of Churchill and Menzies, New Zealand's prime minister, Michael Joseph Savage, took the view that 'freedom, such as we enjoy, breeds the truest patriots, but its genial climate permits also the growth of cranks and ingrates; of dreamers of fantastic dreams; of ideological oddities and ne'er-do-wells; a diversity of creatures having this at least in common, the urge to propagate terror'.[18] The comparison with Churchill's and Menzies' speeches is remarkable. Where they spoke of unity and recognition that a democracy should be strong enough, flexible enough and adaptable enough to include and digest dissent, Savage divided New Zealand society. Here, 'freedom' was much more precarious, it would appear, and needed to be protected not just from the external dangers posed by Nazi Germany and the Axis powers, but also from dissenters – worthless, dangerous, unwanted individuals – within.

But there was no great body of dissent in this country. Opposition was largely confined 'to very small numbers of committed pacifists – members of the Christian Pacifists and Jehovah's Witnesses – probably little more than 2000 in total'.[19] In contrast, 'well over half the adult male population was in the armed forces (154,000) or Home Guard (119,000)'[20] with both Pākehā and Māori populations sharing this burden. Indeed, although Māori were exempt from conscription, Orange writes that 'in 1943 more than 27,000 Maori (out of an estimated total population of 95,000) were in the services or had been placed in essential industries'.[21] Those New Zealanders compelled or expected to join the armed forces did so in overwhelming numbers; the activities of the pacifists were almost wholly insignificant in comparison.

Under 1939 regulations it could be deemed subversive to speak against the recruitment of soldiers, or the war effort in general. A superintendent or inspector of police could prohibit meetings or processions they considered likely to injure public safety and could authorise the searching of premises. From the declaration of war in September 1939 and through much of 1940, pacifist groups and organisations were the main targets of these authorities, as John Barrington noted in his introduction. Then in 1940, following Stalin's non-aggression pact with Hitler, attention was also drawn to communists. Individuals sympathetic to this political viewpoint were prosecuted and the Communist Party newspaper, the *People's Voice*, was closed down. (Its British counterpart, the *Daily Worker*, was banned only from October 1940 to August 1942.)

Clearly, New Zealand had not learnt the lessons of World War I. In that earlier conflict it had enthusiastically followed the British policy of suppressing dissent, imprisoning around 400 whose CO claims were disallowed and, astonishingly, transporting a handful all the way to the front line in France, literally forcing them into uniforms as it did so. Archibald Baxter famously recalled being brutally subjected to this in *We Will Not Cease*.[22] Little changed during World War II. Acting Prime Minister Peter

Fraser (himself imprisoned during World War I for sedition) explained to a Wellington police conference in 1940 that catching the distributors of subversive literature 'had to take precedence over everything short of murder'.[23] *Peace News* was banned from public display from May 1940. As in World War I, New Zealand eagerly committed itself to war on both the foreign *and* domestic fronts. Barrington and his colleagues were arrested, prosecuted and imprisoned for conduct that British authorities would have ignored at Speakers' Corner in Hyde Park, London.

In so doing, the New Zealand state, in a time of 'total war', decided to use important resources to quell and silence its own small number of dissenters. Imprisonment awaited some of those who continued to express their dissent while in the camps. It also awaited those accredited pacifists whose continued anti-war conduct broke the emergency regulations or existing criminal law, such as Barrington and his colleagues.

Barrington and the Christian pacifists, during and after the war

Barrington was serving time at Mount Crawford because he had been convicted of sedition. Through the diary we meet a cluster of leading figures of the Christian Pacifist Society who were also being held there, along with two communists, George Kelman and Sid Harrison, imprisoned for their political beliefs. We catch a glimpse of Connie Jones, the sole woman pacifist gaoled during the war, waving to some of them in the distance while working in the fields at Point Halswell Reformatory, serving her own sentence.

All members of the pacifist group – as far as can be ascertained – continued their anti-war stance after their release. For some, such as John Boal, John Woodley, Jack Hamerton and Ron Scarlett, their time at Mount Crawford was only the prelude to lengthier periods of detention – 'for the duration'. As John Barrington indicates in his introduction, his father and Burton were eventually recognised as legitimate COs. Although this status was denied to Carman, he was excluded from military training because of his poor eyesight.[24] Most of the other pacifists, however, either defied their conscription orders altogether or had their claims for CO status rejected. These and others were sent to the defaulters' detention camps, where they linked up with key figures like Walter Lawry, William Young and Ian Hamilton.

Some among them – Allan Handyside and Scarlett, for example – then became 'absolutists', refusing to cooperate with the authorities in the camps and, as a consequence, spending more time in prison as a punishment. Hamerton, Hamilton and Merv Browne went on what became a well-publicised hunger strike at Mount Eden Prison in 1945 (11, 21 and 36 days respectively), successfully drawing attention to the fact that they remained incarcerated despite the war having come to an end. Barrington himself faced further prosecution and Burton, convicted of sedition, received the indefinite sentence of reformative detention in 1942.

The penalisation of dissenters did not end with the war. As Grant has noted, 'the public service in particular did not want to know [them]. Government jobs for defaulters were impossible … regulations in 1944 banning defaulters from employment in the public service were to remain on the statute book indefinitely.'[25] The nine education boards that controlled primary education decided in 1946 not to re-employ military defaulters, a stance not revoked until 1962.[26] The undischarged military defaulters were also stripped of electoral voting rights until 1952. As individuals, some have left a strong public imprint that includes their own memoirs and records: Burton's *In Prison*;[27] Crane's biography of Burton, *I Can Do No Other*;[28] Hamilton's *Til Human Voices Wake Us*;[29] Lawry's *We Said 'No!' to War*;[30] Young's *Time to Tell of New Zealand's World War II Concentration Camps*;[31] and Handyside's *Indeterminate Sentence*.[32] Arthur Carman also kept brief notes of his time at Mount Crawford in 1941.

Riverside Community provided a home for Barrington and his family after the war, as it did for Merv Browne from 1949–70 and others, including Norm Cole, Chris Palmer, Dave Silvester and Bob Hyland, who had been in prison or detention camps. It provided a temporary haven for Woodley during the war and Handyside from 1970–72. Others found their own niche elsewhere. Hamerton, for example, established a picture-framing business and gallery in Wellington; Scarlett spent many years as a display artist at Canterbury Museum; Connie Jones and John Summers married and ran a Christchurch bookshop together; Basil Dowling worked at the University of Otago's Hocken Library before emigrating to the United Kingdom in 1951, where he joined the civil service and published poetry; Handyside became a Methodist minister. Nor should we forget another leading pacifist, Lincoln Efford, whose ill health spared him from conscription. In 1941 he became secretary of the Fellowship of Conscientious Objectors and, as a writer and publisher, frequently brought the prosecution of dissent to public attention throughout the war. For some years after the war he continued to campaign against military training, worked fulltime for the WEA and was active in campaigning for penal reform.

Available records clearly demonstrate that many COs faced additional ostracism, harassment and barriers to advancement and development that would not have occurred were it not for their wartime 'record'. The only work Burton could obtain after release from prison was as a cleaner at Wellington Technical College; 11 years later he was appointed deputy principal. Expelled from the church in 1942, he eventually became a Methodist minister in 1955 and was finally allowed to return.[33] Arthur Carman had a long career in local body politics, as well as running his bookshop (sold in 1959) and writing prolifically on sport and local history. Walter Lawry worked in his father-in-law's fruit shop in Dunedin but found, some years after the war, that his appointment to the New Zealand-based overseas aid organisation, CORSO, had been delayed. His name was omitted from the Otago Boys' High School register celebrating the school's centenary in 1963. Ian Hamilton returned to his homestead near Kerikeri, but after 'ex-colonials', as he referred to them, tried to burn it down on several occasions, he moved to a more isolated location; he eventually settled in Auckland in 1953 and became a market gardener. William Young had to work as a labourer until he was allowed to teach again in 1949; he left this profession in 1953 to study law and became a well-respected lawyer.

This, then, is the background to how Archie Barrington found himself in prison in 1941, and the subsequent implications for the various dissenters scattered around the prison system for the duration of the war and beyond. The diary has two important functions. First, it provides a wonderful illustration of prison life at the time. Second, it allows us to examine the issue of why Barrington was in prison in the first place: why was New Zealand so intolerant of dissent?

The New Zealand prison system in the inter-war period

There is a very large historiographical gap in our understanding of prison policy and prison life between 1910 and 1950. In an important shift away from the harsh, repressive nineteenth-century approach,[34] in 1910 the formal direction for New Zealand prison policy had been set out in *Scheme for the Reorganization of the Prison System of New Zealand*.[35] In introducing the plan to parliament, Justice Minister Findlay stated:

> [T]he idea of putting a man in gaol simply to punish him for his offence ... was rapidly passing from the public mind. We are beginning to recognise that we not only owe a duty to society in punishing the criminal, but we owe a duty to the criminal himself in endeavouring to reform him ... a better and cheaper system would be to reform our criminals.[36]

Accordingly, prison sentences were to be 'individualised' to fit the prisoner's character and previous history. Depending on the type of offender they were thought to be, criminals would be sent to one of a range of specialist penal institutions. Prison labour would help to rectify an inmate's bad habits: 'the main purpose will be to substitute for the idle habit the work habit. The habit of work will effect the salvation of men and women more than any other habit in the world.' Furthermore, the labour would have a productive purpose: 'we shall not have the soul-degrading nature of work which has prevailed in the past such as shot-drill, the carrying of a heavy shot from one place to another and back ... we shall endeavour to have tasks severe enough, but they will be tasks of usefulness'.[37]

There were no further reviews of this kind until the 1950s.[38] As a result, our knowledge of prisons in this period has been almost wholly dependent[39] on the contents of the annual reports to parliament published by the Prison Department and, in particular, the introductory comments of the controller-general of prisons to them. Sanitised for public consumption, these reports confirmed the smooth transition of policy into practice in three pivotal areas: prison labour, the provision of social and educational opportunities, and the relaxation of security.

Prison labour as a cost-effective means to reform

The *Report on Prisons 1918–19* confidently asserted that 'the old and well deserved reproach that [an inmate's] labour while in prison ceased to be an asset to the State is removed ... every able-bodied prisoner is now as fully employed as our system can compel him to be.' Rather than having to spend their time on utterly useless work such as rock-breaking, prison labour could indeed contribute to community wellbeing, while at the same time preparing prisoners for settling back into society on release: 'this can best be achieved by endeavouring to reform offenders ... by inculcating habits of industry to engender self-reliance and self-respect.[40]

Farm labouring was considered to offer the best employment prospects for prisoners, as was noted in a succession of reports in the 1920s and 1930s, since 'the market is sufficiently large to enable our [agricultural] produce to be easily absorbed without prejudicing other producers.[41] By making most penal institutions virtually self-sufficient, the policy would 'keep the costs of imprisonment down.[42] At Mount Crawford Prison, 'by careful and extensive cultivation we have grown a sufficient feed of mangolds, the dairy herd is in very good condition ... we have increased our number of breeding pigs and they likewise are showing a fair profit.[43]

As well as being productive, farm work would provide its own therapy: 'Work in the open air among growing plants and animals gives a man a new outlook on life and tends to make a better citizen of him.'[44] Rather than using psychotherapeutic treatment that was being developed in similar jurisdictions, prison staff were expected to encourage rehabilitation through 'a good practical understanding of human nature ... coupled with a fair and firm system of discipline and well-ordered conditions.'[45] Although there were references in the annual reports to inmates' 'mental problems', this emphasis on common-sense solutions suited the strong insistence that those who broke the law remained responsible for their own actions, amid warnings that 'There is a growing tendency, particularly amongst sentimentalist doctrinaires, to excuse all criminals on the ground of impaired conduct.'[46] Prisoner classification thus continued to be on the basis of 'age and the extent of criminal experience'[47] rather than any analysis of personality and background.

The provision of social and educational opportunities to make prisoners 'better people'

The reorientation of prison policy towards reform instead of deterrence necessitated changes in the work of prison officers. According to the *Report on Prisons 1920–21*, 'their rifle and baton have given place to a firm but kindly supervision.'[48] Improvements to the everyday conditions of prison life had been introduced, it was claimed: 'for those who are illiterate, we have evening classes ... while a certain amount of recreation is also provided.'[49] By 1934 clothing and bedding were judged to be 'in a reasonably good state of repair ... every prisoner now has a comfortable bed with a mattress, blankets and sheets'.[50] There had been 'improvements in lighting, bathing, accommodation, cooking; eating utensils – the replacement of enamelware and aluminium ware and crockery; wooden beds instead of hammocks; pyjamas and bedding for all; shelves for books; flowers and pictures are allowed in the cells'.[51] During the 1920s improvements to the diet were also introduced: 'a small ration of meat is served with breakfast ... the quality of the institution-made bread has been favourably commented upon by medical officers and visiting officials';[52] it was further augmented ten years later: 'an addition of cocoa and an allowance of extra puddings; wholemeal bread; a liberal allowance of fresh root and green vegetables are provided'.[53]

According to the reports, these ameliorations helped to improve prisoner health:

> [A] large number of prisoners are received into prison in a debilitated condition ... but their health improves with regularised routine and a simple, wholesome diet. In recent years more attention has been given to the provision of fresh vegetables in the diet ... they receive a quarter of a pint of milk daily in addition to the scale allowed with the tea ration.[54]

To provide opportunities for socialisation and further reform opportunities, from 1923 inmates were allowed to watch film shows, wireless sets were installed, and visits and letter writing given more encouragement. In 1930 the Mount Crawford superintendent noted, 'The [Wellington] public library has donated a large quantity of second hand library books which I have had rebound'.[55] By 1935 inmates were able to participate in 'organised sports, lectures and first aid classes'[56] and in 1937 there was mention of 'lectures and entertainments, also evening radio programmes regularly incorporating any broadcasts of exceptional interests'.[57]

Trust and the relaxation of security

After World War I an 'honour system' had been introduced in recognition of the 'greater degree of trust' the authorities had bestowed on inmates.[58] Although providing more opportunities for escape – there were 11 in 1919, for example – this was not allowed to compromise what were now considered the paramount rehabilitative opportunities of prison life. Referring to the escapees of the previous year, the *Report on Prisons 1919–20* explained that they were not a menace to the community: 'It would be quite impossible to build up self-respect and self-reliance of the men committed to our charge if we had to treat them as irresponsible beings unworthy of trust.'[59] The following year's report affirmed, 'It is only to be expected that under the free open-air system that is followed in the management of the majority of our institutions, a percentage of prisoners will fail to respond to [this trust] … [but] escapes do not constitute in any way a menace to public safety.'[60] The approach was maintained throughout the inter-war period. The 1939 report acknowledged that there had been 39 escapes in the previous year, but all escapees had been recaptured; after all, 'under a system in which trust is an essential element a certain number of escapes is inevitable.'[61]

There seems to have been little public concern about the softened stance on security. Even in the early 1960s, George Wilder's[62] escapes turned him into a national hero – a little man outwitting a clumsy government bureaucracy rather than a danger to society. That this was so points to the relatively short social distances between prisoners and the rest of society in this period, as might be expected in the very homogeneous society that New Zealand had become during its first century of colonisation. With immigration restricted almost exclusively to British settlers,[63] the majority of Pākehā New Zealanders shared similar standards of living, values and affectations, without any rigid exclusionary divisions.

As an illustration of this, there was significant community involvement in prison life, and at Mount Crawford the social side of prison life was not forgotten: 'Concerts were given on several occasions. The Presbyterian Social Services club provided Christmas dinner. The Justices' Association provided a small gift for each prisoner on New Year's Day.'[64] Two years later, 'the Presbyterian Social Services Club and several ladies provided Christmas cheer and we are also indebted to them for their efforts in procuring … a number of fine articles for the Christmas concerts. There was a New Year concert by inmates where several Justices were in attendance.'[65]

However, two other characteristics of the prison system jeopardised the possibility of reform, according to the annual prison reports. The first was the difficulty of recruiting suitable staff. It was immediately apparent after World War I that it was 'impossible to keep [prison] staff up to strength … [staff] are expected to interest themselves in the work and lives of the men under their charge and to assist in building up character … unfortunately there is not one applicant in fifty [to the prison service] who is qualified to do so.'[66] As an indication of the continued low status of prison staff, they were still formally referred to as 'warders', in contrast with England where, in 1919, the term had been replaced by 'prison officer'.[67] Barrington himself used the term 'warder' in his diary – there is not one reference to 'prison officers'.

Second, the prisoners themselves seemed resistant to reform. The authorities complained of 'a "stage army" of vagrants and petty criminals who today overcrowd our big city prisons'.[68] Convicted mainly of drunkenness, vagrancy or other petty offences, many of these were 'hopeless degenerates, in whose own interests, as well as the interests of the community, institutional treatment is desirable'.[69] Rather than responding to reform, these men simply kept coming back to prison, serving one short sentence after another. In 1937 62% were sentenced to less than three months imprisonment and 75% to less than six. In 1939 25% of prison admissions were due to non-payment of fines, and 39.3% were sentenced to less than one month; only 0.8% of the prison population were serving five years or more. These trends became even stronger with the outbreak of war. In 1940 35.2% of the prison population were serving sentences of less than one month, and only 0.5% were serving terms of five years or more.

The rarity and value of prison diaries

There had been very little information available to offset these bland reports regarding prison life between 1910 and 1950 – until the discovery of Barrington's diary.

Such documents are extremely rare, and extensive searches have so far revealed nothing similar from that period. This is not surprising: many inmates not only had highly disorganised lives but were also illiterate. For them and others experience of prison was anyway neither novel nor noteworthy. Regulations also prevented writing: prior to the mid-twentieth century, prisoners were forbidden from keeping any such record in the Anglophone countries. In England in the 1930s, Jim Phelan, a writer by profession, was eventually given a notebook with a statement of what *not* to do with it: 'keeping a diary and writing about prisoners was especially frowned upon'.[70]

Although restrictions on diarising were eased from the 1970s, it has only been possible to find four such documents in existence from then:

- *A Prison Diary*[71] – After being sentenced to four years imprisonment for perjury in 2001, Jeffrey Archer kept a diary of his prison experiences for the first two years of his term. It was not written without difficulties, though: pens and paper had to be brought or smuggled in by visitors.

- *The Big Huey*[72] – Greg Newbold kept a daily record of events during the five years he spent in prison, mainly at Mount Eden, in the late 1970s and early 1980s: 'Every day I was in prison I made an entry in a journal which I kept hidden in my cell. In this I recorded events, impressions, sentiments, conversations – anything which I thought might be relevant to the research which I hoped to do when I got out. By the time I was released I had completed twelve volumes of journals, amounting in all to around 2500 pages of manuscript.'[73] Although he informs us that 'diaries as such [were]n't illegal in jail'[74] by then, prison staff were able to manipulate the regulations to ensure that diary keeping could still be regarded by the authorities as illegal activity. Inevitably, what he was writing 'contained material which might affect the discipline or security of the institution'[75] – as he was told. He had to devise ways of smuggling out his writings.
- *The Writings of Bobby Sands*[76] – Sands was a very prominent Irish Republican Army (IRA) hunger striker who starved himself to death while in Maze Prison, Belfast. He kept an illicit record of the first 17 days of his strike. His status within the prison and the ongoing conflicts between IRA prisoners and the British authorities meant he would have been prohibited from doing so. Sands was being kept in isolation, and the consequences of his starvation were beginning to take effect. While noting some of the conditions in the prison, his diary reflects the scaled-down nature of his life. It mainly contains his thoughts on the IRA struggle and also his coming to terms with a long and harrowing death.
- *The Ray Denning Diary*[77] – This provides a very detailed account of Denning's 18-month imprisonment around 1980, spent mostly at Grafton, New South Wales, a prison for 'intractables' – those considered beyond the control of prison staff in 'normal' institutions. Denning makes no mention of how the diary was kept or smuggled out of the prison, but given his placement at the most extreme and restricted end of the prison system of that state, he certainly would not have had permission to keep such a record.

Furthermore, Barrington's diary provides valuable insights into 'ordinary' prison life. In prison research there has been a bias towards the examination of prison life at the maximum security end of the system (notwithstanding some important corrections to this in recent prison ethnographies).[78] Sykes'

1958 reference to the 'pains of imprisonment'[79] – the loss of autonomy, of goods and services, of heterosexual outlets and of security – are still likely to be the determining experiences of incarceration. In maximum security settings the 'pains' will be most acute, the distance between prison officers and prisoners greatest, and the prison culture most entrenched. Denning's diary, for example, provides a vivid account of what, at face value, was a daily struggle for survival at Grafton in the face of systematised brutality from prison officers and frequent conflict among the inmate population.[80]

However, these are far from typical experiences of prison life. By 1940 most New Zealand prisons were designed to accommodate the mainstream prison population who constituted only low- or medium-security risks. A handful of others catered for smaller, select groups: prisoners who were 'old, senile and frail' were held at Whanganui, 'sex offenders' at New Plymouth and 'serious offenders' at Mount Eden.[81] One of the particularly important aspects of Barrington's diary is thus that it describes not the most extreme form of maximum-security imprisonment, but the most typical, which Mount Crawford represented.

Presenting the diary

There are innate difficulties in presenting such a work as a day-to-day account that faithfully follows the chronology of each entry. While the threat of violence is never far away in many accounts of prison life, monotony and routine are much more central to everyday existence. Newbold, for example, wrote of 'the chronic repetition and boredom of prison'.[82] Even for a wordsmith such as Archer, making the constrained little world of the prison and its essential and inevitable routine interesting became an insuperable problem. Eventually resolving to capture only events of particular interest, his entries became more irregular. When moved to another prison, Archer took the opportunity to bring this writing project to an end. Prison monotony and routine had beaten him: 'Although Holleslay Bay turned out to be quite different from North Sea Camp, it was not dissimilar enough to warrant a fourth diary'.[83] For this reason I have chosen to present the contents of Barrington's diary thematically rather than chronologically, the better to illustrate the main characteristics of prison life: the practices, regulations, rhythms and routines, and the lives of inmates and staff.

A few words are due on the way in which the text is reproduced. This is loyal to the prose style, abbreviations and shorthand used by Barrington, except when it has been necessary to provide clarification. The initials he frequently employed to refer to his fellow pacifist prisoners are reproduced here: 'O' or 'OEB' refers to Ormond Burton; 'A' or 'AHC' refers to Arthur Carman; 'JB' refers to John Boal; 'HB' to Harold Bray, 'JHW' to John Woodley and so on. I have also replaced the names of the prison staff with initials to protect their identity, primarily because the diary indicates that many were engaged in illicit practices involving the use of prison labour for private purposes. While this was unlikely to have been illegal, it would certainly have been in breach of prison regulations. What *would* have been illegal, however, is the assault by a warder on one of the prisoners, detailed in the diary and supported in the records of Barrington's colleagues.

Chapter 2 presents Barrington's description of Mount Crawford Prison in 1941 and the myriad regulations covering all aspects of prison life that he encountered there: rules so complex they were difficult to know and enforce in their entirety but also, as he found out, impossible to challenge. Chapter 3 examines his account of the prison living and working conditions, so far removed in all aspects from the descriptions presented in the annual prison reports. Chapter 4 sets out his portrayals of the prison staff: their roles, the relationships he cultivated with them, the disenchantment that most felt with prison life, and the ruses they adopted to make it more bearable. Finally, the two distinct groups in Mount Crawford's inmate population at that time, the dissenters and the mainstream prisoners, are compared in Chapter 5.

Chapter 6 discusses the penological issues raised by Barrington's account. There have obviously been many changes to the prison experience since then: dietary options are now available, the career structure of prison officers has changed, 'ownership' has diversified with the introduction of private prisons from the 1980s, and the prison population has become a good deal more violent. Yet at the same time, the diary also shows that there are a number of timeless aspects of prison life, transcending eras and jurisdictions.

Chapter 7 addresses the question of why Barrington and the other dissenters received such treatment in a society like New Zealand's, famous by then for its egalitarianism, informality and 'fair go' approach to life. Harrop's 1935 guidebook *Touring in New Zealand* warned reserved British tourists, 'It is advisable on arrival in a hotel dining room to ask for a table for yourself and your party, unless you wish to be placed with other people.'[84] New Zealanders did not mind being 'placed with other people' – the British reserve and disdain for those of a different class had gone: this new society was big enough to include all, irrespective of their differences. And the historian Oliver Duff noted in 1941 that, 'visitors to [New Zealand] have often remarked on our readiness to shake hands'[85] – to extend a welcome, to trust and accept others. With cultural characteristics such as these, why was this country so intolerant of wartime dissent?

Chapter 2

Mount Crawford Prison, 1941

Mount Crawford Prison opened in 1927 with capacity for around 140 prisoners and approximately 45 officers and associated prison staff, including a night watchman for the 11 pm to 6 am shift. Other than the superintendent and the doctor, everyone working in the prison was in uniform – it appears there were no ancillary civilian staff. It was a good example of the uncomplicated and under-developed administrative structure of New Zealand prison life in the first half of the twentieth century. Prisoner classification on the basis of age and prior record required only a rudimentary system of formal record keeping, and there was no need for any pseudo-scientific character assessment of prisoners. Outdoor work was to provide its own therapy, and the warders would assist with 'kindly supervision'. These were the intentions, at least, of the prison authorities. What we see in Barrington's diary, however, is the way in which these were undermined both by the structure of the prison and the regulations covering movement and activity within it.

Facilities

Cells

Those who served their sentence at Mount Crawford were accommodated in a cell that was 11 x 4 x 8 ft (3.3 x 1.2 x 2.4 m) – 'a reasonable size', Barrington wrote (12 May 1941). Each inmate had his own cell on a wing that contained 28 identical cells. Barrington's wing – West Wing – housed nearly all the pacifist and CO prisoners, along with two cleaners, two Māori who were let out early each day to tend the cows on the prison farm, and the two communists, Harrison and Kelman.

Furnishings

Barrington provided the following details of his cell:

1 chair. Shelf – table in corner by door for meals. Mat about 3x3 [.9 x .9 m]. Iron bedstead & wire fixed to wall. Corner opposite shelf table is holdall. Top wash basin & water billy. 1st shelf books, 2nd razor etc, 3rd food salt etc breadbag. Below (with separate door) 2 shelves for chamber etc. Small wall bracket above for soap, brush, comb. Illustrated text marked, 1 novel, 3 magazines, all rejects Wgtn Public Library (12 May 1941).

He reported that the cell was badly lit, despite the 'improvements in lighting' that were supposed to have taken place. While this deficiency was a simple technical matter that might have been remedied with ease, the authorities seemed either oblivious to it or uninterested:

… the cell lighting is not good – simply because a low powered bulb is used. Sufficient for large type well printed perhaps. But it could be excellent with a normal bulb. Walls are plastered buff or brown up to 4 ft [1.2 m] then white including ceiling. Grey skirting about 10 inches [25 cm] & massive door grey. Floor wood, dark stained & polished. Shelves, cupboard, chair, brown, meal shelf covered in brown lino (13 May 1941).

As the 1937 *Report on Prisons* had indicated, inmates were now allowed to add to the furnishings and put their personal touches on the standard layout of the cell and its contents.[1] On these points, Barrington noted:

Was in H's [Hardgreaves, the wing cleaner and librarian] cell yesterday and he has an extraordinary collection of objects in it. As [prison] librarian he has license I suppose. A table, elaborate radio and the recess above his corner has been made into a Catholic 'shrine' with crucifix & rosary. The crucifix, he told me, is the only one of its kind outside of a cathedral for it has Virgin Mary on back – says he got it from a bombed church last war (16 June 1941).

As his sentence passed Barrington added to his cell possessions. His collection of books at one point amounted to 76 – the prison regulations placed no limit on the number allowed for the purpose of study. He frequently had a vase of flowers, either brought by visitors or picked from the prison grounds, even though in doing so he was breaking prison regulations regarding 'contraband'. With no internal sanitation in the cell, daphne seems to have been a particular favourite. Its pleasing scent could smother the unpleasant, pungent prison odours that accumulated as a result of inmates being locked in from 4.10 pm to 8.00 am every day.

There was an abundance of New Zealand and overseas periodicals available:

Periodicals: regularly glance at *Weekly News, Free Lance, Observer, Industrial Worker, Methodist Times, Student, New Leader, Left News, War Commentary, Peace News, Zealandia, Sports Post, The Friend, BC Link.*

Casuals: *The Brit, Aust & NZr* (tripe), *Readers Digest, New Horizon, Picture Post, Pix Bulletin, Standard, Vera Brittain's letter to Peace Lovers, New Statesman & Nation.* John A Lee's *Weekly, Illustrated British Weekly, British Digest, Irish Digest, Scientific American, Listener* (24 May 1941).

Inmates were denied local daily papers, however, and this absence of local news added to the sense of isolation that he and his colleagues experienced:

Although this is now Wed. AHC still doesn't know whether he was re-elected to Hospital Board or how many votes he got in City Council election. Indicates how out of the world we are here and how slowly news penetrates. Daily newspapers of course are on no a/c allowed (21 May 1941).

After some weeks and frequent petitioning, Barrington was allowed to have his own radio complete with headset. With this, he could claim back some autonomy from the prison authorities. Prisoners were not allowed to retain their own timepieces but 'knowing the time is one boon of radio. We have to work by guess otherwise' (15 June 1941). The authorities determined what time lights were to be turned off at night; when inmates had to rise in the morning (the rising bell would sound at 6.00 am; cell doors were opened at 6.30 am for the simultaneous 'slopping out' procedure – that is, the emptying of the nightly contents of the cell chamber pot into a communal bucket, and the serving of breakfast); what time they were to eat ('dinner time' was midday and 'tea time' at 4.30 pm); and when they could bathe or shower (Saturday mornings) and change their clothes and bedding (alternate Saturdays).

It is difficult to overstate how important the radio became for him as a vital means of keeping informed about the world beyond the prison walls. It was also a source of comfort:

My evening routine now is: Tea finished and tidy up, transfer radio from head of bed to my chair at 'table' with phones hanging from back of chair ready for London news etc. (phones on ears as I write). Then I make bed as far as possible … My pillow goes on my chair for easier sitting. A folded blanket goes under my feet on top of mat (sit in sox slippers too tight making feet cold). Another blanket goes right over chair cutting off draught from back. Finally another blanket is folded right round me from hips to feet. Thus I keep warm for work at night. But it is a bit complicated if I have to emerge for another book, papers or other necessities (22 June 1941).

Barrington lovingly described this radio in anticipation of the pleasure, knowledge and independence it would bring him: 'the radio is a credit to Colin [the family friend who provided it], neatly arranged in a cabinet with hinged lid and loads of wire' (7 June 1941). Later in the same entry, though, he despairingly pronounced, 'it hasn't uttered a sound yet'. Only after much tinkering and considerable assistance from Hardgreaves (although there was a price to be paid for this, as will be seen later), did he eventually find the ideal spot in his cell to pick up the broadcast wavelengths:

'Hardy' has been hard at work on my 'wave-track' and seems to have made an excellent job of it – but I don't yet know how to work it. The condenser he has replaced mine with seems to be a perfectly good and appropriate new one – minus knob. Had set going well again early this evening, finding I had not adjusted coil contacts to suit my majestic new aerial. I have now combined the huge cable and all other aerial components under bed and think will get great results. Have again spent a good deal of time – 2 hours on this and fitting up board at head of bed to hold apparatus instead of leaving on floor with constant shifts. Packed with paper to fit mattress one end and fastened with wire the board seems likely to serve well and I am pleased with my setting up of it, complete with nail to hang phones on. Hardy has gone to a lot of trouble with extra equipment and has returned surplus wire and I've no cause for complaint or suspicion (15 July 1941).

Hardgreaves also attended to some technical problems with the earphones:

Came in for tea (got very cold in yard) to find H had spent nearly all afternoon at my radio. Had found earphones which had been repaired, connected up wrongly & had put four entirely new connections on to them (14 June 1941).

Variations in the clarity of reception necessitated regular rearrangements of his living space in the cell, however:

MOUNT CRAWFORD PRISON, 1941   45

Have had a glorious orgy of hammering & 'making' tonight, rearranging the bed shelf for my radio, turning it sideways so that one end is not under mattress & tilting every time I move in bed. Now lengthwise between bed & wall, with leg support to floor nails underneath keeping firm against iron bed, either shelf room for phones (for day time use out of way of cleaners) or nail to hook them on for convenient night use (22 July 1941).

Punishment cells

In addition to the four cell wings, Mount Crawford had punishment cells. Being sent to 'the dummy', as this block was referred to,[2] involved a period of solitary confinement for up to a maximum of 30 days, although the term could be extended if there was further recalcitrance on the part of the offender.[3] The inmate would have to get by with 'three blankets (instead of five), no mattress, clothes removed from the cell at night and no books except "educational"' (20 July 1941). Barrington added, 'apparently no one can be committed there except by a JP or magistrate after hearing warder & culprit' (31 July 1941).

The library

There were library facilities, although inmates had no direct access to the room where the collection of books was held. Instead, they were provided with a list of available titles to choose from, after which Hardgreaves would deliver these to their cells. Barrington first came across the practice in the following way:

Today for first time a large board containing a list of library books was placed in our yard and I gathered later one was in each yard. Whether they are sections of the whole or each is complete I'll have to find out. Ours contained 300 books referred to by no., title, description (Novel, Fiction, Mystery, Romance, Western and even one 'Gangster'), author's initials and name – the whole written on paper in ink neatly but with occasional mis-spellings. I began to copy out the catalogue for record purposes in spite of bitter cold. Not quite a 100 listed so far. 'Hardy' is librarian and I understood he was recently being pressed to complete something to do with the library and these boards must be the result (29 June 1941).

The collection was very limited, and the 'rebound' donations from Wellington Public Library mentioned in the 1929–30 annual report remained in particularly poor condition, incapable of generating much enthusiasm among the inmates:

> Such as I have seen of the books are grimy, in practically every case a reject from the Wellington Public Library and most unattractive. I've looked over those scattered on the table in [the] alcove in our wing. I've never seen cupboards open and as far as I can gather librarian sees that there's a book or mag in each cell for a newcomer and supplies a book – his own choice – when appealed to (29 June 1941).

Under these conditions there was very little incentive for inmates to develop their literacy skills, in contrast to the authorities' aspirations for a better-educated prisoner community. Barrington contemplated ways to improve the Mount Crawford arrangements:

> Apropos of library. Why couldn't prison library be expertly selected, the best procurable with a range of light and serious reading of high standard. And new books all, which prisoners may have opportunity of browsing among with a clip on cover for reading in cell. Country Library Service could organise (29 June 1941).

There is no record of any change during his sentence, however.

Exercise yards

The annual reports had made fleeting references to the provision of 'concerts', evening classes for illiterates, film shows and organised sports. The diary reveals, however, that apart from the film shows, these opportunities no longer existed. Instead, when they were not working or locked in their cells, virtually all prisoners idled away their hours in the prison 'yards'. Mount Crawford had a separate yard for each wing. Unless inmates had visitors on Saturday afternoons, or were attending a church service on Sunday in another yard, or the weather was exceptionally bad, they spent every weekend in the one to which they had been allocated – with very little shelter from the elements:

> ... day dullish but fortunately not wet. Good weather at weekends is important for they must be spent in open yards (24 May 1941).

These spaces had only the most rudimentary hygiene and sanitation facilities ('there is piping to the wash basins in the yard and naturally the water splashes one's boots when in use', 1 June 1941), and no facilities were provided for prisoners' use during their leisure time. That Barrington and his colleagues were able to play interminable games of chess[4] or draughts was due to their ingenuity in 'manag[ing] to get sets or scrape the materials for them', as Barrington later wrote in a letter to the *Evening Post*.[5]

The common room

There were no longer any concerts in the common room but occasionally films were shown. While these were popular with the other prisoners they were clearly not to Barrington's aesthetic tastes. He went to the first film shown during his sentence but was not impressed:

> Pictures well attended. Modern projector but sound part of films worn & difficult to hear most of time. We had an overdose of the navy. Two of the pictures were good – a news reel of the approach of war and up to the bombing of Warsaw and a cartoon *Little Boy Blue*. Paul Terry Toons good fun. A Thames picture, *Men of Africa* (Empire colonial propaganda, good in spots like the administration itself). *The British Navy. Heart of the Empire* (St James Park etc) and the Naval Review at Spithead. Nothing really educational and apart from cartoon not even entertainment. Well meant no doubt (29 May 1941).

He had little time for these light-hearted occasions and the opportunities for flag-waving jingoism they provided:

> … there are to be pictures tonight – I believe a war picture to last 2½ hours. I am not going, I prefer to get on with reading (10 July 1941).

The common room was also the venue for lectures from outside speakers. As secretary of the WEA and before his own imprisonment, Barrington had arranged for a weekly lecture to be given by one of its representatives. This was much more to his taste: earnest, educative and political (although he had little time for established party politics, since both Labour and National were committed to defence budgets).

Despite the poor education levels of most inmates other than the dissenters, and the somewhat dry and esoteric topics for discussion in the lectures ('trade unionism', 'housing', 'free speech'), they were well attended. Between one third and one quarter of the inmates were usually present:

> 7pm. Having shaved & washed, attended with 32 others, lecture in WEA series by K. Baxter[6] who brought own chairman. Attended also by Mr L

[the head warder] & a warder who however did not interfere in any way. Men seemed all alert and interested, questions prompt & good (12 May 1941).

This, in fact, was the day on which he began his sentence: but rather than ruminating on its implications, he not only attended the lecture but added in the diary, with a suggestion of disapproval, 'Only I took notes.' Part two of the lecture was offered the following week. There was some decline in attendance but, nonetheless, somewhere between one fifth and one quarter of the inmates were present:

> About 25 present. Including Harold Bray whom we were pleased to see looking fit & well. Introduced to O & others he had not met & supplied tobacco! Baxter good in a racy kind of way – a great flow of words – far too many – but I wish I could flow like that. I proposed vote of thanks to chairman & speaker at close and said it was a real service much appreciated (19 May 1941).

He added, 'we were a trifle late in finishing' and that Baxter's closing remarks were made 'to [the] accompaniment of rattling of keys & appearance of further warders to shepherd us off [to our cells]' (19 May 1941). Prison regulations did not attach much importance to the niceties associated with thanking visiting speakers. The lecture had to finish by the appointed time, otherwise the routine and rhythm of the prison would be disrupted.

The next lecture was on housing, presented by government architect Cedric Firth:[7]

> 8.00 pm. Good WEA class. Dr Bill Sutch[8] came as [Firth's] chairman (probably especially to sight us!) About 30 present and interest good. A bright fire moreover! Firth described the standards of housing as accepted by best architectural principles light air sanitation living & playing space etc and agreed that nowhere in the world was the standard anywhere near generally attained or even attempted & that in matter of spaciousness there had in recent years been retrogression (26 May 1941).

Barrington was impressed by the level of audience participation at part two of the lecture the following week:

> Discussion keen. One member of class referred back in detail to explanation given by Dr Sutch some time back re non-ownership of state houses. Firth brought as a chairman one Beech,[9] another architect who has won prize for design for Savage memorial (4 June 1941).

The next was on 'planned marketing':

Very good lecture by Harold Innes[10] last night on [this subject].
Everybody likes his fresh and direct style based on real experience. Good
attendance too (10 June 1941).

'Uncle Scrim' – the Rev Colin Scrimgeour,[11] Methodist minister,
campaigner for social justice and a notable but controversial broadcaster
because of his support for the Labour Party – was due to speak on 22 June.
However, 'we heard he was in Australia' (23 June 1941). Instead,

H.C. McQueen[12] spoke on vocational guidance in New Zealand
attractively and pleasantly with some really bright stories interspersed. It
was a practical branch of education for a prison audience (23 June 1941).

Naturally, the lectures themselves were of variable quality:

Lecturer was Mackay, returning to lecture on freedom of discussion on
air [i.e. radio] but not a very provocative or thought provoking address (4
August 1941).

… for once West wing [i.e. Barrington's wing] was by the blazing fire. In
discussion I published [sic] subversion in prison! by quoting the piece
about Brit-Emp on p.214 and referring to conservative Government
'made possibly more conservative by addition of people like Bevan and
Morrison and the much greater freedom and public vigilance there'.
'Europe in Travail' broadcasts in wartime. Chairman of lecture Tony
Martin a [Radio] 2ZB announcer – suggested that he is the 6.00 am man
(4 August 1941).

Very poor lecture by Ben Roberts MP.[13] His principal authorities for
support of cooperative idea were Duke of Windsor, the King, Duke of
Gloucester, Roosevelt, the quotations usually referring to co-operation
either within the British commonwealth or internationally and having no
reference to the co-operative movement with which he was concerned.
A very unimaginative address for a life-long co-operator. He could have
made it a very human and vivid story. He must have been using an old
address prepared for a Tory audience (8 July 1941).

While some inmates may have had a genuine interest in these topics, for
many the lectures no doubt simply provided a welcome chance to get out of
their cells for the evening and break up the usual lockdown time of 16 hours.
They also provided an opportunity for furtive trading and the delivery of
messages – as Barrington eventually realised:

... lecture nights are useful for passing papers, books etc around as this is the only time people from all the wings are together (4 August 1941).

Prison labour

The other prison buildings referred to in the diary are a printery and a small soapworks, mentioned only in passing because Barrington, along with most other prisoners, was employed on farm work in the prison grounds rather than in the prison itself:

> There is a prison printery – saw three working there. All prison printing is done I believe and also some forms for govt. offices. Soap-making another prison industry & of course making & repair of prison footwear. Most of the footwear is poor – ill fitting heavy hob-nailed (13 May 1941).

The farm work formed part of the prison department's scheme to make its penal institutions self-sufficient, while at the same time engaging prisoners in work that would be physically and morally good for them, thereby enhancing their employment prospects on release. In reality, these tasks simply formed the 'hard labour' component still attached to most prison sentences at that time (including those of Barrington and his colleagues). There were few rehabilitative possibilities in the work they had to perform:

> 1st couple hours we seven transported trays of prison-made sandsoap from drying shed to room where we packed in boxes. All government offices are supplied (women's gaol does laundering for Govt. offices) (13 May 1941).

When this task was finished, they 'continued on to hillside past women's gaol & resumed attack on broom' (13 May 1941). Six days later:

> On our way out this morning we had to carry each a very heavy log from prison to cow shed. As it was mostly uphill, it was pretty strenuous – in fact a bit of a strain for most of us. Usually have a log (not so heavy) or tools to carry the long uphill way home (19 May 1941).

The routine continued each working day:

> All of us after dinner up at cow sheds carried (in short stages) for about 100 yards over rough paddock, two very heavy iron objects, might have originally been a turntable for railway engines (12 June 1941).

> Morning spent weighing pigs again. AHC & I carried a monstrous wool bale sack of cabbage refuse (from Rongotai) from piggeries to cow byres.

(Air Force food waste is brought here for pigs) and after bringing scales by barrow from prison store to piggeries (2 trips had to be made as storeman was not ready) we weighed pigs, put away the heavy weighing crate and took scales back uphill to prison to be met at gate by Mr A with advice that 6 more had to be weighed – and back we went to begin the proceedings again (16 June 1941).

Jim weighed his first load of mangels this morning and by a fluke I guessed 60 lbs [27 kg] which was within an ounce. Our average load therefore for our half mile climb would be about 56 lb [25.4 kg] and feeding a bag to a cow as we have been doing for the 20 cows in mild [sic] would average ½ ton [453 kg] a day. (We carry more than that of course when we have a straight run.) (31 July 1941).

Regulations

The rules were clear enough regarding how and where prisoners were to spend their time: they were to work during the day; they would be in the yards at weekends (seeing visitors or attending church in a different yard were the most usual exceptions to this); and they would be in their cells the rest of the time. How they were to conduct themselves, however, from the rising bell at 6.00 am until 'lights out' at 9.00 pm, was informed by regulations of remarkable complexity. These never seem to have been explained to the inmates, nor were they ever given a copy of them (many would have been unable to read them anyway). Instead, it was assumed that new inmates would automatically fall in step, either because they already knew the rules, having been in prison before, or by observing the habits and routines of those already socialised into prison life. Commands from the warders had to be obeyed without hesitation and without question:

> Baths. Warder R is in charge and affects an air of brusque militarism and regimentation. Marches us to bath and back again, growls about hats (not being worn – against regulations), says '2 minutes for hot and one for cold shower' (21 June 1941).

Barrington came across a full set of the regulations by accident, in the ninth week of his sentence:

> I began to read Prison Regulations which hang on iron grille at entrance to our wing (but which opportunity to read is practically non-existent) while waiting to be let out to yard after writing today. Found that

searching routine is prescribed, also that with consent of controlling officer we may see not more than two people at a time for ¼ hour during week and may see lawyer or his clerk any time (29 June 1941).

Security

The regulations covered matters of security – in particular to prevent the importation of illicit goods from outside. Provision was made for searching prisoners, including strip searches – despite the prison department's reports emphasising the lack of threat to public safety that most prisoners constituted, and the higher levels of trust that now existed in the prisons. Nominally, at least, a prisoner was to be searched each time he entered or left the prison. Given that most were working on the farm, this would mean at least four searches per day if the regulations were followed to the letter. Barrington wrote,

> On nearing cells tonight we were put thru search routine, I think just as a sample in case 'Boss' (referred to unfeelingly by prisoners as 'the snake' – I don't know why) turns up one night. It is supposed to be done every night. One stands facing cell door. Takes off coat, vest, slippers & sox placing all on floor. One then steps into cell, holds up arms for search then turns about for repetition. Articles left are then searched & thrown after one into cell (14 May 1941).

As it was, the sheer impracticality and pointlessness of security procedures meant that the strip searches were undertaken on a rota rather than a daily basis:

> I had heard that sometimes one prisoner is selected in each wing (probably this could be each night & a different prisoner) and is made to strip for search. My door was locked tonight while others were open & I discovered that was the reason. The warder (McL) said I was the victim but he seemed embarrassed & did not insist on stripping, just running his hands over me (28 May 1941).

The regulations spoke to the way in which the prison value system had the power to overturn everything that was taken for granted outside. Barrington learnt that objects considered innocuous beyond the prison walls had to be rigorously scrutinised for security purposes within. What was healthy or necessary outside could be associated with subversion once inside: 'Stamps are almost always torn off envelopes before we receive them. I thought to save stamps but probably in case of messages underneath' (9 August 1941).

Another innovation to me was that as we lined up to come in tonight Mr L made some announcement about toothpaste. I thought he was offering some prison concoction free but as some of us didn't know about it, it was explained that tubes were being offered at 9d each. Appears that no tube may be brought in by individuals or sent in for them either ... because of experience of contraband being inserted. Mr L mentioned cigarette lighters, money etc. and said that even sticks of shaving soap were a special concession as contraband had been found in them (28 May 1941).

Saluting

The regulations played a broader role than simply policing the prison perimeters. They also ordered and insisted that the most banal, taken-for-granted features of everyday life outside were reshaped to suit prison values inside. What would constitute acceptable behaviour outside the prison might threaten its discipline and order.[14] To conform to prison rules, inmates often had to behave in ways that would be considered unusual outside the prison. Instead of greeting the superintendent with a handshake (that 'readiness to shake hands' that Duff had observed), the inmates were commanded to salute him. The chief warder nearly always accompanied the superintendent to enforce the appropriate regulations if necessary, as if it were beneath the dignity of the non-uniformed superintendent to do so. Following one meeting between Barrington and the superintendent, at which he had to explain why a large pad of writing paper had been sent to him, Barrington recorded 'it was for study purposes & [the superintendent] reminded me that I would have to account for every page & that it was really waste paper from a defunct company'. On leaving the room, Barrington was 'called back by Chief Warder as I had forgotten to salute the Super in departing' (19 May 1941).

Inmates had to salute the doctor as well.

Called in for exam waited with AHC & J & others seeing Dr for some reason or other. Dr Brown seems reasonable enough chap. AHC knew him slightly as member Hospital Board which he commented on. Has to be 'saluted' meeting & parting. Stripped naked & fairly thoroughly examined including blood pressure, eye test etc (15 May 1941).[15]

The fact that Carman had known the doctor outside the prison did not mean this formality could be dispensed with. Saluting the doctor emphasised his status within the prison and the altered social relations there.

Bed-making

One of the consequences of stripping personal autonomy from the prisoners – as if they were incapable of making any decision for themselves – was that a child-like dependency was established between them and prison staff. Rather than deciding for themselves how they would make their beds, for example, the regulations insisted that 'the blanket stays on bed covering mattress with one sheet folded to look like a made up bed' (22 July 1941). Barrington described the necessary procedure:

- 3 blankets each folded in three folds
- sheet folded 3 over fold lapping over top folded surrounding blanket, one blanket enclosing 2 others folded in 3 [sic]
- pyjama trousers folded within outer blanket to give a white line round inner blankets
- pyjama coat folded at foot of bed (22 June 1941).

Clothing

The clothing regulations – when changes would be issued, what must be worn where and so on – seem to have been the one exception to the informal rule that prisoners should be told as little as possible. Following the removal of their own clothes during the admission process, the authorities explained what would be provided in replacement:

Prison handkerchiefs are two (per week), large blue cloth squares, fairly coarse & often looking as if used for painting roofs. At least 12" [30.5 cm] square. Hat which must be worn whenever in sight of higher officials & on parade is more or less indescribable except that it is white (more or less) & sound (so are the trousers). Boots are taken off whenever one enters a bldg. If to go to cell for meal or night exchanged for slippers in pigeon hole (corresponding no. of cell, mine 17) and vice versa on going out in morning (13 May 1941).

Later Barrington added, 'we are not allowed our "private clothes" for two months ([and then] for cell and exercise yards only) and the restrictions are such that the only advantage will be the wearing of an overcoat on cold nights' (21 May 1941).

Letters

The regulations stipulated where and when an inmate could write and receive letters, how long they could be and what they could contain. All letters were checked and censored accordingly:

> As to letters regulations provide a prisoner may in first week write and receive (each) 3 letters, apparently to or from anybody & may be visited by relatives. Then there is a gap of 3 weeks after which each week one may write & receive (each) 6 letters to & from non-relatives ... One is asked Friday how many letters one wishes to write & how many pages ... Was allowed to write them in cell subject to censorship & warned that nothing must be said about other prisoners or the gaol (13 May 1941).

Barrington, an avid letter writer, quickly became aware of the rigidity of these rules:

> When we were mustered this morning a warder asked if I had put my name down for letters (i.e. for letter paper to write weekend). I promptly said no & he put my name down. AHC was puzzled & said 'We can't write this week' (referring to 3 week gap) I said 'Shut up!' But Mr L the head warder said 'What's the use of putting your name down. I'll only have to strike it off.' I said 'You wouldn't strike my name off would you Mr L!' We shall see! (16 May 1941).

Still unfamiliar with the ways of the prison, he hoped his own application would slip through unnoticed and he could begin writing letters immediately. His hopes were quickly dashed, however: the prison bureaucracy, while oblivious to such matters as improving lighting in the cells or library facilities, was much too efficient to allow loopholes in the letter writing regulations:

> Wonder if 3 weeks gap will prevail ...

> After dinner. It did and I write no letters this or next weekend. After that I'll be allowed six to relatives and 1 to non relatives. But the problem is that they must (except at great difficulty) be written on Sunday afternoon in a very short space. Letter paper is not allowed to remain in cells overnight. Apparently it is too difficult to keep check of it and if one can write six letters to the same group of relatives & one to someone else, without mentioning anything of gaol conditions or personalities, in the space of about one hour, I shall be very surprised. O & JD today persuaded officials to let them make a start with theirs today (Saturday) (17 May 1941).

Like everyone else, Barrington had to wait until the allotted day to exercise this privilege:

> My 3 weeks gap will be up tomorrow & then I shall be able to exercise my letter writing privileges The conditions are 3 letters 1st week and then after 1st 3 weeks 6 letters to relatives & one to others each week (24 May 1941).

To make sure his date was not overlooked he approached one of the warders:

> Mr L discussed with AHC papers brought in for him & I seized opportunity of mentioning that my 3 weeks up today & asking if I could write a couple of letters to my family tomorrow and Mr L agreed most heartily (26 May 1941).

The regulations stipulated the number of letters that might be sent or received:

> AHC has had one letter stopped that he asked for weekend (out of 3) on grounds that one he sent yesterday counted as 2 because it included a page for his little boy. Mr B either referred the letter to Mr McG or else in Mr LC's absence Mr McG is censoring & himself raising issue. AHC is naturally incensed. I wrote to my three [children] a special letter each for the three of them. Don't see how they can count that as three (25 July 1941).

> On coming in tonight was called into Super's office (also Jack Boal & Jack Ham) ... Jan's letter had enclosed several others which is against the regulations (& they are all counted as separate letters under quota) (19 May 1941).

There were even rules covering the format of letters. Inmates were not to write between the lines on their sheets of paper – as if by squeezing in extra words in this way prisoners might be gaining some sort of unfair advantage. Presumably such small writing would also have made the task of censorship more difficult.

> Deputy Super L remonstrates with me for writing between the lines of my letters to Jan. Letters must be written on one side of page and *on* the lines only. He said I could have had 2 sheets but I thought I was only being allowed one (21 May 1941).

Finally, once an inmate had qualified for the privilege of letter writing, once the number of letters they wanted to send was correct, once they had appropriately lined paper on which to write and did not write between the lines, there were the regulations concerning what they could actually write about. There were to be no references to other people – prisoners or other – who were considered in any way 'subversive':

> Called in to see Mr L (JHW and I) about finishing time. I rightly guessed it to be about my letter yesterday to Ruth Fry of War Resisters International. I was told I would have to rewrite it. In the first place I could not give the prison address, but only a box number at GPO and I could not mention that I am in prison nor mention the others. (I had been very discreet I thought and mentioned none by name) but as Mr L pointed out I was here for subversion & therefore subject to special censorship & Mr McG [the superintendent] would not pass the letter. JHW piped up that he would not then be able to write to his brother overseas but Mr L said there would be no objection – he was here for holding a prohibited meeting & as apparently the word 'subversive' doesn't appear in the sentence it is not subversive!! Such are the ways & the wisdom of officialdom. Don't think I will now write to Miss Fry, not much point! (16 June 1941).

Inmates were to write nothing whatsoever about the prison:

> Mr B came to me in blue with letter in hand after dinner and said I had referred to a prohibited matter – I said to Jane that university people and the W.E.A. should be interested in this *light business?*, [probably referring to lights off early in cell] also carpenters union, especially W.E.A. with its concern for adult education. Mr B suggested snipping the section off as it was at bottom of page and I agreed to save re-writing (4 August 1941).

> Jack Hammerton [sic] has been taken to task for trying to get [a] 'poem' out in a letter (altering real names & Mr L says the chief won't allow it to go). He mentions 'pot' in it and also 'burgoo' (4 June 1941).

'Pot' was an obvious reference to 'chamber pot' and 'burgoo' was prison (and nautical) slang for 'porridge' – clear enough references to conditions within the prison! No reference to 'Mount Crawford' was allowed, however oblique, subtle or even light-hearted: 'Found from Jane that reference on my drawing for children of "me in my private room at Mt Crawford Monastery" had been blacked out' (21 June 1941). There was to be no mention of any legal proceedings – 'JB & JH were "slated" because of trifling references in their outward letters to Supreme Court proceedings or happenings here' (20 May 1941) – and criticism of politicians or their policies was forbidden, even in inward correspondence. On one occasion correspondence to Barrington from his wife was withheld. When it was released to him, he found it included letters she had forwarded from sympathisers – but there was one missing:

> … received Jan's letter and for all the fuss they've made (including retaining it Friday to Tuesday) it is quite a short note, and encloses very ordinary letters from Mrs Maslen & Lincoln Efford. But now I write I recall that it should also have enclosed one from Rev Jordan which must still be retained. Anyway I've permission to write a note to Jane tonight (20 May 1941).

He subsequently discovered the reason for the missing letter:

> I was called in to the Super today to be informed that I could not have Rev CB Jordan's letter as it contained strong criticism of Mr Mason [attorney-general] and Mr Fraser [prime minister] (23 May 1941).

Here was another reminder that going to prison involved more than mere detention; it involved loss of full citizenship as well, and reduced whatever standing such individuals had previously enjoyed.

Finally, the inmates were not allowed to mention that their mail was in fact being censored, no matter how strange their correspondents might find the clipped and extremely narrow contents of their letters.

Reading material

The regulations extended to the content and usage of library books, periodicals and other literature.

> Books will be checked in and out & exchanging one with another is strictly forbidden. Private books, magazines & papers are not to be exchanged with, or lent to other inmates. All private papers & mags are to be returned to chief warder for the Library or to be placed in the inmate's property … No inmate is allowed to have more than 2 library books and 1 magazine in his possession at one time. This does not include educational books (12 May 1941).

There were severe penalties for the misuse of books:

> Burning, tearing or defacing books in any way is strictly forbidden. (NB I notice that marked New Testament in my cell ends half way through

St James Epistle, remainder having been torn out, possibly for toilet &
cigarette paper) and any such offence will render the offender liable
to forfeiture of books or any other punishment permissible under the
Regulations including payment for damage. 'Remember these books are
your friends and you are requested to treat them as such' (12 May 1941).

The final sentence is particularly ironic, given the dishevelled condition and
banal contents of the vast majority of them.

While giving encouragement to prisoner education, the prison authorities
also took it upon themselves to decide what constituted 'appropriate'
material. Any literature judged 'subversive' was subject to censorship and
prohibition: 'Another book banned? Amongst those Ron [?] brought I learn
was Marx's *Poverty of Philosophy*' (12 July 1941).

Visits

Prison staff appear to have taken a more relaxed approach to the enforcement
of visiting regulations. Barrington, on reception, made enquiries as to when
his wife would be able to see him:

Had talks with two warders about visiting regulations, about medical
care of prisoners & about organising concerts among men. Gathered
that wives are never turned away in spite of regulations and that other
visitors allowed fairly liberally. Apparently earlier 'subversive' cases used
to see about 6 a week & when some restraint was applied to give fairer
treatment to others, representations were made to minister resulting in
tightening up of until then fairly lax regulations (15 May 1941).

Thereafter he had regular visits during the week and at weekends. In
keeping with clothing regulations, at the start of their sentence inmates were
forced to suffer the humiliation of appearing before their family and other
visitors in prison-issue clothing, affirming their new status of 'prisoner'.
After three months they were allowed to wear their own clothes for these
occasions – another privilege that had to be earned. Barrington was delighted
when the three months were over:

After dinner the robing-in, in my clothes. A strange procedure and
feeling after nearly three months. Green sports coat, brown pullover, grey
trousers, silk shirt (cream) open at neck. I carried my great coat out to
yard. O always thinks I take colour well and wishes for like coverage! HB
also in green clothes (19 July 1941).

On one occasion the chief warder warned Barrington about waving to his visitors when he saw them: 'Mr B in charge this afternoon [during visits] and first time I'd known him officious – he jumped on me for waving to visitors coming in. Referred to it as signalling!' (28 June 1941).

While Barrington was never allowed to break the regulations regarding letters, once at visits he noted that he 'had four visitors when, strictly speaking, not entitled to any' (17 May 1941). On some occasions the warders were relaxed about the finishing time: 'Mr Mac in charge and [he] gave us a good deal over time' (19 July 1941).

In the absence of the chief warder, the other prison staff appear to have taken a more flexible and humane approach to interpreting the regulations. Here at last was some display of that 'trust' the authorities had referred to in their reports, at least in the small group of dissenters. This meant, for example, that Barrington was usually allowed to hold his children:

> Warder very kindly said I could take Jezabel [his daughter Janet] in [my] arms & did & kissed her. Also P and J [his sons Peter and John] but Jezabel a little overwhelmed by strangeness of surroundings (13 May 1941).

Why were prison staff so tolerant in relation to visits but not letters? It may simply have been that, during visits, warders could observe what was taking place and saw little need to intervene. It was necessary for them to ascertain and censor what prisoners wrote, however, since letters presented a written record of events that could not be falsified. Warders' and prisoners' accounts of visits could be constructed *ex post facto* to suit as necessary.

Inconsistencies in rule enforcement

The complexity of the regulations meant that many of the warders themselves did not seem to know them all, and thus were reluctant to enforce them, or interpreted them differently, leading to inconsistencies and inevitable frustrations for inmates. Knowing the rules about how long a man could spend under the weekly shower ('2 minutes hot, 1 minute cold') was straightforward enough. Other features of prison life were much more complicated, however – letter writing again, for example:

> The vagaries of warders. The 3rd in command (the genial little bewhiskered man – H says he has been 37 years in the service) unlocked us for removal of dinner things and I asked if I could write 2 letters either this afternoon or tonight. He said he knew nothing about it as he was not

the wing officer. (It was then H[ardgreaves] chimed in with his remark about being 37 years in service & still not knowing anything. A certain amount of 'freshness' is possible for old hands and even for us often.) Anyway some time later Mr McG (who *is* wing officer) handed me the 6 pages & 2 envelopes necessary for my purpose and I was able to complete both just in time for tea (5 June 1941).

The regulations for searching were interpreted at will rather than routinely enforced:

Evidence of shilly-shally methods: at least twice Mr MacC has said we should take off our coat and vest outside cell door for search at night. He said one of these days chief could come in and there would be an earthquake. Mr McG has also at times been emphatic so I thought I would make a practice of doing it. And tonight Mr MacC let me into my cell without the slightest investigation saying 'we never search you unless "they" [i.e. chief warder or other senior prison officials] are in the wing. We could of course.' Another night I'll be roared at for not taking my coat etc off. (If there's a change of warder or if Mr L is thought to be about.) (2 July 1941).

Events out of the very narrow range of the ordinary further confounded the staff – as with Barrington's request to be allowed his own radio: 'Jane brought several books and my coat (which I won't be able to wear for some time), also a crystal radio set from Colin Morrison' (31 May 1941). The subsequent delays and confusion over whether he should be permitted to have it became profoundly irritating to Barrington:

I have asked 3 warders about the radio brought in for me yesterday getting a different reply each time. The upshot is that I have to apply to the Super. There's even a suggestion that radios may be banned as 'there are 2 many wires about the place' (1 June 1941).

Having heard nothing more about it for three days, he then made further inquiry:

I took the opportunity of asking about the radio but Mr L said he knew nothing of that. Did it have an aerial? It was all wrapped up & if he'd known it wouldn't have been left. Apparently rights to radio are hedged about. I'll have to see the Super next Saturday (4 June 1941).

After this clearance he was finally handed the radio, on 7 June (only to find, of course, that it would not work without special tuning).

Challenging the rules

It is likely many inmates – in particular those with poor literacy, few if any visitors, and standards of personal hygiene that meant they did not expect regular baths and changes of clothes – probably felt untouched by regulations in these areas. Barrington did not fit this category:

> Put prepared (carefully) case for further extension of light [to the superintendent]. Said he wouldn't grant beyond 9 but I could write to Controller[-General] Dallard if I wished, which I jumped at – as will enable me to state a proper case through direct channels and possibly secure improvement for all serious students in prisons (19 July 1941).

He discovered that making a petition to the controller-general of prisons – going over the head of the superintendent – invoked a further set of regulations, which required meticulous adherence. These were of a complexity that would doubtless put off all but the most determined:

> Greeted by Mr L at dinner time with news that my two foolscap letters to Controller must be in duplicate – so I've had to copy it out occupying most of dinner hour. Evidently however it has passed the Chief – or perhaps they are not allowed to interfere with a letter to the Controller (21 July 1941).

Predictably, he gained nothing from his application. It also led to him being censured for other breaches of regulations that he had inadvertently transgressed in making it:

> Mr G said Mr B wanted me. I marched to office, took off my muddy boots & was going in with him when he asked what I had in my pocket – I thought of onions which were there but he referred to Penguin book which was sticking out – said it was against regs. to take book to work. I said it was in case caught in rain. He repeated that against regs. & told me to leave it in the hall with my wet hat & hanky I was carrying. His concern was that I should march into office with book in pocket. Announce[d] to Super & saluting as required I was informed of a number of things ... Reply to my application to controller re extra light was read out to me. (a) applications on behalf of all prisoners by one will not be considered but only individual applications (b) as lights on at 6.15 am no necessity for me to rise in dark (c) a copy of *Cosmos* [a pacifist magazine] had been sent to me but it had been suppressed. This was evidently the subject of another letter from Controller from which Super was pronouncing (1 August 1941).

The superintendent then referred to a letter Barrington had written to his wife; he was accused of asking her to bring clothes in for Hardgreaves as payment for repairing the radio.

> My letter to Jan would have to be re-written. Reference to another prisoner getting clothes. I said no request there for clothes. He said there had been in the past. I said not through letter. He said if that sort of thing went on would have to have warder stand over during whole visits. Against regulations to refer to prison or prisoners. They [the prison authorities] could do anything necessary for a prisoner including, I gathered, providing clothes. I was not quick enough to say that regs. or no regs. I must help anyone I found in need, whether prisoner or official – for that is my & our position. Dismissed & saluted & departed not at all abashed (1 August 1941).

It later transpired that Hardgreaves was expecting a woman visitor whom he wanted to impress, wearing his new attire:

> Returning to wing Hardy said his 'date' had been stopped as a result & he would not now be allowed to have clothes – which I disbelieve. As he shut me in, Warder McG said that 'these fellows will get some of you chaps hung yet'. I said 'we can take it' (ibid.).

The superintendent's reaction demonstrates the manner in which any unified representations by inmates were immediately broken up: Barrington could request additional light for himself but not for other prisoners. One way to maintain authority in the prison was to divide the prisoners and individualise them. It is also clear that the authorities had gained some knowledge of Barrington's intention to assist Hardgreaves – presumably one of the warders had overheard his conversation to this effect with his wife and then reported it to his superiors. Barrington's subsequent letter to his wife then provided the opportunity for the authorities to remind him of these particular regulations. The superintendent's claim that they could do 'anything necessary' for prisoners seems particularly hollow. It seems more likely that Barrington took it on himself to help his fellow inmate because they were doing *so little*.

It is clear then, that a very large gulf existed between the aspirations of the prison authorities – to develop a more reform-focused, ameliorated prison system – and the reality of prison life. The annual reports merely acted as a frontispiece for a prison system that was badly run down and that seemed to have little purpose other than maintaining its own continuity. The morass of prison regulations not only reinforced the subordinate status of the inmates and denied the warders any initiative, but also solidified the prison's own impermeability.

Chapter 3

Life in Mount Crawford Prison

In the first few decades of the twentieth century the prison authorities in their reports had regularly enthused over the steps being taken towards prison reform and prisoner rehabilitation in this country. Conditions in the prisons were apparently more civilised and humane, and inmates were undertaking good, productive farm labouring work. The contents of Barrington's diary undermine such assertions, however, while simultaneously presenting everyday details of prison life that the authorities chose not to address, or probably did not even consider.

Silence and noise

The unending noise of the prison during the day and its eerie silence at night made a stark contrast. Barrington greatly appreciated the silence, an aspect that led him to compare his prison experience with monastic life. As with monastic rules, so the silence of the prison after dark was a conduit that brought him closer to God:

> The other night following my usual habit I was meditating at my window after the light had been turned off while I was still reading. I was watching the stars … when the fat jolly warder who had switched light off went by outside. Seeing me gazing through window and still fully clothed he came back to ask 'Everything all right in there?' My yes thanks reassured him (24 May 1941).

Such periods of contemplation and calm were regularly interrupted, however:

> … the march past of a warder in the corridor seems to occur at 10 minute intervals with a rattling of keys, sound of unlocking the great grid which shuts off our wing (24 May 1941).

> Someone in the remand cells repeatedly at nights yawns very loudly – to be heard all over wing. I've never heard anything more expressive of infinite boredom (8 July 1941).

The slightest noise in the dead of night boomed and echoed its way round the whole prison:

> A 'remand' man having been sentenced today was standing outside cell door as we were for tea and close up. Already in prison garb he looks a pleasing kind of chap about my own age or year or two older. He told me he was the luckiest man anywhere for Mr Justice Johnston sentenced him only to a year when he was expecting 3 … Later I heard him call him through cell window – like an animal calling its mate. But there was no answering cry (15 July 1941).

Despite these interruptions Barrington seems to have experienced a nocturnal peacefulness. Of course, there was next to no electronic equipment in the cells such as the televisions and 'ghetto blaster' radios that have since become a regular feature of prison life. The reaction to Barrington's request to have his own radio suggests this was a very rare event at that time. To avoid disturbing others, Barrington always listened to it with his earphones on. Perhaps this display of manners was simply a reflection of his upbringing; it might also suggest a more general respect prevalent in those times, for the privacy of others and the right to live free from annoyance and disturbance.

During the day, however, noise was non-stop: marching boots, jangling keys, shouted orders and, above all, the blaring of the prison-provided radio. As the annual reports had mentioned, the institution had its own radio loudspeaker that was switched on at particular times, for example to hear the war news from England. This facility had been part of the drive to humanise prison life. The effect was exactly the opposite:

> The radio is definitely part of the punishment though one learns to ignore it up to a point. Turned on (2YA & 2YO) just before 6.15 tonight for London news (extended) apart from a brief period – a waiting period – of reasonable music – it has been spoken word practically throughout & unintelligible. At present (since 7.45) some affair is being presented which may be VUC [Victoria University College (sic)] Students Extravaganza. It was heralded by National Anthem (some day I'll make an investigation into the number of *patriots* who stately stand in their own homes when they hear it over radio. That's an acid test.) followed by some ghastly music which may have been a college orchestra. Forget whether I've recorded this story – two Americans were being shown over the prison with super (McG & Deputy L) and seeing the loudspeaker in corridor commented to H that it must be a boon. Says H oh that's part of the punishment. When it's on you can't read, you can't even sit on the chamber[pot] (5 June 1941).[1]

His own treasured radio was drowned out on these occasions:

> Was getting very clear reception of London news until that
> unmentionable loud speaker was turned on after which neither those
> with crystal sets nor anyone else could get a word. I led a roar when it
> was finally turned off but it is back on again with Fred & Maggie[2] & what
> not but improved and bearable at moment (24 July 1941).

Standards of hygiene and cleanliness

There were great contrasts between the arrangements for keeping the
prison buildings clean and the facilities provided for the inmates' personal
hygiene. The standard maintained on the wings and in the cells validated the
authorities' commitment to improving the basic conditions of prison life:

> All cleaning of cell is done by regular cleaners who have to keep whole
> wing spick & span & all floors polished. A hearth brush in each cell
> which one brushes crumbs off meal table & floor crumbs into corner –
> only cleaning done by occupant of cell. On leaving cell after breakfast or
> dinner dirty dishes, spoon, fork, mug are placed on floor outside door
> & are later cleaned & dried by cleaners who bring bucket of hot water
> round with them (13 May 1941).

For Barrington, however, the prisoners' own toilet and washing facilities
were 'the worst features of prison life':

> A tiny enamel basin for all washing purposes. I learn from DS that the
> way to wash in it without making too much mess for cleaners is to put
> basin in centre of small floor mat & get down on knees to it & I find that
> works. But with a bath only once a week & all sorts of dirty work to do
> it is inadequate. Whenever one gets near a tap at cowshed or anywhere
> one makes a dash for it. I am very much in need of a bath now but it
> won't come until tomorrow. Had to be examined by Doctor yesterday in
> unwashed state. Then there are no reasonable lavatory facilities except
> at weekends when one is shut in yard. There are open lavatories there
> otherwise one is shut in a cell from 4.10 pm to 8 am with only an enamel
> chamber pot. My first had a hole where handle should be & I had it
> replaced when I found it spilling. And this morning I find the second one
> is leaking. One has to live with the thing for all those hours. It may be put
> in bottom compartment of cabinet with separate door but one's food is
> in compartment immediately above and as John says the smell is liable to
> permeate the wood. So at his suggestion I am leaving it in further corner

near window which opens less than usual bungalow fan light. There is no opportunity of using lavatories on way to work in mornings for there is always a rush to get us marched off to a central place where all are publicly searched & assembled in working gangs. Sanitary arrangements are furtive accordingly! (16 May 1941).

Not only were bathing and showering greatly restricted, but these activities and others, such as stripping in front of the doctor and strip searches on the way to and from work, were undertaken with a total lack of privacy. As Barrington put it, 'baths under Mr McK's eagle eye' (19 July 1941).

A bath or shower might be followed by a haircut or shave, depending on whether or not one was willing to risk the skills of the prisoner-barber – whose level of ability was entirely a matter of luck. George Kelman was on hand to do the work for Barrington on one occasion: 'Good hot and cold shower and scrub and haircut by Kelman' (24 May 1941).

Despite the prison being relatively new, the meagre and broken-down facilities were inadequate for maintaining good personal hygiene. Barrington reported, 'The towel which is changed once a week is [the] size of [an] ordinary tea towel [and of] the coarse variety' (15 May 1941).

The performance of bodily functions became a particularly demeaning and degrading aspect of prison life. Two months into his sentence Barrington observed,

I am a big and clumsy person, never used to 'roughing it', either by camping or otherwise. It accordingly took me longer than most to accommodate myself to some of the conditions here. For instance I have only recently adopted a satisfactory technique for the use of the 'pot' or chamber, which I have not used since infancy and bigness and awkwardness aggravated the difficulty. Probably this accounted for some of the internal difficulties I experienced. The solution was not accomplished before a lot of discomfort and agitating (3 July 1941).

Inevitably, there were accidents in the rush to dispose of the pot's contents at the allotted time:

Started the day very badly indeed. As soon as the cell door is unlocked after breakfast one has to rush out to buckets in yard to empty chamber if used during night. Rush because one has to get back to cell then out again to exchange slippers for boots and be on parade some distance away with all the prisoners for search, detail etc (19 May 1941).

Bedding

Barrington considered the bedding to be adequate but of a low standard and infrequently cleaned, despite the authorities' 'improvements'. On admission he was issued with 'fleecy lined pyjamas, two sheets coarse but clean and a pillow slip, pillow, four upper blankets (most fairly thin), three used doubled on mattress which [is] poor but reasonable if freshly teased' (12 May 1941).

> [T]he blankets get no airing and though I've very little sense of smell, I loathe the smell of the blankets when I tuck myself in at night. I am assured that one gets used to it! We take our blankets into the yards once a week just for a shake, not a real airing (15 May 1941).

He devised his own solution: 'to give more airing, I spread my blankets around the cell floor on arising and don't make my bed until after breakfast'. As for the sheets,

> … one is changed about every three weeks. I've had to adopt a private marking system to know which one to exchange for a clean one. Some of them are pretty worn & I've put a foot through one. Making my bed I've to be careful to put the hole at head end for fear of widening the hole. Both my pillow slips were ripped right down – the material is quite rotten & putting one's washing in them at weekends does not improve them. My laundry no. is 93 & my [allotment] of shirts, underwear, pillow slips, handkerchiefs, bread bags, pyjamas, sheets are all supposed to be numbered & the same ones returned. But there is a good margin of error. I suppose the intention is to track down wilful damage but it would be pretty hard. Men tear off pieces of sheet or blanket etc for their tinder boxes. How they are expected to light their matches, I don't know (22 July 1941).

Clothing

Prison-issue clothing – manufactured at Mount Eden – was of a similar standard. Although described in the reports as being in 'reasonably good state of repair' (although so cautious an endorsement from the authorities should have immediately raised suspicions), it was threadbare and seemingly distributed at random. According to Barrington, the prison boots were 'pitiful objects' (31 May 1941).

Clothing was sent to the laundry once a week, apart from trousers, which were changed fortnightly. What was issued in return was very much a matter of luck and sometimes cause for mirth:

... all clothing changed except pyjamas – trousers especially snowy white (button missing) though underpants too small and my shirt has buttons this time though it would choke me if they were fastened (31 May 1941).

My underpants this week were designed for Fatty Arbuckle (a hint of things to come?) and in the meantime they tend to descend to my knees (13 July 1941).

My underpants had no button & my clean trousers were too tight for my knees to bend or for buttoning up (27 July 1941).

Occasionally fortune favoured Barrington:

... today with clean clothes after bath, I received for first time one of the nice grey flannel shirts with buttons that button right up to the neck and long sleeves which also button (21 June 1941).

It was left to the inmates to remedy the deficiencies themselves, if they were so inclined:

Today borrowing needle & thread from JD I sewed two buttons on trouser fly (which has been a gaping cavity most of week) & another on my waistcoat. Only need to find 2 large buttons for my coat and I shall be a much more presentable person (21 June 1941).

Yesterday at the laundry JD negotiated a coat exchange for me and I have a coat which though it is a little smaller, short in the sleeves, greasy at the cuffs and dirty on one side, at least has pockets which are intact instead of ripping from their bearings (to say nothing of a hole in one) and there are no holes in sleeve (29 June 1941).

Barrington paid the laundryman's bill: 'I gave Davey six matches by way of turning other cheek for loss of coat' (5 July 1941). Laundry workers had limited power to provide more suitable or better-fitting clothing, however, as there simply were not enough warm items for everyone:

Had to take cotton shirt after baths today. Silly but I suppose they haven't any woollen shirts to go round. Wore my other for two weeks. Laundryman was saving me the cook's coat after wash, too, as one I've been transferred to is smallish, but when I went to collect with clean clothes this morning, it had gone (5 July 1941).

Keeping warm

The debilitating effect of weather conditions on the prisoners' strength, vitality and health did not feature in the prison authorities' plans and aspirations. Apart from setting the fire in the common room for WEA lectures, the Mount Crawford authorities do not seem to have done anything at all to warm the buildings. As a result, there was little refuge from the cold inside:

> Most men feel cold here terribly. To offset it they sleep on blankets instead of the sheets, using sheets for extra weight. One blanket is folded on mattress and the others are folded double save the last which enclosed the whole at night (13 May 1941).

> Cells are very draughty. Though doors are massive there must be at least ½ inch gap most way round on each & with window open (it only opens slightly) there is a pretty strong current most of the time. Difficult to sit anywhere at nights to avoid and the current is really necessary for fresh air (15 May 1941).

> I am standing to read, shifting weight from one foot to other in a kind of jig, or sitting hugging both hands, under my arms & rocking myself!' (21 May 1941).

Not only did the sub-standard clothing make a laughing stock of those compelled to wear it, it was often quite inadequate for Wellington's climate. As there was no issue of pullovers, the best the prisoners could hope for was a woollen shirt, which they then hung on to long after it was due to be laundered. Even the dissenters who, with their mainly middle-class backgrounds, would probably have been more fastidious about personal hygiene than many others, tried to do this:

> A very cold day with spots of rain or snow. Impossible to keep warm in yard even by steady walking … Baths were first item on programme and my change of clothes included a return to sleeveless cotton shirt. A bad change in any case in winter from warm full sleeved wool shirt. So handed back the clean one and kept my dirty shirt. With cold [I was suffering from] I thought I'd at least be as I was (28 June 1941).

> JHW was lucky with shirts being handed 2, one cotton, one wool. He kept the wool! He too had retained previous one two weeks rather than change. Found he sleeps in his (presumably plus underwear) finds it necessary to keep warm. Customs here for warmth must be very varied. Past F. Redemption chap I noticed in bathroom had pyjamas under his clothes (5 July 1941).

He subsequently reported:

At change of clothes yesterday it was established that my woollen shirt
of 3 weeks ago was an accident and I am doomed to cotton shirts
throughout. I can take it better than others as I don't feel the cold so
much. I haven't wrapped up for a week or so, though it is sometimes chilly
at night and a long sleeved pullover would make one less conscious of the
body while reading (13 July 1941).

Barrington prepared carefully for his evening's studies:

I have discovered a new and warmer way of wrapping myself up for work
on cold nights. It makes me like a monk, and I have to take up my skirts
when I want to move. But it is easier than loose blankets wrapped around
me. I enfold my trunk and legs in a blanket wrapped right around and
falling over feet and fasten it with my belt on outside. Another folded
blanket goes under feet, and another over shoulders if required (2 July
1941).

When eventually issued with his own clothes, he used these as sup-
plementary bedding and finally found some comfortable degree of warmth
at night:

Very snug & warm on cold nights now with 1 sheet, 3 blankets folded
double, 1 unfolded blanket enclosing the others, my overcoat & my prison
clothes on top of me! (2 August 1941).

Food

The cold and damp gave added piquancy to the prison diet – 'talk turns much
on food here' (27 May 1941). Indeed, food is the diary's most prominent
theme, signifying the extent to which inmates' wellbeing was in the hands of
the prison staff. As meal times approached, they were like helpless animals
waiting with tremulous expectation for feeding time. Food fantasies and
discussions became a way of temporarily transporting themselves from the
prison, at least in their imagination:

JD told me yesterday that where he was boarding in Tauranga for 6 months
his cut lunches were made of bread & marmite & though he likes marmite
that was too much. AHC says they are practically vegetarian at home –
they have meat 3 times a week and only tripe liver and pressed tongue.
Oysters on Sunday. JD mentioned that once only his marmite sandwiches
had meat as well and the combination was good (27 May 1941).

When journey down precipitous tracks with pump yesterday nearly completed & we were resting, breathless & hot, I thought of ice cream & asked Mr MacC whether we were allowed it at Christmas. He said C was a long way off. We discussed raisins, chocolate – Ron pined for dates. AHC usually runs to oysters which he mentioned earlier in the day & as a final choice I essayed a couple of pounds of licorice allsorts (27 July 1941).

That said, food rations were actually remarkably generous, a reflection of the vastly superior diet that many settlers commented on after emigrating from Britain.[3] In fact, Barrington and his fellow inmates each received eight times more than the weekly allowance permitted for the British population as a whole during the war:[4]

Johnson [the] storeman commented yesterday on fact that our ration of butter is 1 lb [454 g] a week & some complain because they get dairy instead of a factory butter (which now supplements the prison supply & there is competition for the small proportion available. H offers it to me as a delicacy.) whereas people in Eng. are now cut down to 2 oz [56 g] a week. We should not complain. (& don't) (20 June 1941).

Barrington also commented on bread-making innovations, intended to make loaves healthier and more wholesome: 'An experiment is being made with what is believed to be wheat germ bread. It is very good' (18 June 1941). He regularly praised the main meal of the day at Mount Crawford:

A fine Sunday dinner. Two chops in addition to a great slice of roast beef. Numerous potatoes (boiled and none of which I ate), cabbage and gravy. And the plum pudding generous and good (17 May 1941).

When working some distance from the prison, inmates would have a picnic lunch in the form of sandwiches; 'dinner' would then be served as 'tea':

Hot tea good tonight too. Cocoa (hot & prison mugs equal about 2 cups) Copious stewed steak, with very copious gravy containing carrot, swede, 8 potatoes. Plus very nice and plentiful apple pie! All hot. Tendency owing to getting 2 courses plus drink all together, to gobble in order to consume all while still hot (13 May 1941).

Initially the authorities also supplemented the diet with a daily apple. However, this was stopped in line with the general food rationing introduced in New Zealand in 1941:

The reduction to one raw apple a week as our sole supply of fruit is just too absurd in fruit producing country whose export has been cut off. Women's Food Value Leagues' Report to minister on wastage of fruit in N.Z. revealing. Speaks of fruit dug in for manure, carted away for pigs or thrown over gulley to rot and instances an institution of 1400 which could profitably use a ton of apples a week over what it can buy (9 July 1941).

For a while their diet was supplemented by pears from the prison gardens, which were liberally distributed:

We were waiting to go into cells with porridge when we were called out again to find that a whole van load of cases of pears had arrived & needed to be brought in. We fell to with a will in spite of cooling porridge. Took at least 20 minutes. One case was broken and we were allowed 2 each. The storeman had already authorised me to have 2 so that made 4! We'll have the remainder cooked tomorrow (29 May 1941).

I've eaten too many pears today! But the opportunity once again was too good to let pass. 6 were issued with dinner but besides eating I should think a couple of dozen during the day I've still 11 in my locker. In the course of the day's travels I was also able to give some to the two warders on 'Lofty lookout' duty, one to Davey of the laundry, 2 each to the men in the soap works, a couple to warder McL and to warder C, OEB & Basil & 1 each to the men in the printing & some to the warder on the gate! And we left a few in a basin in the yard & Mr L coming in helped himself to some of those. And a near full case was carried away I think for Mr McG (19 June 1941).

The main problem with the diet, however, was its inevitable monotony. While the authorities were correct to say the diet was 'plain and wholesome', what they did not say was that the same food was served every day. The standard menu included:

Breakfast: porridge, bread and butter, hash and tea

Dinner: stew (usually made of stewing steak, carrots, swede/turnips and potatoes); dessert (for example, plum pudding); tea

Tea/supper: porridge, cocoa, bread and butter (13 July 1941).

There were sometimes changes to the main course at dinner – chops were once served instead of stew – and at weekends or on Mondays corned beef would replace the stew, much to Barrington's displeasure on one occasion:

'Dinner today was unpleasant for me – cold scraps of corn beef with much fat (others had ample meat)' (26 May 1941).

Nor had the authorities said anything about the unsatisfactory methods of food preparation. The drinking water, for example, was frequently contaminated:

> There is often very thick sediment in the bottom of my (& others) water billy or dipper. As far as I can work out it is not the fault of the cleaners but [it] is impurity in the water. This morning it was so thick that I drew Mr McGs attention to it and suggested a filter (one might as well suggest the moon) I have a drink of water last thing at night & first thing in morning and after shaving and washing I use the last of my water for brushing my teeth before going out in mornings – the only decent cleaning usually possible. But when the sediment is thick I am reluctant to use the last of the water. & could not this morning (3 August 1941).

Barrington also had an aversion to the porridge and initially ate little of it. The reason he found both this and the tea ('so-called', 'foul') so unpalatable eventually became clear:

> … the kitchen has only two boilers, in which porridge, stew etc as well as tea has to be made and no matter how well scrubbed, various fragments and odours combine in the tea. Tea bags are put in the boiling water and presumably stew for a while (15 July 1941).

Food hygiene was also poor, as reflected in the grotesque *pas de deux* that occurred on the wings each morning: a prisoner carrying the slop buckets, into which the overnight contents from the chamber pots were emptied, was immediately followed by another serving breakfast:

> One warder unlocks, slop man passes door. One lets him go if one has to empty vessel oneself later. Take porridge and hash (good) from bearers. Then mug of tea. Another warder locks me in again (14 May 1941).

Health

Even though Barrington was of robust health – he had passed the standard cursory health check at the beginning of his sentence – he eventually succumbed to illness. The cold and diet played their parts, but so too did the conditions in which he had to work:

> 6 pm. Very hard afternoon. Pleasant at first warming up in brilliant sunshine after frost. But then we were more or less slave-driven with

heavy loads of earth on rickety old wheelbarrows, each journey being a considerable distance part up part down hill & part flat – from near pig sties away behind prison right round side to glass house nurseries. The warder (Mr MacC – quite decent out in the hills) I think driven by fear of the 'boss' whose house adjoined the glass house, drove us hard and our unaccustomed muscles were taxed and tortured and we got so hot that now in my cell the cold is intensified as another frost settles in. This will harden us up but we would prefer the process to be a little more drawn out (21 May 1941).

Initially he became physically stronger, no doubt as a result of the manual labour fuelled by substantial meat and potatoes servings in the middle of the day. He even became anxious about putting on weight:

This morning, unloaded a lorry of flour – carrying 7 or 8 200 lb bags off lorry and a short distance then up about 20 concrete steps and into the store. First time I have carried anything of that nature and did it easily – some found it difficult. Definitely getting stronger and was relieved to find at pig-weighing that I am not gaining weight as I thought I was (16 May 1941).

Over time, however, he became progressively run down. He tried to keep his deteriorating health at bay as best he could, even eating the detested porridge:

… with an eye to the vitamins … I even, coming from the so hard toil, sampled a little of the everlasting porridge liberally covered with sugar. I ate some only of the small sample but will try it again whenever strenuous exertion seems to demand the extra nourishment. The mighty are falling indeed! Had bread with my cocoa (and 2 apples later) & am shortly going to indulge in some more bread for supper (21 May 1941).

Inevitably, he succumbed to illness:

Monday night had a buzzing in left ear for hours and have noticed a slight suggestion of ear ache occasionally which I don't remember ever having before. Have a sore developing at corner of mouth and lip slightly ulcerated. Prison diet having its effect I suppose (4 June 1941).

Dinner – Too much meat, potatoes, cabbage. Plum pudding 'tea'. 5 pears issued. My innards still seem out of order. I should probably fast but the coldish weather & hearty exercise outdoors make me eat heartily (8 June 1941).

Developed a sore right eye while at piggeries and it is painful. May be a cold (10 June 1941).

He eventually suffered an attack of influenza:

A most gorgeous day, but I apparently heavy with flu carried on work (hay and cabbage leaves to cows) but easing up and sitting in sun now and again. Afternoon I was put to finally clearing up piggeries muck. Heady, with idea of taking it easy in sun, but it required fairly steady pegging all afternoon, and wind got up chillily later. Managed to get 4 good onions (1 of which I've given to Dave) and JB got me an ample supply of parsley (plus a piece of thyme!). So I've had onion and parsley sandwiches for tea and have onions and parsley for weekend. But I've a thoroughly blocked nose, aches and pains and fever. I've some concoction Mr McG got for me – flu mixture – which I am sipping after tea. I asked for it this morning but I think he'd have forgotten it if Hardy hadn't reminded him for me at dinner time. (4 or 5 weeks ago I asked for ointment for a sore mouth. I haven't got it yet but I've still got the sore mouth (27 June 1941).

The virus left him unfit for work. As he discovered, there were even regulations for illness, primarily intended as a check for malingerers – evidence once again of the authorities' lack of trust in the inmate population, despite affirmations to the contrary in the annual reports. Illness was not to be an excuse for 'rewards' (a comfortable day in bed with a book, for example) and elevated levels of comfort:

A day in bed! and very cosy too with rain and cold outside. It looked like a day off but we were called to parade as usual, in spite of heavy rain in night and continuing drizzle and black skies. I suggested to Warder McG that though my cold was improved a day outside in the damp would not be the best for it so he said to 'go sick' and stay in … I assumed I would just stay in my cell and read. But [the warder] said I had better get into bed and after parade he would bring me some dope. I was reluctant about bed it seemed foolish but I got undressed and abed and he brought a flu mixture and two aspros. I put books and writing materials by my bed ready to make a good day of it, but was disturbed later by Hardgreaves' announcement that under regulations a sick man had his books and clothes put outside door. I promptly hid two books under my mattress just in case … I also learn that the sick go on half rations, but by design or accident only my bread was affected (30 June 1941).

Barrington excused himself from a WEA lecture because of his illness.

I shall miss the lecture tonight. Afraid there would be an uproar if I appeared after being 'sick' all day, though I wouldn't have to go outside and there would probably be a fire (30 June 1941).

In prison, one was either fit for work, or sick and therefore bed-ridden – there was no in-between stage, either in the gestation of illness or the recovery from it. Barrington was well aware that, in the eyes of the authorities, if he was well enough to attend the class, he would be well enough to get back to hard labour the following day.

Work

The physically demanding labour proved too arduous for many mainstream inmates whose various disabilities, infirmities and frailties were often exacerbated by the nature of the lives they had led prior to admission. The dissenters, by virtue of being among the fittest and healthiest of the prison population and with the requisite work ethic as a result of their backgrounds, were often called on for the heavier tasks. The work still proved physically challenging for them. Barrington commented on one new CO prisoner who was at the start of his sentence:

Like us at the start his muscles are not accommodated to loaded barrows & bags of sand etc. Fountain pens don't leave us primed for that class of work (28 July 1941).

Barrington's physical frame (1.8 m tall and over 76 kg) was more suited to labouring. However, it also meant he was regularly singled out for the most demanding jobs:

About 10.15 I was called off by Mr L as a 'strong' man and JH & JB were recalled from woodcutting to go off with Mr B, Price (the prison smith) in a PWD [Public Works Development] truck as far as Borstal. There we found a dynamo weighing anything from 6 or 7 cwt [300 or 350 kg] up. We had to transport it from the top of Mt Crawford by a small sledge over precipitous tracks & open paddocks ½ way down to sea level. There we left it at the power house used for pumping the water supply. From there we took a similar dynamo down to the road at sea level & climbed back up hill in time to be late for dinner which was kept properly hot for us. It was warm & strenuous work (19 June 1941).

Frosty but sunny day. Carried heavy fencing posts up hill to cowsheds. Then loaded pigs. (But I was more fortunate than others & didn't load my trousers with pig [droppings].) Then I collected 6 sacks of big & little beef etc bones scattered all over paddocks by seagulls – some of them of weight hard to believe carried by gulls. No doubt they have spread them abroad by now again. Then mangolds again (24 June 1941).

Furthermore, although the agricultural labour regularly involved very dirty work, there were few opportunities to clean up afterwards, and then in only the most rudimentary of facilities:

We were no sooner out to work than heavy rain set in continuing almost all day, but again holding out until we were out after dinner. Some of us had an indoor job and a dirty one. Transferring fat from huge oil drums to other drums and any containers that could be found – the fat comes from air force Levin and they want drums returned. There is quite an accumulation of them – far more fat being supplied than can be used in making sandsoap. The pumice man was given one whole drum full to help his fire along. The job was dirty, smelly, greasy and steady. JH and HB helped to load more pigs and were given a change of clothes. Ron S. and JW had job of cleaning drums (empties) with hot water at pig sties and they were given change of clothes. AHC also who got thoroughly wet at cowsheds (9 July 1941).

On this particular occasion they were allowed to shower and clean themselves outside the allotted time. In a demonstration of how inflexible the regulations could be, however, they were not allowed to change their wet and greasy clothes:

We also had use of bathroom for hot wash at dinner time short shower at tea time to get grease off … [but] JD, AHC etc were refused new clothes by laundry men although sent by Mr MacC (9 July 1941).

Nevertheless, there were occasions when the work seemed pleasant enough, and the pastoral setting brought its own pleasures and sense of satisfaction:

A beautiful afternoon. AHC, JHW & I broom cutting in a valley. Sun so good we soon had shirts and singlets off and basked in it for couple of hours (15 May 1941).

Sometimes the work provided a temporary sense of solidarity and bonding, and little 'treats', as it were, that pushed to one side the immediacy of imprisonment:

Independence Day! Although showery, a pleasant picnic day for us. We took our lunches (our bread and butter plus a 'ration' of cheese) down to pines where we were cutting before and had an industrious day. AHC worked at wool sheds but joined us for lunch. JB remained at jail carpentering. We made a roaring fire to boil the bucket and had very good cups of tea and much toast. We were sitting round fire enjoying these things (having stopped early) with Mr Mac having his some distance off, when the big road gang under Mr McK came marching up the hill – they had much further than us to go but were returning for dinner. They cast envious eyes at our enjoyment and we exchanged verbal fire, even to offering Mr McK a cup of tea which he declined but politely (4 July 1941).

As with other specialist jobs such as in the prison laundry and kitchen, some of the agricultural work required particular skills and brought perks to match:

Afternoon on pigsties & very little progress owing to feeding & need to keep sties dry for night. The pig men have a copper [kettle] always boiling & owing to special hours they are allowed to make a cup of tea. HB & I had one with them, sugarless but good. They also have extra rations of tobacco as [do] head cleaner, soap men, yard man (29 May 1941).

More often, however, the onset of winter not only made labouring difficult but also ensured that prison life as a whole became more uncomfortable. In addition to the penetrating cold, there were no facilities for drying clothing:

Once more it has rained heavily all night and now holding off after breakfast (porr. hash tea bread) We did get half or ¾ extra inside though – and then as we'd settled down for the morning we were called. Carted hay all morning, the cowshed being empty. We'd suggested to no avail that it should be filled while weather and hay were dry – to no avail. So we carried wet hay. Now the rain is coming down – for once at the appropriate time – just as we are due to go out after dinner. Later: nevertheless, we were called out as usual for line up and search and then put in yard to see if weather would clear – and remained there all of a wet and windy afternoon. Most of us wet with boots on (10 July 1941).

At times the work became physically dangerous, although the prison authorities seem to have been oblivious to this:

Engaged all day digging up and carting by barrow the piggeries manure heaps ... Had to take through garden fence and down steep path whose natural slipperiness was increased by previous night's rain. The barrow raced away & had to be braked by own velocity – with bearer sliding with it (25 June 1941).

Furthermore, they were given no protective clothing:

My hands are quite sore tonight from toiling with the dynamos & then carrying the cases of pears the long distance by wooden stretchers and they're grimy with oil from the dynamos. It is very cold tonight and that accentuates soreness of hands especially cuts & scratches. A knuckle of my right forefinger, which has been in trouble on a number of occasions since coming here, was gashed & bleeding again today (19 June 1941).

Farming practices, prison style

The authorities had claimed that prison-farming efficiency 'compares favourably with free labour standards'. At a time when maximum productivity was obviously needed for the war effort, however, much of the farming was wholly inefficient and haphazard:

Jim D says with proper farming the prison farm could be made self-supporting – apparently no system at all. An occasional bag of super [i.e. fertiliser] whereas a good quantity required per acre. Acreage of paddocks not known even (15 May 1941).

We also loaded a lorry with pigs today … Lorry could not back into load, so had to catch and carry the heavy pigs by four legs upside down and lift over rails into truck. Pigs have a pretty muscular kicking capacity … Yesterday talked to P.W.D. man who suggested from his own observation that lots of improvements could be effected in work here (8 July 1941).

Even to those with little knowledge of farm production, it was obvious how efficiency could be improved:

Continued hand weeding the plantation this afternoon … We employed sharpened little sticks to help extract the weeds – with tools we could have done three or four times the area (20 May 1941).

Inefficiency and wasted effort typical with the weighing of the pigs. It would be simple to mark them with a number and keep a tally of each weighing. The methods are most cumbersome and roundabout (3 June 1941).

Afternoon – first finishing paddock of turnips for cows – most stupid was going minutely over the field picking up decayed pieces and stale turnip tops & adding to store for cows instead of leaving to be dug in. Then the others went to another turnip field beyond vegetable gardens and again carried turnips by bags on their backs a ¼ mile [400 m] uphill. Meantime I again scraped the floor of the hay shed and sifted the remains for grass seed! (11 June 1941).

Noon. A hard morning but with collective hand-cart instead of individual wheelbarrows. Very cumbersome & too heavily laden with the good earth and a much longer uphill than yesterday. A reasonably good horse & cart could accomplish six times as much with ease. But no horse is kept on this 80 acres and I suppose manual labour is always available (22 May 1941).

When tools were provided, they were often hopelessly antiquated and broken down. As Barrington notes, 'all tools and other equipment & outbuildings here of the most primitive character' (21 May 1941). He also records some warders expressing complete disinterest in farm work; others had no farming background at all:

Mr McC referred to labour spent on Mr McGs car etc and road approaching his place and impossibility of getting anything done for farm, even to a sack of bran for cows. He was not interested – the milk and butter had to be produced that was all (8 July 1941).

The warders' lack of affinity was reflected in their treatment of the animals they were tending:

AHC & Ron S afternoon removing the offensive manure heap (product of pig sties) from outside to inside veg. garden precincts. AHC nearly sick with odours. Even a dead pig had been thrown in with offal instead of decent burial (14 May 1941).

Twice today Mr A displayed evidence of bad temper. When dealing with the pigs, their habit of biting stronger pigs seemed to infuriate him (as it had the other day when he went into a sty & savagely kicked the pig which had been set on by the others apparently thinking it had caused the trouble). Today he not only kicked savagely but also laid on with his fists (not that they could make much impression on a pig's hide) and in one of his thrusts caught a pig's teeth which scored his hand somewhat (4 June 1941).

... at pig sties to help with a sow being separated from sufficiently mature litter & objecting strongly. Had trouble with her & added to it by young pigs from another litter being put in with hers & then she breaking into them. Danger of her killing others. Very difficult to deal with the monster. Mr A & Mitchell got at her with staves, but my ruse of a bucket of food succeeded & later we got her safely to new quarters (11 June 1941).

Inevitably, these poor farming methods were manifest in the quality of the livestock. According to Barrington, the cows were 'a very scraggy mixed lot of all breeds & none' (15 May 1941).

Overall, everyday life at Mount Crawford was far removed from the impression given by the authorities – of a thriving and efficiently run farming industry that also restored prisoners to health and vitality. In many ways, it was exactly the opposite: the farm functioned *in spite of* the broken-down machinery, antiquated methods, wasted energy and disinterested prison staff. The prisoners had plenty to eat but the monotony of the diet proved debilitating and dispiriting, and they performed their work in ill-fitting, unsuitable clothes in conditions more conducive to ill health than good. If the weather was sufficiently inclement to disrupt the working day, the inmates were still made to spend their time huddled together in the exercise yards, which were open to the elements. The annual reports conveyed nothing of the drab monotony of prison life, where every day was entirely and deliberately predictable. Any departures from the routine in which everyone had a set place and set tasks to perform, from the point of unlocking in the morning to lights out at night, would immediately cause suspicion and investigation:

Last night while others at [the lecture] I heard warders K & W open a cell door on the opposite side of [the] wing and ask someone about a dozen times, 'What were you doing up there? You must have been doing something up there', without seeming to get any satisfaction (1 June 1941).

Despite the intended reforms of the twentieth century, the prison had in fact lost very little of the uniformity and predictability associated with its late-nineteenth-century administration. Incarceration was no longer designed to terrify prisoners away from crime and relentlessly crush any recalcitrance they might display, yet the underlying traditions and conditions were still in place, corrupting, narrowing and diminishing the supposed reform initiatives. Any real prospects for reform were negated by the debilitating environment: a cold prison made colder by the unrelenting dampness of the Wellington winter; ramshackle farming practices; spilt or overflowing chamber pots; tea that tasted like porridge and porridge that tasted like tea; and disinterested warders supervising work about which they knew or cared little.

JESUS OF GALILEE

By
F. Warburton Lewis

1931
IVOR NICHOLSON AND WATSON
LIMITED   LONDON

Archie Barrington in 1949.

PAColl-10354-1, Alexander Turnbull Library, Wellington

Left and following pages: This copy of *Jesus of Galilee* by Warburton Lewis (1931) contained Barrington's diary notes from 12 May 1941 to 13 August 1941.

MSX-8144-Cover, MSX-8144-150, MSX-8144-152, Alexander Turnbull Library, Wellington

i

they had not known it was true ; they would not have believed it to be true if they had not known that the man who was telling the story knew all about it ; it was an impossible story to invent, and, if true, it was an impossible story to tell unless he had the evidence on the spot. He had only to turn aside his tunic to show the wound marks. They all knew that the story was history.

It was only a month or so before that he had passed into a Samaritan village and out again because they would not receive him, but you cannot indict a nation ; a nation consists of men. Jesus was rescued from death by a Samaritan, and here Jesus holds up the deed of this man from a nation that was accursed in their eyes as an example in the art of religion.

And he is a business man to boot. There is in the narrative a word that indicates that he is going on a business journey ; he is going to a market ; but that sight in the ditch there, that wounded man, makes him forget all about his market. And he does not just leave him there and report ; he attends to his wounds, takes him to the inn, spends the night with him, sees him come back to life, and leaves a " blank cheque "—" whatever you spend more, I will repay when I come next time." Evidently a man of known probity, this, whose word is as good as his bond. And when he went back to those other things he had left, it was to a sweeter market, and a sweeter heart that he took there. He " felt good " all the next day, because he had " wasted time " on a man who had no claim, because he had lost a market and had gained a friend.

The story ends at Martha's house. It was with Martha that they left Jesus at the end. The seventy were afield preaching the Gospel. Jesus sent word to the nearest, and they carried him away to Martha's house. "A certain woman named Martha received him into her house," and nursed him back to health and strength again. Do not forget Martha. She may be dense, I know, but she received him into her house and cared for him.

I wonder what those two men said to each other when they parted. I wonder what Jesus said to the Samaritan before he left the room. He said something, for the Samaritan went to the innkeeper and said : " Take care of him." The Samaritan had discovered something. Jesus was alive enough to make that Samaritan know that he had found a friend whose life was needed.

Luke x. 38.

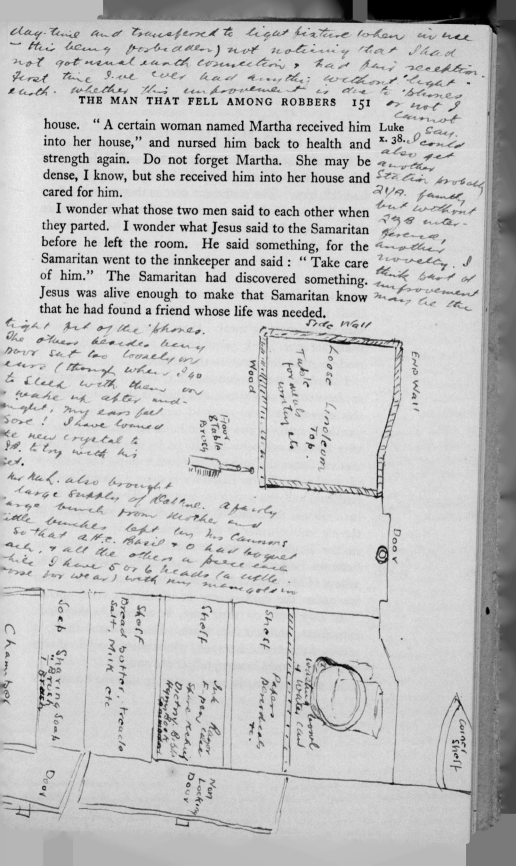

Ormond Edward Burton.

½-152915-F, Alexander Turnbull Library, Wellington

Barrington with his young son John at an anti-war meeting at the Basin Reserve, Wellington, 1940. *PAColl-1035-4, Alexander Turnbull Library, Wellington*

Barrington leading a pacifists' march in Nelson, c.1945.

216382, Geoffrey C. Wood Collection, Nelson Provincial Museum

Barrington (second from right) meets Indian Prime Minister Pandit Nehru at Government House in Delhi, 1949.

F-37733-1/2, Alexander Turnbull Library, Wellington

Barrington meeting Chakravarti Rajagopalachari, Governor-General of India, in 1949. *PAColl-10354-2, Alexander Turnbull Library, Wellington*

A typical cell in Mount Crawford.

Dylan Owen, PADL-00814, Alexander Turnbull Library, Wellington (32050894)

Opposite: The prison's exercise yard.

114/105/01-G, Alexander Turnbull Library, Wellington (22839389)

Mount Crawford Prison, Wellington, where Barrington kept his diary.

EP/1958/1411-F, Alexander Turnbull Library, Wellington (22776398)

The prison's extensive vegetable gardens, maintained by prisoners.

114/105/02-G, Alexander Turnbull Library, Wellington (22738307(1))

Two Mount Crawford Prison officers, 1950.

114/104/04/21-F, Alexander Turnbull Library, Wellington (23209778)

The censors took exception to Barrington's reference to 'Mt Crawford Monastery' in this drawing Barrington made to send his children.

MS-Papers-5312-01-1, Barrington family, Scrapbook of communications from A.C. Barrington, Alexander Turnbull Library, Wellington

Pages x–xii: A selection of Barrington's prison drawings for his children.

MS-Papers-5312-04-1

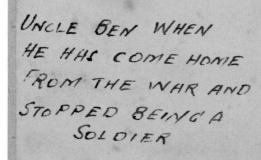

UNCLE BEN WHEN
HE HAS COME HOME
FROM THE WAR AND
STOPPED BEING A
SOLDIER

MS-Papers-5312-01-4

John Peter & Jezebel playing in the band for Daddy coming home

MS-Papers-5312-03-6

POOR MR. WORLD
HAS BEEN WOUNDED
IN THE WARS
HE FEELS VERY
SORE AND SAD
AND MISERABLE
AND WORRIED
HE DOESN'T
KNOW WHAT WILL
HAPPEN TO HIM
WITH PEOPLE
FIGHTING ALL OVER
HIM.

MS-Papers-5312-05-4

Chapter 4

Prison Staff and Officials

How did the prison staff and officials go about their work? The annual prison reports say little about the accomplishment of these tasks, only raising periodic concerns about the poor quality of warder recruits. Barrington's diary illuminates this hitherto hidden aspect of prison life in this period. We see the rigid class and status distinction that existed between non-uniformed and uniformed staff and officials; we see the arrival of members of the Prisons Board to make parole adjudications and the disruption this caused to the routine of the prison; and we see the warders, nearly all of whom were unenthusiastic about their work and who also participated in an illicit working culture using prison labour for their own private purposes. Yet we also see little hostility between the prison staff and the pacifists – indeed, the latter were treated as a 'better class of prisoner'. Much to the distaste of nearly all the warders, one violent incident did occur. This appears to have been a highly unusual event in Mt Crawford, so much so that an inquiry was immediately set up to look into the matter, only to effectively deny it had ever happened – thereby ensuring that the prison system could continue to meander along its dreary course.

The superintendent

Described by Barrington as 'a very self-conscious, shy looking man … am told he has no conversation – in other words finds it difficult to express himself' (15 May 1941), the superintendent's status was signalled by his lack of uniform. The prison service provided his accommodation:

> … we were working close to the Super's house and main entrance to the prison. The house has naturally very well kept grounds and a magnificent harbour view (20 May 1941).

The superintendent was heavily engaged in front-line interaction. With no broader managerial responsibilities to perform (his budget, for example, would have been determined for him by central administration), he was very visible to staff and prisoners and was regularly involved in the minutiae of day-to-day decision-making. He routinely visited inmates who had reported sick. Barrington was warned of this in advance when he became ill (although in this instance, the superintendent's deputy stood in for him):

> H said that when the Super and L came on their round at 10.30 that would happen. However today the Super didn't come – Mr L strolled in and demanded loudly at my open door 'what's the matter with Barrington?' I said just a cold but unadvisable to take it outside. He asked if I had had some stuff and I said I had been nicely fixed up and that was all (30 June 1941).

The superintendent's proximity to the front line seems to have contributed greatly to the warders' tendencies to refer any ambiguities in the all-pervasive regulations upwards for adjudication, as we saw in Barrington's application to have a radio in his cell. In this way, the immediate presence of the superintendent perpetuated the warders' lack of initiative as they went about their work:

> Jack H had a birthday recently & his fond aunt sent a large square of iced fruit cake for him. The night Mr L gave me my pencil, he taxed J about the cake. Said he 'a cake has come for you.' J grinning 'that's very nice.' L 'yes nice to *think* about it. It's not allowed.' J 'what's to be done about it?' L 'I'll ask [the superintendent]', possibly as to whether J could have it. But later he says no and what about it. All they can do with it is put it with his belongings. J asked if he could see it & it was carefully unwrapped & shown to him (6 June 1941).

> Last night Basil's light failed about 6.20 pm and he was in darkness remainder of evening and morning. Warder was sorry but apparently has no power to supply a new bulb (27 July 1941).

The visit of the Prisons Board

Once a year the rhythm of the prison was interrupted by the arrival of the local Prisons Board. Its purpose was to adjudicate on early release applications (on the basis of good behaviour), and parole applications both for those serving the indefinite sentence of reformative detention and those who had been declared 'habitual criminals' (another form of indefinite sentence, made available under the Habitual Criminals Act 1906). The board comprised a judge of the Supreme Court, the controller-general of prisons, a doctor, and two or three other members of a non-official nature appointed by the governor-general.[1] Barrington noted the change in atmosphere when the board arrived at Mount Crawford. Showing due deference to their superiors, both inmates and warders were appropriately clothed and coiffured in a bid to ensure they appeared 'at their best' in front of board members – although as soon as the inmates had been interviewed, things immediately returned to normal:

> There was great commotion when we came in tonight. The Prison Board was in session reviewing sentences – in the meeting room which separates our wing from administration office. There was Mr L in resplendent blue outside door & a row of prisoners. The prisoners who went before Appeal Board on Friday were carefully cleaned up first, exchanged their dirty trousers for clean ones and after changed them back again! (10 June 1941).

The warders were usually oblivious to the everyday noise of the prison and the prisoners' demeanour. Now they were anxious: extraneous sounds from outside the room or insufficient gravitas shown to the board could be interpreted as a lack of respect for such high-ranking officials, with likely detrimental effects on those making their applications:

> We were kept outside until the way was fairly clear and the position was explained to us by Mr T who impressed upon us to be very quiet. I asked should we not go in sounding very happy & Bluey (as the red haired lad is called) pouring out my cocoa said H was in trouble for 'something he said in there'. His tongue probably gets well away with him (6 June 1941).

There was a two-stage process to the board's adjudications. First, the applicant made a cursory appearance before the officials, something Burton[2] described as akin to 'shelling peas'. When Barrington was in Mount Crawford there were six applicants; each had on average less than 10 minutes to convince the board they should be released. The decision hinged on how much of his sentence the applicant had already served and the impression he gave during the interview. In an era when prison 'paperwork' was kept to a minimum, it is not surprising that the board was able to get through its business so speedily: decisions required no elaborate written justification, as the applicant had neither the right of appeal nor any right to see the papers.

The second stage involved publication of the results. When these were posted on the prison notice board, the inmates gathered round to note the respective successes and failures before exchanging congratulations or commiserations:

> Excitement in the precincts today because some have been given 'a date' – that is Prison Board have granted a remission fixed date of release. Davey (whom I thought was Ashton but he is the nurseryman) the Presbyterian helping the laundryman will go in 2 months & learns at same time that a friend in High Commission Office has agreed to act as escort for his wife & daughter from England. Bill Mitchell the pig man is very pleased because his remission is one half and he will go in October (he works long hours with the pigs). Harold Hardgreaves may go as soon as he can get a job with overseas boat, so now he is moving heaven & earth – we've all to try to get in touch with friends & he is busy writing to Mr Butler – justice & what not. Difficulty is to know what recommendation one can give. I asked Mr A and he advised to leave matter alone. But will do anything I can. He says the authorities will get him fixed up. But I expect they move very slowly … Of course there are disappointments too. Sid Harrison did not get a date but possibly because it came too soon and one of the Maoris [sic] hoped to get one but did not. The other of the two working with the cows, a nice looking lad, comes from Wairoa & is here for three years (20 June 1941).

Some were resigned to the news, as in Barrington's description of one man: 'The lanky & lean and staggery looking hard shot who staggers in and out with washing for the clothes lines, didn't expect a date because his record is too bad, there is breaking & entering on it' (20 June 1941). Such inmates might put on a fatalistic show of disinterest to conceal their disappointment, like another whose application was declined: 'He was telling us yesterday the last war made a wreck of him so that nothing but liquor matters to him' (20 June 1941).

Uniformed staff and their work

Beyond the concentration of authority in the superintendent, there was a lengthy model of uniformed line management in place: the deputy superintendent, the chief warder and the front-line officers or warders. Promotion to the two senior uniformed positions would have been on the basis of length of service and a rigid, unblemished compliance with and enforcement of prison regulations – however illogical, contradictory or unnecessary these were on occasion. Rule enforcement, which effectively stripped warders of initiative and perpetuated their inability to engage in reform tasks with the inmates, was paramount. For example, coats could only be worn at certain times, no matter how cold the weather might be:

> On the wild & woolly day which was yesterday Jim was among those who decided to brave the elements in the yard for a while. He is also one of those now permitted to have own clothes. So naturally he put his heavy coat on to go to the open yard. But the warder (Mr W) said private clothes were only allowed at weekends and waited for him to take it off & go to yard without it! J elected to change his mind & stay in cell (6 June 1941).

One man's refusal to remove his coat when outside the permitted times led to a spell in the 'dummy':

> Today our 8 was amalgamated with another gang to make 14 under the rather genial Mr A. He is a warder who visited Webb St Church after OEB was gaoled last year with relatives and came in for supper afterwards. A man in the gang who has served 3 months of a year's sentence & whom I discovered to be pining for Opotiki, said that Mr A had put a man in the 'dummy' today (solitary confinement, bread & water, no bed clothes) … The reason given was that the man wouldn't take his coat off (23 May 1941).

Even small, harmless and comforting acts were subject to control, such as feeding the birds that fluttered around the cell windows or on the prison lawns. Barrington had begun to throw bread to sparrows shortly after commencing his sentence, but later wrote,

> I saw Mr McL blowing crumbs from my window sill outside so later his request that I stop putting bread outside the window … was not unexpected. It makes a mess. I continue to feed sparrows in the yard. In any case my window is too public to befriend birds. There is usually someone rushing past. Sid Harrison's on the opposite side opens on to a deserted area and yesterday a sparrow came right into his cell (1 June 1941).

There is no further mention of feeding birds. The bird droppings would obviously have tarnished the standards of hygiene in the prison – the same standards that permitted the morning's slopping out in conjunction with the serving of breakfast.

Similarly, warders rigidly enforced lights out at 9 pm. Barrington complained, 'Warder A is on night duty & our lights are turned out with disgusting but efficient promptitude' (30 July 1941). Inmates were also forbidden to talk to members of the public who came by when they were working outside, and were prevented from doing so by the warders: 'Our work lying on the road through veg gardens was full of incident. Occasionally men or women passing to visit gaol ... late afternoon Mrs Lane stopped to talk to Basil but was shooed on by Mr C' (26 June 1941). Even waving to distant passers-by was frowned on: 'Hailed schoolboys away below on road to Massey Point, but found from Warder that any such contact even at a distance strictly forbidden' (13 May 1941).

In such ways, the warders remained preoccupied with enforcing and policing rules and regulations that were petty but at the same time essential to the administration of prison life at that time. Not only were the inmates separated from the outside world, but their living arrangements also had to be different from and more restrictive than any found beyond the prison. Unsurprisingly, given the nature of the warders' work, Barrington was in concurrence with the prison authorities, finding the warders to be 'a fairly undistinguished bunch' (24 May 1941).

Characteristically, however, the tone of the diary is one of empathy rather than scorn for them. Barrington frequently commented on what could only be the miserable conditions of the warders' employment. In addition to tasks such as supervising and watching male adults bathing themselves, warders also had to maintain intrusive surveillance on them even while they were in their cells. This remained the defining feature of the warder's job, irrespective of the more productive role the prison authorities had envisaged for them:

> 8.05 pm and the peephole has just been employed but I waved my pen [to indicate that I was writing letters] and the warder passed on (13 May 1941).

> All my last two conversations with [Warder] H have taken place through peephole – only one of his eyes being visible! Who would be a warder? (5 June 1941).

Like the inmates, the warders also had to live with the deficiencies and shortcomings of the prison environment. In the mornings they had to accompany and supervise the prisoners tasked with bringing the slop buckets along with the breakfast trolley. When Barrington dropped his full chamber pot, the duty warder supervised the clean up:

My rush with a full chamber caused it to catch the iron door in passing with disastrous results – all over my floor & corridor. I had to set to work & clean up a very nasty mess. I was locked in with the freedom of corridor & cell while the others paraded. The warder (W) was decent & did not complain beyond saying 'Jesus!' and saw that I got clothes for the job (19 May 1941).

Indeed, sometimes the warders had to endure even worse conditions than the inmates, as Barrington noted on a day when the weather was so bad it not only forced the abandonment of work but also allowed for an optional retreat from the yards to the cells:

From my window I have just seen that one [warder] is on duty on the exposed platform above the exercise yard in this blizzard (5 June 1941).

And while inmates were in the yards the warders had to watch them, with even less shelter than the prisoners and with nothing to help pass the time:

Amongst AHC's mail yesterday was a copy of the *Annual Rugby Guide* which he has edited or co-edited for years. We passed it up to the yard – watching warder up above us. His is a most miserable job up there even in fine weather. He has to record the fact every time a prisoner is let in or out of a yard (keeping a stock a/c), keep watch over the whole eight yards, not reading or conversing with prisoners. Prisoners have a better time than he! The first Saturday I was looking at *Auckland Weekly* in yard & he asked me to turn round so he could see the pictures too from aloft & I read the titles out to him (18 May 1941).

For some warders, discretion became the better part of valour when the weather made conditions utterly wretched for both the workers and those supervising them. They simply wandered off on the pretext of having other tasks to complete, leaving Barrington and his colleagues to perform their work as they liked. Presumably, and in keeping with the assurances of the authorities in this respect, the warders did indeed trust the prisoners not to follow suit. In reality though, their actions were a demonstration of the thin attachment that they had to their employment, and the shabby, cheerless nature of much of it:

A very wet day but Mr McC has us out as usual. Even [the superintendent] said to him at parade 'It's pretty wet to have them out this morning isn't it?' Mr McC: 'It is a bit dark.' Mr McG: 'See that they don't get wet.' When Mr McG unlocked us I said: 'we're not going out today are we?' He said 'Mr McC can't do without you.' I said: 'He doesn't like working inside.' Mr McG: 'That's just it, dodging jobs.' And what a job for a very wet day with tracks to cow shed just a morass & bog & through a hill top water lying everywhere: we had to fill & carry to outside prison ten sacks of cow manure (well pressed) from most ancient section of manure heap. When we were all loaded, Mr McC disappeared inside saying he had to do his books, telling us to carry cabbage leaves to cowsheds after. We had about 16–20 sacks of cabbage & cauliflower heads to take up the same muddy way & put in cow bins (1 August 1941).

Despite sharing the prison deficiencies with inmates, warders would also regularly remind them of their respective positions in its power structure with key jangling and other signs and symbols of their authority:

Warder R in charge & affects air of brusque militarism & regimentation, marches us to bath & back again, growls about hats, says 2 minutes for hot & 1 for cold shower etc but I think is all right under the façade. Told me not to 'sir' him but to call him 'officer' (21 June 1941).

Another way of demonstrating this was to put prisoners in their place, quite arbitrarily and preferably in front of a crowd of their peers for maximum impact, as during one of the WEA lectures:

One bad break came when Mr L stood up in all his blue majesty and interrupted the proceedings to threaten men in the back row that they would be put out. They could either ask questions or he would boot them out. Evidently they were talking among themselves a little, possibly about the lecture, though they were not disturbing the class. The way it was done was bad, especially for the lecturer and chairman (4 June 1941).

On other occasions warders used their authority to cause maximum irritation to the prisoners, sometimes without any apparent thought to the consequences of their action. While an extra 10 minutes with their own families in the course of a day probably meant nothing at all to the warders, it was a much greater matter for inmates to be deprived of 10 of the 30 minutes they were allowed to spend each week with their visitors:

Warder McK arbitrarily decided to shorten visits because people were waiting – must have cut us at least 10 minutes out of 30 we are entitled by law (5 July 1941).

There is no evidence in the diary of any warders having the military background usually associated with the role at that time.[3] If they had, perhaps this would have given them more of an affinity for wearing the uniform, saluting and so on. Instead, they came from an assortment of nondescript civilian backgrounds. Barrington learned, for example, that:

> Mr A was with Mr McG at National Park. His wife I think must be second for they were married only 1936 & that would explain why his daughter lives with her grandmother. Said they lost a baby and Mrs A is only now recovering. Told AHC that when depression started he was running a billiard saloon & making £15 a week (12 June 1941).

The warders, observing Barrington and others busying themselves with education in their spare time, responded with bewilderment, suggesting they had little experience of such activity in their own lives:

> Tonight it seems the friendly Mr W has gone off and Mr S one of the newer warders has come on with Mr K. After the peephole inspection by Mr K I heard Mr S. ask 'What are these jokers studying? and the reply was 'Goodness only knows' ... The question may have been 'What are these jokers studying for?' (2 July 1941).

The dreariness of their working days was no doubt exacerbated by fielding regular questions from inmates regarding the omnipresent and apparently illogical regulations, over which the warders had no control, and about matters that would have been inconsequential to them even though of importance to the inmates:

> HB bailed up Mr L this morning about his clothes and is to be given them this weekend. He will have been here eight weeks on Monday. It appears that gloves are not permitted. O was refused his but got a warm scarf. Sid H got his gloves by accident as they were in an inner pocket of his o/coat (11 July 1941).

They also had to deal with complaints from prisoners, which no doubt only brought home to them the wretchedness of the prison conditions and the environment in which they had chosen to work.

> In the yard alone with Mr L, Jim D apparently bearded him about the impossible tea which Mr L said he would look into, though he said he usually tastes it. Jim also made the bright suggestion that the skim milk (or part of it) after separation of morning cream for butter be used for making the evening cocoa instead of water. And it seems that Mr L agreed to try this, to the extent of a gallon or two (19 June 1941).

Although they were supposed to police the all-pervasive regulations vigilantly, to actually seek out and react to every infraction would have made their work impossible. Most, it seems, chose not to pry too deeply into what the inmates were doing, as long as security, safety or prison routine were not ostensibly put at risk. When the head warder, Mr L, came back to inspect the cocoa,

> … that made things slightly embarrassing as he being present the warders expected us to take off coat & vest for a search & JH had 3 fair sized onions as well as pears in his pockets! I too had pears and a small onion I'd found neglected in dug over patch. So I had onion sandwiches for my tea! Good again. The embarrassment passed as Mr L was engaged in conversation! (19 June 1941).

On another occasion Mr L, on overhearing a new inmate's request to trade Barrington's tobacco ration, simply gave voice to his indignation rather than commence any formal proceedings:

> Waiting in line for our tea tonight a newcomer not yet changed into prison clothes with Mr L standing right alongside breezily asked if I had any tobacco I'd like to trade etc, to Mr L's interested amazement. Mr L said what do you think you're in here for 7 days for and he replied a holiday! 'Trading' is of course strictly forbidden but a good deal of swapping goes on. Even our swapping of books and papers is against the rules (7 July 1941).

It often seemed that the rules and regulations that were supposed to hold prison life together were simply not worth bothering with – as if the warders themselves had little faith in their validity.

'Perks of the job'

Another factor discouraged the prison staff from prying too deeply into the under-life of the prison. Nothing at all was said in the prison reports about the perks and bonuses that prison work afforded the staff. The warders and superintendent alike participated in and were at times compromised by these 'extras', which existed at both formal and informal levels. For example, staff were given the option of living in prison department houses close to Mount Crawford at very low rent, although not all of them took this option:

> Asked Warder MacC if he lived at prison but he was scornful. Spoke as if having to work there was quite enough. Said he wouldn't have his

wife looking out on gaol all day. Living, of course is cheaper – rental for warder's house about 11/- ... but one would be at the beck and call of heads. He had built a home in Miramar within walking distance (15 May 1941).

They were also able to purchase supplies of vegetables, milk and other prison produce at very cheap rates, presumably as part of some agreement between themselves and the authorities regarding their pay and terms of employment:

> The warders get a bag of vegetables a week for 6d and SH says that Friday's bag consisted of 2 cabbages, 1 small pumpkin, 12 carrots, 12 parsnips, 6 beetroot & 12 onions – good ones (2 June 1941).

There was nothing untoward about these bonuses. However, there was certainly no formal approval from the Prison Department for what had become, as the diary records, the routine arrangements at Mount Crawford, whereby staff regularly made use of prisoner labour for their own personal advantage. In some instances, the fact that inmates were working on improvements to prison department houses or assisting warders in legitimate activities meant the ethical or legal issues raised could be somewhat blurred.

> While carting hay [a warder] ... came for us [and] we learnt that it was to shift furniture into a prison house down road for a warder, Mr K, down from Waikeria. Jack was not about when Mr L came for us so Ron replaced him. He'll be disappointed. We unloaded the 2 NZR [New Zealand Railways] lorries and will return after dinner to unpack (11 July 1941).

On numerous occasions, however, the inmates were put to work manifestly for the private benefit and gain of prison staff:

> Carried bag of rotted manure a distance for warder at close of day – he generally has some such task and I think collects it later to take home to his own place (16 July 1941).

That Barrington uses the word 'generally' on this occasion demonstrates how routine this practice must have been. Indeed, it appears to have been systemic. Similar practices on different occasions involving different warders are noted during the course of the diary:

> Mr McC decided to have carried a heavy railway sleeper all the way

uphill. He was careful to explain that it was not for firewood (which I believe a gratuitous fib – for I had to put it with the heap he keeps for firewood.) Likewise he got HB to go amongst pines & bring up a sapling – both he said he wanted for blocks for the fencing, but at piggeries he had HB cut up the sapling into small pieces and fill a sugar bag for him to take home. For a fundamentalist [Christian, as this warder professed to be], these fibs or fictions are scarcely credible (31 July 1941).

These practices were not confined only to the uniformed officers, however: the superintendent was also involved and frequently used prison labour to his own benefit:

After taking shelter we were once more put to rolling Mr McG's lawns, though the ground was obviously too wet. Continued all the afternoon though parts could not be done (4 June 1941).

JH afternoon washing and polishing super's car. Whole week we have worked practically without a warder once being in charge of us (18 July 1941).

… called to the super's lawns to aid JRH, AHC & JB who were finding the ton or more roller tough work. Continued all afternoon (30 May 1941).

Gathered two fairly heavy bags of cones for super's private supply and carried homewards up the hill (6 June 1941).

One of the prisoners was selected to perform a kind of manservant or personal assistant role at the supervisor's residence, earning the title 'the Super's "house prisoner"' (6 August 1941).

At no point does Barrington mention any opposition to such practices from other warders. Indeed, a set of protocols and tacit understandings had developed between staff and prisoners in relation to them, illustrative again of how widespread and routine they were. The warders colluded in these practices, covering for one another when mishaps occurred that went beyond the well-prescribed code that regulated them:

A little porker was killed & was being fixed up – I understand for Super. There is also an apocryphal yarn that yesterday one too large for the purpose was killed by mistake of the warder and to cover up his mistake (so fearful are they of the higher officials) it was to be buried! Seems scarcely credible (16 May 1941).

Prisoners involved in such work were given 'tips' or other bonuses, which took the form of food and tobacco rather than cash:

After dinner was better as we were in pines, cutting more down & up & carrying. I mostly knocked off & gathered cones, one for super and one for Mr A. He provided HB & RJS with a cigarette each. (smoking not allowed while at work) (17 June 1941).

JB was collected by Warder W for a carpentry job for a couple of days – probably at G's house. For he came back boasting of real tea & crockery (26 May 1941).

Had half a chocolate wheaten biscuit (received from JH who must have had afternoon tea at the Super's for whom he is building a garage (5 June 1941).

After carrying the sack of tomatoes for Warder A from the prison to his house, Barrington remarked: 'Mr A got from his wife a paper bag of "goodies" which he told me to put in my pocket' (11 June 1941). On another occasion, when he and his colleague Ron Scarlett helped the new warder to move his furniture into the prison house,

Ron was given a Capstan [cigarette] by Mr K. When asked if we smoked Ron said no he didn't smoke gaol tobacco. He is more fastidious than most smokers. However he enjoyed the Capstan. Legs were broken on a sideboard and dressing table and the carriers took them back to make new legs in the railway workshops … we [then] had two very nice cups of real tea at the house and 5 or 6 wine biscuits. Ron had another Capstan (11 July 1941).

The food would have provided a welcome break from the prison diet:

JH meanwhile, in return for cleaning Mr McG's car, had a nice cup of coffee, before that at the fort he had fried terakihi! and there's a tale that he frequently has curried sausages there! (26 June 1941).

This illicit use of prison labour with its attendant rewards and tips was not confined to the dissenter group, as if they were particularly amenable and cooperative. Any prisoner thought sufficiently trustworthy and reliable appears to have been co-opted. It also seemed to be understood that those in receipt of 'rewards' would, when possible, later share them with other inmates, rather than consume them alone or trade them to the highest bidder on the open prison market:

The lads all had a piece of very fruity fruit cake provided by the Maori boys who get titbits when delivering milk to warders' houses (24 June 1941).

Maori lad again appeared with two little cakes in his billy (as he did yesterday when JW & I had them.) & I enjoyed them. The Maori boy has a good job! When he delivers milk to warders' homes & to the fort he collects something at each (26 June 1941).

Here, then, were demonstrations of the 'trust' the authorities had referred to in the reports – except that it was manifested in the illicit working practices about which both staff and inmates had come to informal agreement. Rather than checking or suppressing deviancy, prison life was actually creating it – among the prison staff. Devoid of any closely monitoring central regulatory authority, and separated by the physical and moral boundaries that existed between the prison and the general public, the staff appear to have taken any opportunity to gain a little more from their low pay and low status employment.

A better class of prisoner

These arrangements are indicative of the relatively short social distances between most of the warders and many of the inmates, without which it would not have been possible to have inmates working in and around the warders' houses. Although the regulations forbade prisoners from speaking to or even acknowledging anyone from outside the prison, the dissenters and the families of prison staff inevitably bumped into each other. Such meetings appear to have caused little anxiety or embarrassment, however. Barrington recorded several such occasions:

Miss McG [the superintendent's daughter] looks not unattractive and gave us a pleasant 'good morning' (30 May 1941).

Had interlude when Mr A got me to carry with him a case of tree tomatoes in a sack from gaol to his home down hill (on Fortification Road overlooking harbour entrance) – I learnt that this house and another nearby are also gaol properties though further away and access to gaol by long winding (& slippery) path up hill. Mrs A was on point of going out in fur coat etc. A pleasant looking woman whom I met nearly a year ago at Webb St [Methodist Church] (11 June 1941).

Mrs K and two little children arrived just as we did for afternoon work (11 July 1941).

The willingness of most of the prison staff to accept prisoners as legitimate members of society, rather than degraded outsiders, was mirrored in the short social distances in existence between prison inmates and significant members of New Zealand society in the outside world. The WEA lecture programme was a further demonstration of these links. Most of the speakers were from public sector organisations, and some were particularly prominent 'celebrities' in the context of 1940s New Zealand – most notably 'Uncle Scrim', Bill Sutch, and the 2ZB radio announcer Tony Martin.

Barrington and his colleagues chose to be cooperative with the authorities, excelling at their work rather than refusing to cooperate as some of the COs and military defaulters held elsewhere did.[4] This is not to say, of course, that they were entirely quiescent in their approach to the prison authorities. Barrington frequently challenged the prison rules, but he did so through the formal channels rather than by undermining or threatening the authority of the warders. Once their willingness to cooperate was established, their pacifist status ceased to present any barrier to the development of these generally cordial relationships. Indeed, for the warders, Barrington and his colleagues clearly represented a 'better class of prisoner':

> Harold says when he was brought in Mr L said to escorting detec. 'It's a shame to bring these chaps in here.' Detec. thought appeal court decision a foregone conclusion – in our favour (20 May 1941).

> Mr A again very conversational & pleasant this pm. Told AHC that he is always put in charge of worst men(!) as he is best able to handle them – they have to be dealt with firmly and severely! – it was a pleasure to be in charge of men like us (12 June 1941).

The group's backgrounds contributed to the cordiality and respect showed to them by many of the prison staff. Their social status outside the prison and the power of the warders within it seemed to establish a relatively harmonious equilibrium. Both groups in their separate ways, were social 'outsiders', which allowed them to put their differences aside and work together without friction. Despite the formal requirement for Barrington to salute the superintendent whenever they met, there was also an informality to their interaction, and Barrington observed the superintendent had even used his nickname: 'Mr McG has, twice, accidentally, I think, called me "Barry"' (3 August 1941). As far as the warders were concerned, these men were not 'real criminals'; they possessed social attributes that made everyday conversations worthwhile and interesting, and added something of value to the otherwise featureless monotony of prison work:

> Mr A talked about all manner of things as we worked & coming home discussed our views in relation to changing human nature, danger of easy drift to communism (or Fascism as I pointed out) of those who readily followed Labour for selfish purposes (6 June 1941).

> Learnt that others spent a good part of wet yesterday 'arguing' with Mr MacC on his fundamentalist beliefs – the powers that be being ordained of God we should always obey them, but even he admitted that if it came to the point of being ordered to kill someone he would have to refuse. To my surprise he has been 15 years a warder here. Does not seem to be popular with other warders and is as afraid of the bosses as a new recruit. He is no bother to us though (1 July 1941).

> I offered Mr W a book & he has taken it though he says he has little time for reading nowadays as he is trying to build own house on a section he has – that is why he is staying on night shift. Must be pretty strenuous. Had long yarn through window (12 August 1941).

Some of the warders maintained a show of reserve and suspicion, but this began to thaw as the two groups became acquainted and accustomed to each other:

> Good old Mr MacC improves daily, becoming more genial. His searching becomes a mere touch with one hand and now he is on duty for the night and has just been around leaving on the lights of those of us still up. He said genially through my peep hole, 'now this won't do you know. Too much study is a weariness of the flesh!' I said 'it can be other things' and on he went (17 July 1941).

One warder held out against any overtures made to him, however:

> Again no response from the grim McK to my good morning. Reading *Since Calvary* yesterday I was reminded of the story told here about him – that he not only goes through ordinary routine but also has a broom with a huge needle stuck into it with which he pierces the mattresses in the cells to discover hidden objects – a perfectly natural precaution. I'm told he has been a warder 'all his life' and prides himself on never having let anyone or anything slip through his fingers. Must be a foul job & probably his trust in human nature, if he ever had any, has been killed by betrayals – for given the gaol system, warders even if they have the idea

of kindness & sympathy would not be permitted to carry it through far enough for reasonable chance of success (19 May 1941).

But after delicate probing and grooming, Barrington detected flickers of warmth behind McK's icy correctness:

Mrs Blake [one of Barrington's visitors] wanted to know if she could bring apples etc but Jane told her no. However she was determined to bring me something and it was a spray of daphne & to my surprise Mr McK the stern warder in charge said it could be left with the gate warder for me & with much amusement (& pleasure) all round I received it later at the hands of Warder C (gardens) whom Jane described as 'the dear old man' on the gate. Warder also let me hold Peter & Jeb, Peter again stroking & fondling my face (21 June 1941).

Whether it was simply in Barrington's nature to treat all fellow human beings with civility, courtesy and politeness – Christian fellowship in practice, as it were – or whether there was some more Machiavellian intent to break down officer reserve in the hope of winning better treatment and privileges, is not clear. The evidence strongly points to the former, however, and the affinity that he established with the prison staff began to bring its own rewards:

Tonight I asked the 'locking up' warder (a very decent one named W – usually asks if everything is all right before locking me in for the night & adds a smile) if he could ask 'them' to tone the radio down a bit as it was nearly driving us mad. He said it wasn't in his province but he must have passed the word on for after unintelligible London news the radio was switched off & we are at peace! When it stopped loud cheers in which I joined, could be heard from cell after cell! (16 May 1941).

Had baths this morning also and Warder McL when I mentioned loading pigs with my filthy trousers kindly saw to it that I got a clean pair (7 June 1941).

[Mr A] also said he would get us work inside if we wished. AHC said preferred open air but if had to go inside wd prefer printing (so'd I!) & Mr A said he could arrange if he liked (12 June 1941).

Mr MacC kindly asked about my cold and whether I wanted more 'dope' and it is here for me with two aspros (28 June 1941).

Whenever their 'chief' was not around, the warders were even prepared to relax some of the regulations for this 'better class of prisoners':

Wedding cake in prison! Lined up to come in for dinner, Mr B (in blue, 2nd in command during Mr L's absence) beckoned me in passing, pointed to the pencil on my waistcoat & said it was absolutely against all regulations at the same time handing me a wedding cake container for postal transmission. When I exclaimed 'wedding cake' he again cautioned me that it was against all regulations. There is humour and grace in prison (30 July 1941).

Barrington reciprocated the gratuities and kindness shown to him:

Ginger [Barrington's sister Gladys] brought jonquils – early ones costing ¼d – a great bunch. I persuaded Warder McG to take some for his wife as there are limits to the capacity of my cell for flowers (26 July 1941).

I have handed through the window a *Picture Post* & two NZ mags to Warder W, a slight courtesy for several hours of light (27 July 1941).

These reciprocities did not appear to be extended to the main body of the prison population. From the brief comments Barrington provided of interaction between warders and the mainstream prisoners on East Wing, it is apparent that the social distances there were much greater:

When carrying sandsoap the other day we were taking it from a room at end of west wing and through open door I got glimpse of two long rows of prisoners stretching into distance receiving Mr McK's stern order: One step forward. March. And I realised that with the much greater number in east wing a certain amount of strictness would be inevitable or there would be great confusion. Including people on remand or maximum – rarely attained – is 28 – and then remands are in a definite category and dealt with separately after working gangs have departed (3 August 1941).

Clearly the warders understood that acceptance of Barrington's little gifts, kindnesses and attempts at friendliness would not expose them to manipulation or coercion by 'getting too close' to the prisoner. With Barrington at least, they knew they could afford to drop their guard without fear of later exploitation. It also seems evident that most of the warders favoured the opportunity the presence of Barrington and others provided for a more harmonious life in the prison. From his comments, it is clear that many warders did not like the disciplinary and punitive powers associated with their work:

We ambled down-hill slowly & I got Mr C talking by reference to his being on the bridge this morning. He referred to a man in the 'dummy'

& said he had already been there 21 days. Apparently no one can be committed there except by a JP or magistrate after hearing warder & culprit. [A war resister if not yet a fully fledged CO] was in yard this morning & Mr McC referred to Mr McK's treatment of him or attitude towards him as disgraceful – browbeating & abusive sufficiently to make a man go for a warder. (Mr McC could survey all yards & such actions from his loft.) He said it shouldn't be necessary to send any man to the dummy. He had done so twice & that was in [the] first five years of his 15 years service. He gave Mr McG credit for not snooping round looking for culprits or doing anything to provoke trouble (but regretted his indifference to anything beyond his own immediate concerns) & compared him more than favourably to D the previous super who must have been an unholy terror & would think badly of warders if they were not keeping dummies full (31 July 1941).

Prison violence

Lack of personal security is a largely taken-for-granted feature of prison life. Barrington was not subjected to any 'standovers' from other prisoners, however, and as we have seen he also worked hard to ensure relationships with prison staff were as cordial as possible in the circumstances. And while different standards of discipline were in place on East Wing, Barrington gave no indication that those prisoners were involved in violence or intimidation either.

Given the mix of inmates – a group of pacifists, and a collection of men many of whom were aged and infirm and with apparently little history of violence – the lack of conflict in this prison should be of no surprise. Nonetheless, there was one incident – an assault by a warder on an inmate – that occurred at Mount Crawford during Barrington's incarceration, although it seems to have been aberrational rather than systemic.[5] The reaction to it confirms the very rare nature of violence in Mount Crawford at this time. It involved the inmate Parsons, imprisoned for failing to register for conscription. Following verbal abuse and bullying from chief warder McK, he was ordered to the dummy for disobeying a command. Barrington recorded what followed:

> Witnessed a little drama of passive resistance this afternoon. Warder K's gang were loading & carrying bags of cinders. Bob Durrant & the lad [Parsons] who came in with him in gang. The lad was given a month

for not registering. Seems as if moving towards CO position by degrees & without reasoned and calm convictions, more of stubbornness – as is probably often the case. When having deliberately not registered he found the authorities after him, he registered but too late. Today I saw from haystack what looked like refusal to lift & carry a bag at cinder stack. I saw warder K point & gesticulate & appear to threaten. Then I saw him line his gang up & march them round to front gate & I assumed a man was going in for the 'dummy'. Later learned from Bob that it was the same lad (29 July 1941).

This seems to have been too much for Parsons to bear:

During tea heard a man howling. Could see nothing from window but seemed to be a lot of warders about including K. Wondering if it was the lad who refused to work for him last week. A JP was here today, possibly in order to deal with him (5 August 1941).

In a conversation with Barrington, another officer at first denied that anything untoward had occurred:

H told me P wants to see me about dummy incident. Gather man beaten up allegedly by McK and has a terribly black eye. Could not see P before dinner but hoped to get facts. I asked Mr McC if there was trouble last night and he said someone was sick in west wing. But I'm pretty sure that was not what I was referring to (5 August 1941).

Barrington's suspicions were well founded, however:

Have been pursuing enquiries about beating up incident. It is naturally hard to get exact particulars. I have asked Sid, Bill, Harry, Aston, the Super's 'house' prisoner, Dave, Mr MacC and others including (1) the young lad Parsons – in for one month for not registering – was yesterday sentenced to 3 days in dummy by Rad [sic] J.P. (2) He refused or may have refused to enter last evening (3) The following warders are alleged to have been present or [to have] participate[d]: MacK, A, C, K, K. (4) I did not see Mr A or Mr C at time I heard the cries I did see Mr McG? Also Mr S looking towards D from bridge. (5) Parsons is alleged to have one eye badly blackened and a face cut and bleeding (6) A blood soaked towel is said to have been brought up today (7) One of the cooks is said to have seen the incident and to have seen Parsons just afterwards. (8) A [a warder] is believed to have said he got out of it – wasn't going to have anything to do with it (9) W [another warder] is said to have said it was disgusting and justified warders being called 'bastards' outside (10)

I sounded Mr McC this afternoon and he first expressed surprise but later said he had heard something of the kind but hadn't enquired. Said it shouldn't be and wasn't right. But he could not say anything of course. Referred to Mr McK as having something of a reputation. (11) P the big genial smithy seems genuinely concerned and militant over the issue. He also says that McK gets his wife to wait down the road on visiting days and follow people up to watch 'plants', tobacco for Knowles from Mrs K being discovered in this way. (12) according to P, Mr McK at Mt Eden got a plate of hot porridge on his neck, which still has the scar, and that an enquiry declared he deserved what he got. Of course I cannot vouch for all these details but it looks as if a case for enquiry – urgently – has been made out. I referred it to OEB at dinnertime and he was making enquiries too. Fortunately he and Basil had clergy visitors and may have been able to solicit their aid (7 August 1941).

The meticulous detail of this particular entry is illustrative of the fact that, in this small institution, it was very difficult to have any secrets. At the same time, that Barrington went to such lengths to record these events indicates how atypical they were. His account also suggests that a number of the warders were trying to distance themselves from the officious Mr McK. They appeared to think that he operated a different moral code, deliberately seeking out breaches of regulations that others would have ignored. Meanwhile, the incident clearly stirred the generally quiescent prisoners and galvanised resistance among them – another reason why such incidents were so unwanted by most prison staff.

Both Burton and Barrington, the two most prominent COs, decided to take the matter further, as they revealed to each other at a Holy Communion service the following morning:

There must have been over 20 at service conducted by Rev Squires in priestly attire – with wafers for bread and silver chalice for communion cup. Mr A assisted and they were going on to Borstal after leaving us … Mr B, acting deputy chief was present in blue and made a real community of it by communicating, kneeling at form alongside J.H. We were pleased. I announced my intention of speaking to Mr McG [the superintendent] about 'beating up' rumours but O asked me to hold over until dinnertime. After breakfast he produced a letter he had in meantime written to Super and proposed to hand in. This rather makes any action by me unnecessary. Twice this morning I saw Mr McG in grounds and if I had been near enough would have raised the matter then and there (7 August 1941).

By making a written complaint – or 'papering' as the term is now known in prison jargon – Burton had raised the stakes. As we have seen, this was an era in prison administration when formal record keeping was kept to a minimum. As a result of Burton's letter the superintendent was compelled to act: the written record confirmed the incident and it could not be ignored. His letter was not appreciated by the superintendent:

> OEB was called to Super as we came in tonight and as we were being locked up he stalked by with news that the Super can manage the prison without O's assistance. Which sounds like the retort discourteous to his letter (7 August 1941).

Barrington reported the content of the letter and the exchange that occurred between Burton and the superintendent:

> O's letter to Super was: 'On the evening of Tuesday August 5th I heard a man shrieking as though in great fear & pain. I did not think a great deal more of the matter until I found next day that a bloodstained towel was passed in to the washhouse from the punishment cells. Since that time very many circumstantial rumours have been passed around the gaol – no doubt many of them utterly without foundation. However it is clear that either a brutal assault was carried out on a prisoner, something which I'm sure you as Superintendent would not condone – or that a very grave injustice is being done to a warder. Under the circumstances I would respectfully request that an enquiry be held before Justices. At such an enquiry I would be willing to give sworn evidence that I personally heard sounds such as I have described above. Yours faithfully, O.E. Burton.' His account of interview with Super yesterday is: S. Do you wish to make complaint of any officer. B. It is hardly for me to do that. S. Presuming a bit aren't you? B. I don't think so. S. I can run this gaol without your advice. B. I am making no suggestion about that. You have the document before you. It is for your information (8 August 1941).

Not only had the assault disrupted the tacit and informal consensus that had been established between the warders and the dissenters regarding their respective roles in the prison; in addition, Burton's written complaint had disrupted the preferred mode of informal prison administration.

Arthur Carman, acting independently of both Barrington and Burton, also made verbal representations to the superintendent, who then attempted to intimidate and silence him in the obvious hope that he would not take the matter any further in the form of a written complaint:

AHC not having heard of O's experience put his name down yesterday to see Super and saw him this morning with same result. S. You've been listening to rumours. A. I myself heard what I have described. S. You should keep your eyes to yourself. You are only concerned with what happens to you. A. I only wished to explain what I had heard as I thought you might not know and would want to enquire into it. I am concerned with it for what happens to one is the concern of all here. S. You'll be getting yourself into trouble if don't keep to own affairs. Have you a complaint against any warder? A. No (10 August 1941).

With relations between the pacifists and prison staff disrupted, the superintendent revealed a previously hidden level of personal animosity towards the men whom he now clearly considered to be members of a 'contemptible intelligentsia':

S[uperintendent]. You people seem to think some of us dead from shoulders up. We've got a brain as well as you. It's my job to run this gaol. What do you think I have officers for but to keep me informed? (9 August 1941).

Nonetheless, the assault did become public knowledge, sparking reactions that were remarkable but quintessentially characteristic of New Zealand at that time. Recording this, Barrington began his diary entry with the comment: 'Today [Sunday] has been another exciting one!' (10 August 1941). This was one of only two occasions when Barrington used the term 'exciting' to describe what was happening in the prison (the first being the arrival of the Prisons Board), demonstrating again the highly atypical nature of the assault on Parsons and its power to disrupt the prison rhythm and routine:

JB took our service in yard. Good lad. Had got half a letter written when Salvation Army [SA] service started and we all went to that with Colonel Burton conducting and Bernice and Doreen [SA choir members] singing a duet and solo! Then dinner finished I was just preparing to continue writing for remainder of dinner hour when Hardy said through peephole there was a visitor for us. O., A. and I were called out & put in yard. Mr McC informed us that Minister of Finance and Mr Jones were the visitors. We were shown in and greeted by Hon. Mr Nash Acting Prime Minister & had a private chat! He asked after our health and sentences. Asked if we had any complaints (evidently leading up to Parsons – we knew Parsons had been interviewed) and we said what we knew. I also seized opportunity to put in a plea for light extension for study (to which he was definitely sympathetic) and referred to apple a week fruit position. When Presbyterian service came on we were asked to remain in yard as might be wanted. A. beat me in a game of chess. Just as we were called in for tea, A. and O. were sent for and were away quite a while and it is pretty clear a proper inquiry is proceeding – we heard that the Inspector General of Prisons [B.L. Dallard] was coming and I saw Read JP and I think Collins going with Super towards 'Dummy'. Whatever result is, action will be salutary and [will] tend to restrain abuses. The underdog hasn't usually strong people to stand up for them (10 August 1941).

In fact, Nash had been accompanied by 'Mr Mason, Attorney General and Minister in charge of prisons. Mr McC later told us that after Parsons had been interviewed he told him that he had refused to give the name of the witness who saw him kicked down stairs' (10 August 1941).

How had the complaint escalated so quickly and so dramatically? At Visits on the day following the assault all the pacifists had told their respective visitors about the incident. Because of their high-level contacts, Burton's in particular, the information then found its way into government circles. It still seems extraordinary, though, that senior ministers should then choose to become involved. The only plausible explanation for this is that the treatment of wartime dissenters remained politically sensitive. Ministers feared the damage that revelations of this kind could do to the government's attempts to promote a completely united front for the war effort – and what publicity it would give to opponents to spread dissent and promote pacifism. Nash – himself a Labour politician who had taken a pacifist position in World War I – seems to have been the member of the Cabinet most sympathetic to the dissenters.[6] His own conscience may have been disturbed when the reports of violence reached him.

Following this intervention, the prison authorities conducted an immediate inquiry:

> The whitewashing [of the dummy] was a point of interest. There were a lot of Warders in [the] offing while inquiry proceeding – apparently in case required for evidence. There are rumours today that inquiry is to proceed this evening. I understand Inspector General conducted inquiry & that Collins is also the JP [who is going to] be doing most of the questioning. The Controller is said to have arrived about 10 pm having been away all day. Naturally there is a lot of interest among prisoners. Especially old lags who welcome any possibility of warders being 'straightened up' (11 August 1941).

Perhaps the authorities assumed the inquiry would act as a palliative for the prisoners – both West and East Wing inmates had an interest in the matter, as the assault was a reminder to all of them of their own powerlessness and vulnerability. At the same time, an internal investigation might be able to prevent further adverse publicity. Barrington and his colleagues were summoned to give their evidence:

> … about 11.30 four of us called away to carry logs up a precipitous
> path from halfway down hill to Super's place. A tough proposition with
> stomachs already feeling empty. Jim was called away from that inside &
> we believe may have been for inquiry. Believe young Barton (cleaner)
> was called before Super and B [his deputy] yesterday and questioned.
> According to Price, a man for the dummy is usually taken down by
> two warders before working parties come home. On this occasion
> it was not until after all came in for tea that 5 *warders* did the deed.
> [Later], finished bundling up and tying pohutukawas this afternoon. JPs
> returned and inquiry proceeding. (During tea they passed my window
> with B and W going towards dummy.) For nearly an hour after dinner
> we were put in yard until Mr MacC arrived. Usually we are turned
> out to work on our own. It was pleasant in the sun and we amused
> ourselves with deck quoits which we found there. Parsons who is being
> kept in solitary was in adjoining yard and we were able to get a cigarette
> & matches to him. It is scarcely a proper inquiry & warders are asked if
> they wish to give evidence (12 August 1941).

It was inquiry enough, however, to reassert and reaffirm the authority of the prison staff:

> Davey [the Presbyterian laundryman] has just come to window &
> suggested that inquiry is being ditched & that Parsons has been given 3
> more days in Dummy for swearing (13 August 1941).

How the laundryman could have found out so quickly is something that we never discover, but it was symptomatic of the way in which news was able to spread so quickly around the prison. As for the findings of the inquiry, the authorities could not publicly concede that a violent assault by a senior member of their staff had occurred. A discussion between Barrington and warder MacC confirmed, however, that the rest of the prison staff wanted to distance themselves from McK. Gratuitous brutality not only caused difficulties for them within the prison but also in the wider community:

We discussed inquiry, lights, education etc He referred to terrific 'corruption' last week – said it was terrible and as he says McK is not known in Wgtn and when he goes out goes in private clothes. Whereas men like W are known & if things like this get in papers it is pretty unpleasant for them (12 August 1941).

These comments remind us not simply of the low status of the warders, but also of the more general public antipathy towards those *employed* in the prisons.

Such matters aside, the diary illustrates that the prison staff were working in an institution that bore little resemblance to that described in the official prison reports. Overall, the prison functioned not by rigorous enforcement of regulations but by a relaxed and often scant regard for them. Staff and inmates developed illicit working practices that advantaged both groups but these were, of course, in direct breach of the very regulations that staff were meant to police.

Chapter 5

The Inmates

The inmate population consisted of two groups: the mainstream prisoners, for the most part serving short sentences and with strings of similar previous convictions; and those serving a sentence for their opposition to the war: the Christian pacifists who refused to be silenced, those whose claims to CO status had been denied and who then refused conscription, and two communists. Housed in separate wings, the two groups met only during work or at the WEA lectures.

Mainstream prisoners

Barrington has told us little about this group or their crimes, partly because, due to his religious beliefs, he was interested more in the men themselves than in what they had done. Furthermore, it was not common practice for inmates to enquire about another's crimes; this information would be disclosed only if an individual chose to. After reading an article in *New Zealand Observer* by James Moriarty, who described coming into contact with murderers and 'sex perverts' during a sentence he served at Mount Eden, Barrington observed that Moriarty 'would not have known what they were unless he had asked them – a thing not usually done' (26 July 1941).

There is no evidence from the diary that warders deliberately 'set up' prisoners for retribution by disclosing to the rest of the prisoner community any particularly distasteful offence committed. On one occasion, Warder MacK did ask Barrington if he

> ... could lend a prisoner front and back [collar] studs as he had to appear in court tomorrow. I had none but said one of the lads with clothes would lend ... Mr MacK explained that the man was charged with rape – I don't know whether he thought that would influence me in [the] decision to lend or affect [the] probability of the court decision (12 July 1941).

The context suggests the reason for the disclosure on this occasion was indeed the latter: the warder wanted to ensure that the prisoner appeared in court dressed to a reasonable standard in the hope, probably forlorn, that this might have an impact on his sentence.

The great majority of Mt Crawford inmates had anyway committed minor crimes that were of little interest to their peers. Of those for whom Barrington provided quite detailed description, two were serving indefinite sentences as habitual criminals. Over a cup of tea at the piggeries during a break from work, one of these, known as 'One-Eye', related the details of a particularly undistinguished but highly typical criminal career for prisoners then serving such sentences:

> He is 61, twice declared habitual criminal (referred to as 'Lac' and one remains [so] declared until it is lifted). He has had over 13 years in prisons. Serving about 2 months at present. Bob Semple [the government minister] got his 'Lac' off. Safe robbery his principal exploits also petty thieving. £60 most he ever got. Got him started by asking his experience of gaols. A safe is called a tank. When Bob Semple asked what he could do for him, One-Eye said 'get the lac wiped off me'. And Bob said right. One-Eye lost his eye only recently in a brawl. First occasion have got an old lag in a position to and willing to talk. Asked him if he had his life over again he'd go same way and he declared not (16 July 1941).

During the same conversation, One-Eye revealed,

> [Price,] the pleasant looking gentle big fellow who is more or less blacksmith-engineer here, is also a 'lac' and is serving 2 years and 3 months (so One-Eye says) for failing to report. Apparently until [the] lac is wiped off one must report regularly to police – and in prison may be detained simply at will of controller (16 July 1941).

In other words, Price had been released from his previous prison term on conditional licence. His failure to comply with the conditions of this had led to his recall to prison.

There were also two sex offenders in Mount Crawford. Barrington had come across both outside the prison, indicative again of the 'small world' nature of New Zealand society, especially at that time. He described the first of them:

> A man I recognised [as] a little chap whom I've often noticed as a dapper little man smartly dressed & always at entrance to Grand Central Private Hotel as if employed there. Jim D tells me that he is here for 2½ years for

interfering with a girl of six years – taking her into St Mary of the Angels & being discovered by nuns. Jim also says he belongs to the [Exclusive] Brethren but they have cut him off from all recognition and contact (19 May 1941).

Despite the man's offence, he seems to have been able to mix freely with the rest of the prison population; there is no indication from the diary that he was living in fear of retribution as a result of his crime.

The second came from an altogether different background and circumstances, and was a soldier who had disrupted one of Barrington's (prohibited) street meetings. Barrington then met him at Mount Crawford after he had been remanded in custody:

Remand men were released from [the] yard while we were still waiting for our porridge. Among them was a tall handsome soldier, whom I recognised as one who blithely pushed me off my stand at Manners St Reserve several times on one of my 'big' nights. Connie [Summers] gathered him & others in later & they were sitting at Webb St when I arrived for supper. Had spoken to him once or twice since (a Fort Dorset man). When I spoke and smiled tonight he had sudden surprise in recognising me & said 'I take my hat off to you now!' Goodness knows what he is charged with (30 July 1941).

Typically, Barrington's first instinct was to offer assistance to the soldier, despite the man's earlier conduct and irrespective of what he had done to get himself remanded.

When he got to his cell, I was able to slip across with a *Readers Digest* for him and later after I was locked in DS called through door to know if I had a match 'for your soldier friend'. I pushed four under my door & D conveyed them to him (30 July 1941).

Barrington had not asked about the soldier's offence, of course. He later wrote, 'according to DS my soldier friend is on remand for a week for rather nasty sex affair – sounds like some messy business amongst Fort Dorset soldiers' (31 July 1941).

Of the other prisoners, Barrington had struck up something of a friendship with Hardgreaves, the wing cleaner. The diary goes on to reveal, however, that this man was somewhat delusional; the prospective female visitor for whom he wished to be suitably attired may have been nothing more than a fantasy:

Hardgreaves was just yarning at door before I was locked in again. Started discussion as to whether I could strike a woman with a child & argument developed when I said I would not strike anyone. He is (qualified to 'was') a staunch RC but thinks the church all wrong. Referred to angels being turned out of heaven of which I said I knew nothing. He has been keen to get a first aid class started – has 15 who will co-operate. His idea is that it is his only chance of a job when he emerges; as being 59 is too old to get work at sea [he previously worked as a merchant sailor]. He is serving 29 years he says for taking an overcoat from a hotel when drunk. Says he has a letter from [British Deputy Prime Minister Clement] Attlee saying there must be something wrong with the sentence (5 June 1941).

Barrington also described 'Ack Aston', the superintendent's 'house prisoner', who was apparently also a 'swindler'. There was Collins, who 'robbed the Ford Company of £600 and who works in the soap shop', and 'someone serving 9 days for an income tax offence'. There were also 'the Maori boys' who regularly brought Barrington a share of the food they were given during their milk rounds. Another Māori prisoner asked Barrington to write a prayer for him:

A near middle aged Maori asked about Basil. I gave he & another Maori a few matches & cigarette papers. After dinner when lined up in mass formation & ordered to break off for working parties, the first Maori handed me a piece of toilet paper folded into the tiniest possible space. I put it in my pocket as it could not be examined there and did not get an opportunity for some hours. When I did [I] found this pathetic message. 'If you don't mind I would like you to write me out a morning pray and also night pray.' A trusting request which I hope I can fulfil adequately (4 June 1941).

He wrote the prayer: 'Evening seemed to race away last night. Drafting and writing out morning & evening prayers for Maori friend took quite a while and I have copied out this morning for reference' (5 June 1941). Events took an unexpected turn, however.

Was grieved to find my Maori 'friend' missing this morning, evidently he was one of those shifted to Wi Tako and as we were not out at work yesterday I had no chance of giving him his morning & night 'pray'. Fortunately my sending a copy to mother will serve well as now I will be able to ask her to try to get them to him. I've yet to discover his name. The Maori dairyman did not know. H has promised to get it for me (6 June 1941).

We never find out whether Barrington learned the Māori man's name and was able to send him the prayer. Once the latter left Mount Crawford any contact could only have been through Barrington's mother or some other intermediary, as prison inmates were not then allowed to correspond with each other. But the fact that he heard nothing further from or of the Māori prisoner should be of no surprise. For most inmates at that time, there were no farewell parties, 'graduation ceremonies', or even simply opportunities to say goodbye:[1]

> I always regret not knowing when men are departing – we don't get [the] opportunity to say goodbye properly. The men (who are getting extra remission) usually don't know themselves until after we have gone to work on the day they are leaving (4 July 1941).

They left only the faintest reminders of their presence there: 'the tall, fair, curly haired cook departed this morning, as usual without any warning – he was around 6.45 with the breakfast team' (2 July 1941). Some needed no farewells, however, as it was highly likely they would be back before long:

> While working Friday morning I met … John Fitzgerald, a deaf meths drinker. We passed quite close and I shouted out 'goodbye John. Mind you don't come back again.' But deaf John with gaze fixed straight ahead neither saw nor heard me. And Mr R replied 'Even if he could hear you it wouldn't make any difference to tell him that' (29 June 1941).

As the warder had predicted, Fitzgerald was back soon after: 'a frequent & likeable if funny inhabitant of O.B. wash house making his third appearance since we've been here' (24 June 1941). Barrington next saw him working in the gardens, which were 'very exposed', one cold winter's day. Fitzgerald knew the conditions well enough to make some rudimentary attempt to protect himself from the elements:

> He would not be able to get enough steam up to get warm at all. Noticed when he was at open 'lavatory' that underneath his clothes he had on a very long nightshirt! (3 July 1941).

The few prisoners who stood out and left memories of their presence behind were those whose skills the inmates valued, and whose departure left a gap that nobody else could fill. The barber, Kelman, was one of these:

> [He] was to have been released on Monday but would not sign the 'double probation' apparently required for extra remission and so he has to stay until tomorrow. He was all ready to go & would be disappointed.

A nice little chap. We'll miss his genial barbering (12 June 1941).

Barrington was transferred to Kelman's cell following his departure, after weighing up the move:

> Advantages and disadvantages. Removed me from next door neighbour to [Arthur Carman] with whom I'll be staying 8 or 9 months. The cell is much dirtier (walls seem to have had blacksmith's hands scrubbed over them!). Won't get as much light after lights out and view is much restricted. Nearer entrance which is handy for the morning rush [to the toilet] but one is locked up later, tea getting colder! Cell is about 18" to 2 ft [45–60 cm] shorter (13 June 1941).

In the new cell he found items that bore testament to the value placed on Kelman's role in the prison: 'a pillow about twice as thick as mine, his much better enamel mug, enormous enamel mug for holding water instead of clumsier billy & better knife fork & spoon' (14 June 1941).

Barrington described assistance he and his colleagues gave to an unknown inmate in the dummy while they were in their exercise yard:

> Yesterday a prisoner in the next yard leapt up and clutched top of our wall while overhead warder was not looking and asked for cigarette as he had been in dummy (and no ration). Basil and HB put tobacco in envelope with papers, someone else supplied matches and the envelope was thrown over to him. We cannot see over walls of course or converse with prisoners in other yards (20 July 1941).

There is no further mention of this inmate and his fate, but his is a typical example of Barrington's descriptions of the mainstream prisoners. Most of them resembled little more than flickering shadows of life, more likely to be in prison than out of it. We fleetingly meet 'an old Maori', an 'insubordinate husky Maori' also in the dummy, and a 'one handed man (Gordon) who works industriously about the residence, [and] whom we learned from Mr A, lost his hand blowing up trout'. We read of 'the taxi man who goes out Thursday [who] left his coat hanging over sty today & pigs got it and made a nice job of it with their snouts & the muck of the sty! He has more than had enough of pigs' (16 June 1941). Barrington described 'a little old man in 2 weeks out of six months & packing sand soap' (16 June 1941), and an 'old, little, whiskered man, who has taken the taxi bootlegging man's place assisting with the pigs'. There was a 'lean and cadaverous laundryman' who was denied parole, and One-Eye, of course, who liked to boast of his unpleasant lack of personal hygiene:

Old One-Eye is down with garden gang today & will be a packet of trouble for poor Mr C whom I heard ineffectually growling at him today. Says One-Eye as we passed referring to his previous job at piggeries 'I shit my nest up there' & seemed to think it a great joke (23 July 1941).

Most evocatively of all, Barrington provided a sketch of an 'old chap with one arm [whom he] saw scratching with a hoe [on a day when] those working in veg gardens had full blast of bitter southerly & felt it' (30 May 1941). All the inadequacies and futilities of the prison system as it then was are encapsulated in this brief description; this was what the old man's existence had been reduced to. But he was just one – if one of the most enfeebled and utterly defeated – of the collection of short-sentence recidivist prisoners in Mount Crawford, complete with their disabilities, addictions and delusions – and their profanities, much to Barrington's distaste:

The men on remand recently seem to be comrades in crime for they yell loud communications to one another through cell windows on opposite (off) side of wing, and pretty lurid language. 'f this and f that'. When Scrim was speaking Sunday night they shouted at the radio 'Shut up you bastard.' Warder K heard one this morning and called him by name, Ashcroft, to cut it out (15 July 1941).

Most of these men would have known how to get by in prison, but not outside of it. The importance that Barrington and colleagues attached to wearing their own clothes as a way of reclaiming and proclaiming their own identity probably meant very little to this group. Given their backgrounds, it is likely the recidivists' own clothes were in much the same condition as those issued within the prison; or the men were so far gone in their acceptance of their prison identities that they had no inclination to pretend otherwise. They presented few redeeming features and little hope for the future. Most received no visits or letters which, as Barrington reflected,

… makes one realise how extra difficult must be the lot of the majority who haven't folk or friends to take an interest in them – no one to do little services & provide a radio, books, periodicals, some sort of contact with outside world (21 June 1941).

Yet it was primarily for these 'forgotten men'[2] that the prison existed at this juncture. Nothing was done to prevent them returning after release; instead, the gates were simply reopened to usher them back in. The prison's main purpose was to provide a sanctuary – albeit a tawdry and shabby one,

one that stripped men of their dignity and autonomy – for those whom society had discarded.

The war dissenters

Given the country's overwhelming support for New Zealand's involvement in the war, it is little wonder that opposition to it brought fame and notoriety to some of the more prominent war dissenters. They were already well known locally and nationally – particularly Burton, the much-decorated World War I hero, and Barrington who, as the national secretary of the WEA, came into regular contact with the Wellington intelligentsia. They found themselves being recognised in public, standing out as obviously as they did both in terms of the strength of their religious beliefs and even their physical appearance: healthy young men, for the most part, wearing civilian clothes at a time when the majority of their contemporaries were in uniform:

> AHC was taken into Somerville Dentist yesterday with Warders Kerr and Griffiths the pumice man. The young nurse, finding his name was Carman, said to AHC excitedly 'Are you one of the pacifists?' and was greatly interested in us (9 August 1941).

Seemingly oblivious to his fame, Barrington was hailed by a stranger:

> While carrying marigolds a military motor brought an officer who went in main gates. His military chauffeur called out to me '& how's Mr Barrington?' Do I respond all well or words to that effect? I replied cheerily as usual but haven't any idea who he was (14 July 1941).

The fact that they wrote and received a good number of letters and had the support of their families also differentiated them from the mainstream prisoners. As we have seen, one of the first things Barrington did at the start of his sentence was enquire about visiting times for his wife. His mother accompanied his wife and children on the first visit:

> Mother herself always anxious, dubious and apprehensive about line of action. [Nevertheless, she] said, 'I'm proud of my boy' after attending trials & is writing friends accordingly (13 May 1941).

Family visits on Saturday afternoons were treasured moments for him and he recognised his own good fortune in this respect:

> Pleased to have my family back today looking well. Jan & mother & John, Peter & Jezebel – nursed P & J & kissed all three goodbye. Jane talks of

'working' half a day a week at Webb St & concerned about taking further money from Stuart in view of his marriage. They brought (or mother did) violets, daphne, *Listener*, *Empire*, *Peace News*, Shaw plays, *War Resister* which Mr McK asked if I had received before. I hadn't although as I said I had received some of their material. He decided to hold it & refer yonder. I expect I shall not see it again (2 August 1941).

Throughout his sentence these visits were joyous, if somewhat chaotic, occasions:

Yesterday Jezebel was trying to tell me something I couldn't understand across the counter until Jane interpreted it as 'Daddy's in gaol'. Peter caught it up with a grin and gleefully shouted 'Daddy's in gaol'– suggesting that it's a new kind of beautiful slogan held up to their friends! (29 June 1941).

He was also regularly visited by a wide range of supporters:

My visitors today were Jane & Mother, John, Peter & Jezebel for half an hour & then Mrs Blake, 'Smithy' and Trig (AC Tregurtha lawyer I worked with many years ago and then again for 8 or 9 yrs in Wgtn). The prison must have been delaying our outward letters – I suppose they've never had such a team with such a mail & they are definitely delaying some of the lads' inward letters (21 June 1941).

There was obvious relief when a letter informed him that his family was coping competently in his absence: 'Jane is to get £2.9 a week from Social Security Dept & seems to be getting about £2 a week from other sources which will keep things going well' (23 May 1941). Jane had supported him during his campaigning and would no doubt have been well aware of the inevitable consequences of his actions. His feelings for her came to the fore on two occasions in the diary, the first in response to a poem by Basil Dowling, who displayed a penchant for writing during his sentence:[3]

I have copied out some of Basil's poems written in prison. He lent me his ms book for the purpose. They are beautiful. 'The aged oak' reminds me of mother and I'll send it to her and his Margaret. One to Jane [Barrington's wife] for though ours is a steadier maturer love and ever growing, the idea is the same … I have not copied the one in which Basil describes his pleasure in the patch of grass outside our wing until he learnt that there the scaffold is erected when a man is hung (29 July 1941).

The second was in the following reflection:

Jane's birthday. I hope the mumps [she was suffering from] have flown. It's a miserable day and even seems to be raining at the right time [that is, to prevent them from going out to work] but expect we'll be dragged out. Jane should get a letter from me. She is a game & loyal lady. I asked Ginger [his sister] to get her stockings from me and mother & mother to get her a book. I believe silk stockings are a rarity. They come only on Fridays and are rushed [i.e. purchased] in a moment (29 July 1941).

As well as being an indication of the effects of wartime exigencies on everyday life, these are tender comments in the context of the highly masculine, emotionally reserved society of 1940s New Zealand.

His three children remained a source of great joy and comfort to him, and while in prison he did the most he could for them, writing to them and sending drawings. When they visited they hung on to him with great affection:

Mother, Jan, J, P & J to see me looking very well and I was able to nurse all three much to my pleasure. Even big John was keen to crawl over counter for the purpose & Peter stroked my face very affectionately. They showed me snaps of them all which were to be left for me but I haven't got them yet (7 June 1941).

On one occasion he noted his daughter in particular was missing him:

Roughly copied from an ad for J, M & Peter. Saving up things like that to copy for the little chaps. Jan's letter says Jezebel misses me most because the boys are able to understand. She asks for me and even pushed a letter under my den door the other morning. She was two on 8th (my birthday too) (21 May 1941).

Apart from an occasional brief insight, Barrington scarcely mentioned the hardships his pacifist beliefs imposed on his family, or the level of physical and emotional strain that his wife was experiencing. Quite apart from anything else, it was a walk of some three miles (a good part of it uphill) each way from the family home to the prison, unless transport was provided by friends.

A fine day. Most had visitors. Jan did not come. Last Sat. with no relief from holding heavy Jezebel must have been too hard and she's feeling a reaction from the period of tension & strain. Next Sat. Mother will mind Jeb. But I had 4 visitors when strictly speaking not entitled to any (17 May 1941).

The cause of Christian pacifism was paramount, however, and family life had to co-exist with this, often on an unequal basis. After he was reprimanded for trying to help Hardgreaves, Barrington explained in a letter to his wife how he would remain steadfast to his Christian beliefs, irrespective of the consequences:

> Have written a fresh three pages to Jan commencing thus: 'I wrote to you last night but I have to try again. You see I have more than you to please at present. And hindrances are encountered in trying to continue being a Christian, that is in helping anyone, high or low. Of course I shall go on trying to help people. There could never be any excuse for a Christian ceasing to help one another and I don't intend to. Naturally one doesn't force help on anyone (1 August 1941).

Even when he began the diary, while on remand awaiting sentence, he did not reflect on the certain outcome. Instead, he listed a series of 23 new words and their definitions that he had discovered in a dictionary which, presumably, he had been allowed to retain during the remand period:

> ... ontology: concerned with the essence of things or beings in the abstract ... iconoclast: breaker of images – especially 8–9th cent against use of images in religious worship in churches of [the] East ... psitticine: of parrots, parrot like (psitticism – talk by GBS [George Bernard Shaw] about benevolence in Stalin – he ends by referring to leaders etc formerly shouting for slaughter of communists and Bolsheviks as psitticism. What on earth is ps. you ask? A useful rhyme for witticism. Look it up in the dictionary. I have! (11 May 1941).

What, though, of the separation of the pacifists, COs and communists from the mainstream prison population? It may have been to protect them from exploitation (or worse) by the other prisoners: as we have seen, Barrington and his colleagues had a good deal to learn about prison life, as the following extract again shows:

> On Sat we were marching around yard to warm up. The warder up aloft suggested we needed a band. So I started up with Onward Christian Soldiers. We hadn't really got going properly when the gate was unlocked & swung open and in stalked the returned Mr L [the deputy chief warder] with stern mien & reproving finger. 'Enough of that,' he cried 'or you'll be separated.' I said 'we're not allowed to sing?' 'Certainly not' says he & stalked out. I don't know how seriously. But we sang hymns at our service this morning though with restraint & order (24 May 1941).

However, while Barrington came perilously close to being exploited and entrapped in his dealings with Hardgreaves, he was not at all intimidated by the other prisoners. He made this clear to one, Peebles, who had quickly sized him up as a trading partner for cigarettes:

> A cleaner this morning asked if I'd swap next tobacco ration for half a jar of jam & ½ a ration of butter. We were on march so I couldn't discuss but sure enough the jam was put in my cell (to be found during unexpected cell search while I was away but I was merely told to empty the jar as two are not allowed). The jam apparently is allowed to those on remand (if for long enough) and this was some unused. I didn't want to barter ... but this chap is very insistent upon a weekly swap of some kind (23 May 1941).

Barrington was not interested in bartering or trading – the standard practice in prison culture. Although Peebles was clearly under the impression that some sort of 'formal' agreement (in prison terms) had been secured, Barrington subsequently explained to him that his Christian beliefs dictated the cigarettes should simply be given to the needy without any reciprocity: 'Have broken news to Peebles that after this week I want to be free to give my tobacco ration away without bargaining for it' (7 June 1941).

Of course, it may be that this separation from the other prisoners was to prevent the dissenters from proselytising their views and attempting to recruit others to the pacifist cause. Barrington had leapt into action to attempt this early in his sentence: 'While waiting with a lot of men in shelter to come in for dinner today, the warders being at a safe distance, I suggested a meeting and stood out in front & answered one or two questions!' (4 June 1941).

There are no further reports of such activities, though, as if he realised both the naivety of attempting to secure converts in this way, and the need to concentrate on getting through his prison sentence. The way to do this was by building up the solidarity and cohesion of his fellow dissenters, rather than recruiting newcomers to the fold.

Nonetheless, his beliefs remained unchanging and unflinching. His view – that both Britain and Nazi Germany bore equal culpability for the war – explains his dispassionate and equivocal reactions to war news he periodically received:

> John Boal reads a satirical article about Hitler. From warder we hear confused story about Hess (deputy to Hitler) landing in Britain by plane

and surrendering. Some sort of peace move it must be. Wish they could
see reason and make some sort of end to it. Then we could get on with
the job of re-building (14 May 1941).

It is clear that Germany has declared war on Russia! What next!
Churchill declares that Britain is determined to destroy Hitler & whoever
is at war with Germany is an ally & all possible aid will be given Russia. A
topsy turvy world (23 June 1941).

Subsequent revelations of Nazi atrocities were proof, for Barrington, of
the evils that stemmed from war. (That a country should deliberately seek
war to enable it to pursue such atrocities did not seem to occur to him.)
And while he quickly gave up on open air 'soap-box' style harangues during
his sentence, he did record various discussions held with warders and other
prisoners about his beliefs:

> Starting off Mr B & I had difficulty in getting appropriate ropes from
> Johnson the little storeman (chivying each other about the war we are
> becoming quite friendly – as opposites do!) He heard Menzies the PM of
> Aust. on air the other day & thinks Menzies is the man to settle people
> like us (19 June 1941).

While there was sympathy for the pacifist cause from one or two (and
quite strong opposition from others), there is no evidence that Barrington
had any success in converting anyone else. The pacifists anyway kept largely
to themselves, both as a result of the spatial arrangements of the prison and
their own preference:

> Sid Harrison (communist) asked if I would help him from tomorrow
> with the gardening gang (especially pig food transport by barrow &
> digging in of surplus). Have left it to him to ask for my services if he
> feels like it. I may not be allocated of course. I was puzzled as to how to
> respond, not wanting to be separated from our own gang, yet realising
> need to mix with others as far as possible (18 May 1941).

In fact, there were insurmountable divisions between those opposed to
the war on religious grounds and those politically opposed to it:

> Often have discussions with Sid Harrison at piggeries when we're
> sheltering there. Day before yesterday he said surprising things: That
> fellows like us would certainly be welcomed & appreciated in Soviet and
> in a communist state. We'd be put in charge of education etc! We would
> be needed. Fellows like himself were ignorant & *brutalised by war*. He

knew that and we're hopeless from the point of view of educating the people along right lines. He was disgusted with me for refusing to admit that I'd rather live under Soviet than capitalist regime at present and still more disgusted when I said that if in Soviet I'd be dead (30 July 1941).

The responses of the two distinct dissenter groups to the prison authorities were also very different. While the pacifists were generally quiescent and respectful, the communists continued their opposition:

Sid Harrison was janitor at Weir House (Victoria College) and was imprisoned for having copies of *Peoples Voice* in his possession. He takes the line of most resistance here, disgruntled against officials, doing as little as possible & generally I think being difficult. Quite a decent fellow but that line can't make him any happier or advance his cause (17 May 1941).

The prison's strategy of keeping the religious dissenters together understandably helped them to maintain a sense of solidarity and unity – unlike elsewhere in the prison:

... pilfering in East Wing. In bath-house, Aston, Knowles and Griffiths (pumice man and very strong) were considering a joint deputation to chief about pilfering ... Knowles mentioned sugar, but I should say he is unreliable, probably barters it away – wouldn't be surprised if he doesn't receive some pilfering proceeds. Radios are interfered with. HB lost a week's tobacco ration, RS two pencils etc. We are free from that also in West Wing (9 July 1941).

It has become very rare for inmates to steal from those on the same wing.[4] On Mt Crawford's East Wing, however, where most were short-sentence inmates with little to gain from any kind of bonding, such conduct was probably fairly common. In contrast, the West Wing solidarity could dramatically change the prison experience and alleviate its pains. The thought of what they looked like in their prison clothes, for example, had allowed Barrington and colleagues to laugh at themselves collectively, rather than recoiling in individual shame. After another weekly change of clothing, he mused

Clean trousers (a bit tighter round the legs & Jack H's at half mast), flannel underwear (pants without a button ...), a shirt somewhat worse than the last, sox ditto, and 2 handkerchiefs one of which huge and obviously a piece of shirt (17 May 1941).

This solidarity also helped them to maintain faith in the validity of the pacifist cause. They accepted their imprisonment with equanimity – hence Barrington's comments when some of the COs' appeals against conviction were to be heard in the Court of Appeal:

God is taking our little plans out of our hands and projecting them with his own matchless skill. Could anything better have happened? Whatever the verdict the cause will have gained much. I said earlier this morning that we didn't mind cleaning pig styes for the love of God! Harold Bray's turn tonight to speak and we're thinking of him & praying for grace & wisdom (16 May 1941).

'Students', not prisoners

Belief in the righteousness of their cause and that they were part of God's mission on earth also gave the pacifists a sense of 'difference' from the other prisoners. They might be in prison, but they were not prepared to accept the label and status of 'prisoner':

Jack Nightingale had visitors at same time – two lads from Ch[ristchurch]. One had a camera and asked warder McL (in charge) if he could take a photo of Jack (who was heavily unshaven). Afterwards Mr McL asked why on earth he wanted to take a photo – said he couldn't understand the mentality of some people. Jack piped up that he didn't regard himself as a criminal though in here and was not ashamed to be here (3 July 1941).

On two occasions Barrington referred to himself and his colleagues as 'students' rather than prisoners:

Gathered from AHC that he had rather given Mr A the impression that we were more favourably treated than others which I think not correct except as far as inherent in our position as students (22 July 1941).

And on being told to write to the 'controller' (of prisons) to seek permission to have his cell light on for longer, he noted that he jumped at this opportunity – 'as will enable me to state a proper case through direct channels and possibly secure improvement for all serious students in prisons' (19 July 1941). Indeed, Barrington's cell, filled with the books he collected as he pursued his studies, was not unlike a study with its own library:

At dinnertime too, I received three things brought in for me on Saturday. Vol 1 *Historians History of World*, *Jean-Christophe* (R Rolland) a comb, fountain pen ink, blotting paper and a large scribbling pad of 200 pages. (I have to account for every page) I am getting fairly complete! (20 May 1941).

He planned to maximise his prison time for study purposes: 'Finished *Under Fire* & commenced *Student's Guide* by Prof John Adams view to learning something about systematic study which I've always lacked direction in' (16 May 1941). His efforts, however, were eclectic and haphazard:

> During the morning I read 33 pages of *Historians History* besides a little writing and odds & ends and a few pages of *Three Men in a Boat* whose humour is a trifle laboured. I also counted words of five pages of the History & got an average of 564 so that the 1st Vol 627 pages was about 372,000 words. I am up to page 240! (5 June 1941).

> Wet morning. Finished also this morning third vol. of *Historians History of the World*. Making rather heavy & laborious job of it and I don't feel that it is especially profitable but I'm persisting (29 July 1941).

This entry also demonstrates how, apart from the tokenistic evening classes for illiterates that the authorities claimed they provided, education featured very little in the organisation of prison life. In fact, rather than helping to socialise inmates or stimulating their behaviour – which was 'vital', they had stated – it strongly militated *against* this. The prison routine and timetable constantly broke up the day and interrupted any periods of time free for study; unless the weather was exceptionally bad, inmates were forced to spend their weekends aimlessly in the yards rather than studying in their cells:

> We were turned out in the cold about 10 am – not to work but to spend remainder of morning in yard – to my disgust. I had begun *History of Greece*. However I took community supplement from *Peace News* & *Readers Digest* with me & read all of former to two or three. AHC, JB & HB played chess. OEB by some special favour was allowed to remain in cell (29 July 1941).

Barrington – and others – were determined to make imprisonment a liberating experience, one to be welcomed rather than feared. Their ascetic, cellular confinement was conducive to the monk-like qualities of pietism, contemplation and study:

> Will be glad to have light till 9 pm tonight. Asked for it Sat. I have been hopefully sitting up to find the peephole used 8 or thereabouts & the

light inexorably switched off no matter what I am doing with books on knee & pen poised hopefully. I mutter 'blighters' but don't really cherish hard thoughts. Pace cell for a while & meditate – and last two nights consumed a buttered crust for supper (13 May 1941).

Light on early & good spell [i.e. of bible study and religious contemplation] before breakfast. Hymns, St John, Prayers, *Penguin Political Dict*[ionary] (14 May 1941).

Solidarity through religion

When out of their cells, the Christian pacifists maintained their solidarity and sense of unity with daily commitments to their religious beliefs – particularly so in the yard at weekends:

This morning started a group study of Acts of Apostles led by OEB (17 May 1941).

Had our Bible class in the morning which was crowded out, then visitors (7 June 1941).

This morning, Saturday, it is raining as hard as it can … B[ible] C[lass]. Study of Acts in yard, very wet and seats had been left in the rain. The only dry spot was the wash basins shelf (26 July 1941).

On Sundays they held their own church services: 'Ormond conducted a fine little service. Experimented with hymn singing (instead of reading together) with results felt to be satisfactory and to be developed' (18 May 1941). He added somewhat optimistically, 'it may be helpful to those in the other yards'. On other occasions they broke off their own services to attend those provided by the prison; it would seem their presence was required to prevent an embarrassingly small attendance (demonstrating again the gulf that existed between their fervent beliefs and the rest of the almost wholly irreligious prison population):

My service this morning was interrupted when the sermon was well begun in order to attend a Minister's Association Service for a young and reasonable Baptist. If we hadn't gone, there would only have been about five there (20 July 1941).

They routinely shared any providences, gifts and 'finds' that came their way:

Tea tonight was again fine. Stewed beef & potatoes, large quantity plum pudding (same as Sunday) with plentiful sultanas & cocoa. Also 1 shiny red apple. O gave AHC as he passed & A halved it with me. So then I have 1½. I passed a small piece of cheese (15 May 1941).

I have nearly double milk ration tonight as H had some left after he had distributed & I'm well in hand with butter as Jim D has given me half a ration (21 June 1941).

3 onions which I gave to Dave, Jim and Harold. AHC and I had two nice biscuits each from Harry: one of mine I gave JW and JD also introduced by Harry to a tin of boiled mussels and had about 4 without distress. I suppose in this place I could acquire a taste for anything! (9 July 1941).

Putting my milk bottle out for washing at breakfast ready for evening ½ pint [284 ml] I found it full (½ pint) at time. A 'remand' did not want his & S passed it over. Harry passed a ¼ jar of golden syrup through window & I passed him some matches. Ron also brought his full jar to yard so I kept that & gave AHC the ¼ for he had already had a full jar from Harry (26 July 1941).

In ways such as these (and completely against prison regulations), they tried to ensure that none of their colleagues was left hungry while at the same time allowing each to have more of the food they enjoyed the most:

> The foul tea is supposed to have milk in it but I add a little to tone it down and use milk for cocoa & if any left drink it so as not to waste. Gave some to AHC last night. O again foisted today's apple on me. (I'll quarter it in yard). Dave gave a generous helping of butter which O gave him! I now have a reserve supply. JHW was going to give me some but he can give to Dave. Not eating porridge I use more butter than the others. We have discussed possibility of getting authorities to provide a lb [453 gm] packet of raisins as a weekly substitute for those who do not smoke. Retail it would cost only 9½d compared with 1/1d for tobacco, papers & matches & would be very acceptable (18 May 1941).

The sharing extended to flowers as well, so that all could enjoy the pleasure of their colours and aroma in the grey world of prison:

> Mr McL also brought a large supply of Daphne. A fairly large bunch from Mother and little bunches left by Mrs Cannons – so that AHC, Basil and O bouquet each and all the others a piece each while I have 5 or 6 heads (a little worse for wear) with my marigold in vase (13 July 1941).

Barrington provided Burton with some of his own bedding:

Yesterday when giving our blankets their weekly shake in yard I noticed that O had some more indescribable than most. One especially was an extraordinary colour very thin & with a great hole in centre. I got him to exchange for one of my good ones. He feels the cold a lot. I gather that he and others have paper under their mattresses to keep out the draught (1 June 1941).

Collectively they assisted Ron Scarlett, a vegetarian:

Ron appeared during the proceedings & was duly welcomed and told the 'inside' routines necessary for comfort etc. He is practically vegetarian, doesn't drink milk and doesn't eat hash or golden syrup. I have arranged to relieve him of the latter. We'll soon dispose of that for him! (10 June 1941).

Vegetarian provisions were meagre at best; Kelman, also a vegetarian, lived on 'raw carrots, swedes, parsnips and baked onions' (24 May 1941). To ensure Scarlett did not suffer unduly as a result, Barrington wrote, 'took half ration of cold pudding out for Ron & told him I'd bring the other half this afternoon & if I'd known we would not be searched I'd have brought it all at once (28 July 1941). The generosity of the food servings facilitated the assistance they could give, as did the food bonuses given in return for work undertaken for the warders:

Ron Scarlett ... is not getting enough bread. Nearly everybody gets too much though with the wheat germ loaf some of us are eating all ours. But Ron eating no meat (even hash) using no milk and no golden s. [syrup] probably has a very deficient diet. Discovered about bread as he was worried about prospect of 'picnic' lunch tomorrow as he would have no bread, eating his whole loaf at night. We reassured him that we would bring plenty. But JB arriving from work down at warder's house brought nearly a loaf of dry bread and we soon had it passed to Ron who then and at cowshed devoured it as it was – seemed to take it in great gulps. JB also brought brown sandwiches of which I had one and spoke of celery soup and hot scones produced by Mr A.! (3 July 1941).

In return, Scarlett's unwanted weekly ration of Golden Syrup was quickly targeted by the others:

O gave me an apple & a small quantity of treacle per JH. RJS after several attempts was too nervous to bring out his jar of gs to pass on to AHC though we 3 times during weekend took our jars out hopefully to yards! Though not difficult it is complicated by R being in east wing – as also HB (15 June 1941).

Although very hesitant about participating in such activities at first, Scarlett gained in confidence and no doubt also became aware that the warders were not inclined to look too carefully for breaches of regulations such as these – particularly among a group of prisoners with whom a level of trust had been established:

Ron S. actually braved all dangers and brought his treacle (wrapped in paper and a spare sugar bag!). AHC and I are dividing (12 July 1941).

Similarly, Barrington and colleagues gave support and encouragement to new Christian pacifist arrivals:

Found on emerging that Basil in our wing & was able to give him a welcome through peep hole in passing & again when passing his window. He had to stay in for finger prints etc and then was in exercise yard until dinner. JH & I were able to give him a wave there from cow shed hill. After dinner he was assigned to gardening gang which if sustained will give O a working mate (4 June 1941).

… new CO – looked after – Harry handed me a piece of cheese at lecture & I gave half of it to Bob Durrant with whom I sat. He had been shifted from our wing to east (28 July 1941).

If an opportunity arose they also proffered what they had to other needy prisoners, without any expectation of reciprocity. This contravened not only prison regulations but also prisoner culture, with its insistence on repayment on pain of huge debts otherwise occurring.[5] Barrington noted,

While waiting in the yard yesterday O produced an apple for me but we shared it among the 4. Cold corn beef, potatoes & a nice beetroot, plums, rice & milk & cocoa for tea. Plus an apple (bruised) given me by cleaner Hardgreaves. For lunch 2 apples were shared between the 7 of us. JMW has been offered all one man's allowance & is taking the apples but only because the man cannot eat them. I was reserving my tobacco for old Maori but Harold Bray smokes & we'll be seeing him in the morning. He won't get any until Sat. & the others have given theirs away. I am keeping pieces (the fat piece) of corn beef & 2 large potatoes to take out to the boys' lunches tomorrow (19 May 1941).

It is possible their values sparked a response from some mainstream prisoners, who occasionally shared items also: 'The Presby laundry man handed me some Pix's & a *New Horizon* through window' (12 June 1941); 'Harry (Maori) gave Arthur two biscuits each for him and me' (3 July 1941).

The inescapable impact of prison

But whatever their intentions to the contrary, Barrington and the dissenters could not help being affected by the values and environment of the prison. This was reflected in the way in which *everything* in the prison – no matter how small or insignificant or how worthless outside of it – came to have value, or was put to use in some way. Anything at all – even half a chocolate wheaten biscuit – that made the prison experience more bearable, made it a shade brighter, broke the monotony and provided some level of enrichment, however tenuous and brief, became precious.

The continual search for useful objects turned Barrington and his colleagues into scavengers. This was particularly evident in their endless hunt for food to supplement the prison diet:

> And I had this parsley heaped on my table making a sandwich when Mr A called on some of us to see if we would help with some pears which had just arrived. I bundled my parsley into cupboard & we went to with a will. Many I'm afraid were over ripe. But for carrying we were allowed to help ourselves & I had about 8 of which I ate 3 for tea (18 June 1941).

> … Jim and I had substantial raw carrots which he got and washed in the garden. This afternoon I got a couple more onions for myself and some for AHC HB and JH and again I've supplemented porridge and tea by onion sandwiches with some reserved for supper and a small onion over for tomorrow (26 June 1941).

Such smuggling practices did not have to be particularly sophisticated to get past the half-hearted scrutiny of the warders:

> A luxurious bed of parsley attracted me & I collected a liberal handful & put it in my shirt – an unnecessary precaution as there was no search tonight. I took some for my innards and after porridge for tea I had bread and parsley sandwiches with salt! Two sandwiches of a double slice each and I've ample parsley left for supper & breakfast (18 June 1941).

At times they went to remarkable lengths to salvage any food they could find, however dubious its quality and origin:

Basil Dowling gave me a pear which he too retrieved from garbage tin! E said he and Sid came across about a dozen perfectly good ones (1 July 1941).

Had cup of tea at piggeries. They had out to dry large smoked fish (3) recovered from garbage which they had washed and intended to cook (18 July 1941).

… a large cooking apple thrown clear from Air Force garbage today only damaged by a gashed side, I operated upon it with a piggeries knife and extracted a perfectly sound & clean segment from its innards! (24 July 1941).

We helped clean the pig sties and weren't they slushy! … Found one whole cauliflower intact and we ate the heart. Mr MacC (warder) said, 'you don't know what's been at it.' But I said it would be alright washed (28 July 1941).

The prison diet alone was simply not sufficient to sustain the health of men expected to perform exacting and physically demanding hard labour, nor to help them to fend off the effects of the cold. But the fact that they were prepared to eat anything they could scavenge was not simply the result of such deficiencies. As Ugelvik[6] has argued,

[Prison] food can be seen as part of a complex melange of identity threats experienced by prisoners as attacks on their acquired status as adult males who can eat what they want, when they want it. On the other hand, food can also be an area for resistance, aimed at the individual prison, the larger prison system it is part of and the wider … society it represents.

As well as adding variety and vitamins, boosting their diet in these ways allowed the men to reclaim this cardinal part of their life. In addition, food sharing was a way to ensure that it went to each according to his needs, rather than the standard measurement for all that the prison worked to: 'big & little men, big eaters & little eaters all get the same quantity – liberal for main foods but decidedly short when it comes to the "extras" like milk, butter, golden treacle, fruit' (21 June 1941).

Scavenging extended to objects as well as food. Barrington found a tobacco tin, 'and having become possessed of an extra cake of soap I can now carry soap in pocket near a tap' (3 June 1941).

At piggeries today the pigman produced spoons and knives from a cubby hole and started polishing them. They were superior to prison ware, good quality. Six bread & butter knives and as many teaspoons & dessert spoons and an apple corer & what not. I learned that these are all recovered from air force garbage. The pigman trades them for tobacco, presumably with the carrier (18 June 1941).

Recently I secured a piece of blanket about 20" [50 cm] square I found in paddock. It may have blown away from washing lines. I carefully washed it at cowsheds & left overnight in a tree to dry. Next day I halved it with AHC to provide for each of us a cloth to wipe our little meal tables after meals to make writing & reading at them afterwards easier. I keep it with my floor brush – he under his mattress (19 June 1941).

Boler producing a piece of wood cut to the requisite 15¼" [38 cm] for my radio support. I brought it in up my trouser leg and down my sock & will work at it tonight (22 July 1941).

They demonstrated a remarkable inventiveness in putting such treasures to use:

JD made splendid coat and trouser hangers for AHC and me this morn – out of galvanised iron. Promptly hammered in a nail under blanket shelf and hanger holds trousers sports coat and overcoat comfortably (18 July 1941).

JB with practical turn of mind for community conceived the idea that fishing would be important food producing aspect and we would need to make our own nets. So he has fossicked around to discover correct knot and found Bill Mitchell of piggeries fished and made nets in depression. JB has learnt the knot and carries a littler spindle affair he has made and practices net making. Good work (21 July 1941).

By virtue of working outdoors most of the time on the prison farm, Barrington and his colleagues were well placed to do this: the hard labour part of their sentence, intended to punish them the most severely, also presented them, ironically, with the most opportunities to alleviate some of the pains it caused. The thrill of smuggling back into the prison what they had managed to scavenge also enlivened their predictable and regimented world:

My concern about getting 4 onions past search was solved beautifully. For late afternoon I had another visitor, resulting in entry to cell ahead of others and dispensing with search! (27 June 1941).

The rudimentary searching practices ensured that the risk of being caught in possession of contraband was slim. At the same time, given the reasonably cordial relationships between warders and COs, it would seem unlikely that the discovery of a few leaves of parsley or some rotting carrots would have produced much response from the officials. The men could embrace the excitement of smuggling without being too concerned about its possible consequences.

'Everything means something in prison'[7]

Just as the slightest deviations from the regimented system of order and control provoked immediate suspicion and speculation from the warders, so it did among the inmates too. They observed everything, missed nothing and speculated wildly over the meaning of every departure from the anticipated norm:

> The doctor must be going on holiday as he was in attendance today [rather than later in the week] & those requiring his services were rounded up (27 July 1941).

Similarly, after the assault on Parsons in the dummy, anything out of the ordinary seemed to recall this incident to mind:

> Since tea there has been a banging of the gate down to 'dummy' & Warder K, who seems to be on night duty with W tonight, came to Storeman's cell window and got his keys which he returned in a little while. Whether this has any significance or connection with dummy incident I don't know (7 August 1941).

> While in soap [works] A and J saw McK mixing whitewash and story is that he has been whitewashing dummy (9 August 1941).

In a world stripped down to this minimalist form of existence, in just the same way that pieces of chocolate biscuit assumed exotic qualities, so the tiniest departures from the norm of prison life became matters of great magnitude and the smallest incidents noteworthy:

> Sharp frost. Breakfast: porridge, hash, tea, bread. The fiery anti-pacifist storeman Johnson, returning the second of my *Picture Post* [magazines], offers to give me an eye shade for reading at night and called me Barry (23 June 1941).

> Tea: rather stodgy rice pudding (without fruit) cocoa, bread. At lecture AHC gave me a fair lump of cheese (24 June 1941).

By the same token, reveries of life beyond the prison – and how much this was missed – could be conjured by the slightest connections to it that the men came across inside:

From my green sports coat last weekend I collected a woman's hair – presumably Jane's! I have preserved it. It is an unusual occupant of these stony masculine walls (26 July 1941).

To a degree, the dissenters succeeded in establishing their own culture within the prison, undercutting and undermining the more usual prison values. Their belief in the justice of their cause also provided a sense of righteousness and solidarity that lightened the pains of their imprisonment. Unlike the 'forgotten men' in East Wing, they also gained support from letter writing and visits. Yet in order to survive in prison as they did, they could not avoid being touched by the experience of it. With the other prisoners, they became skilled in the art of scavenging, making the most of any opportunity, however minute, to brighten their threadbare existence.

Chapter 6

Prison Past and Present

The last entry in Barrington's diary was for 13 August 1941:

> Warder A on night duty poked a jovial friendly face at my window & had a few words. Davey has just come to window & suggested that inquiry is being ditched & that Parsons has been given 3 more days in Dummy for swearing.

The official version of events had been confirmed. The assault on Parsons 'never happened': he was in the dummy for swearing at an officer – there was no more to the case than that. This adjudication closed the matter and brought to an end the interruption it had caused to prison routines and inmate–staff relations. The prison returned to normal. Barrington was greeted, once more, by the friendly warder's face at his window. He had his inevitable breakfast of 'porr[idge], hash, tea, bread'. The prison radio became a central issue again:

> Loudspeaker to 9 as usual last night, though somewhat restrained. Mr T yesterday claimed credit for fixing up the relay system when it was broken & neglected for a week or so earlier. I said if he fixed it up that was the only thing we had against him. It was a surprise to him that it was regarded as a menace to sanity (13 August 1941).

But on this day Barrington, having had to battle the elements for much of his sentence wearing ill-fitting flimsy shirts and trousers, had some good fortune at last. For once, the weather had come to his assistance, granting him a day in his cell: 'Rain persisting [and] we're shut in with gladness.' We take our leave of him as he reflects on Irving Stone's 1934 novel, *Lust for Life*, which he had finished the previous night:

> A strange tale of a strange man, Vincent Van Gogh … The book is raw but mightily moving. The fine frenzy of the artist writing to create burning himself up, possessed by his craft – there is something sublime and terrible in it. My own Dad had something of that same 'lust for life' (though that expression is faulty) and its disappointments.

As we have seen, the diary fills an empty historiographical space by revealing scenes from everyday prison life in 1941. But it does more than this. Through its images of the past we also gain further understanding of prison today. It draws our attention to the discontinuities between prisons of the past and present, and the continuities that link the past with the present. Irrespective of modifications to prison buildings or changes to the formal aims and expectations of incarceration, imprisonment has certain timeless qualities.

Before we can make any such generalisations, however, we need to assess the typicality of Barrington's representation of prison life at Mount Crawford: the more accurate we can gauge it to be, the more authoritative the diary becomes as a testament to prison life at that time.

Corroborating the diary

Barrington's contemporaries have validated his Mount Crawford experiences on numerous occasions. In his 1945 memoir, *In Prison*, Ormond Burton also complained that the library was 'a scandal. The greater part of the books are rejects from one or other of the public libraries … there is quite a fair sprinkling of the stuff which some years ago was considered to be nice for little girls between the ages of seven and twelve.'[1] He confirmed the strong work ethic the dissenters brought to prison: 'Hard and willing work enables a man to keep his self-respect in a place that is largely designed to kill self-respect.'[2] And he too wrote of the cordial relations between select prisoners and the families of prison staff:

> The superintendent's wife [at Mount Crawford] was a very kind person, always on the lookout for anyone, convict or post girl, into whom she could infiltrate a cup of tea. Her husband unofficially approved of this practice … there is a fairly widespread tradition in the prison service that if a convict has for any reason to go to a warder's house, as is often the case with vegetables etc, he should be offered a cup of tea.[3]

In addition, he referred to the atypicality of violence at that time: '[prison life] is as peaceful and as ordered an existence as one could very well desire. It would be an ideal life for a great scholar provided he could have an extension of lights until midnight.'[4]

Arthur Carman's notes confirm the routine prison menu. In addition to the 'porridge and hash and tea' for breakfast every morning, porridge would also be served for the evening meal five days per week, the exceptions being

'Mondays (rice and cocoa) and Fridays (rice and apple)'.[5] His account of the assault on Parsons is very similar to Barrington's: 'on Tuesday night as I was having tea I heard sudden cries as of someone in terror and then loud crying – together with a coming and going of warders from the "dummy". I found out later that it was young Parsons, one month for failing to register – and McK had apparently battered him and a blood stained towel was handed in to the washhouse next day'.[6]

The memoirs of dissenters imprisoned in different institutions confirm Mount Crawford as a typical example of the prison system as a whole. Describing the backbreaking, pointless and inefficient work, Allan Handyside wrote that at Rangipo, 'much of [this] was grossly uneconomic or intended to simply provide hard labour'.[7] Ian Hamilton, imprisoned at 'Wenukai' (his pseudonym for Hautu Detention Camp), wrote, 'the farming is just a joke, or it would be a joke if it weren't so excruciatingly cold. As it is, the stock on the farms is a walking indictment of the government and also the jails'.[8]

On the subject of prison-issue clothing, Walter Lawry wrote of being given a uniform at Paparua that 'may turn a tall man into a scarecrow as the moleskin pants end several inches above the ankle and the coat sleeves reach to the tips of his fingers'.[9] William Young recalled, 'as to the underclothes and shirt I was issued with, you could spit peas through them, a condition I found to be a common factor of practically all prison issue clothes'.[10] Nor was Mount Crawford the only cold prison with insufficient bedding: at Paparua, 'the blankets, grey and rough, don't look anything like the ones I am used to at home, and the frost air drifting through the window into an unheated cell doesn't make for comfort'.[11] Similarly at Mount Eden, 'they give you two coarse sheets but you never use those, you put as many thicknesses of blanket over you as you can arrange and then tuck the canvas sheets round your feet to keep the draught out'.[12]

Like Barrington, it was the monotony of the diet rather than any particular lack of food that Hamilton remembered: 'look at what the prisoner must have, it's in the regulations. So many ounces of meat per day, so much butter, sugar, vegetables ... [but] until you've been in jail, its almost impossible to realise how a certain type of food routine can get you down'.[13] The poor food preparation at Mount Crawford was also observed at other penal institutions: 'after the cooks fill the tins they put them in the oven to keep hot, which explains the solid crusts on each. And the tea, which has been left boiling for up to half an hour after infusion, beggars description'.[14] With an aversion similar to Barrington's, Lawry wrote, 'can that grey-looking solid lump with a crust on top be porridge?'[15]

This does not mean that all New Zealand prisons were identical, of course. By 1941, each superintendent seems to have had considerable local autonomy. During the war, there would have been even less monitoring of local prison administration than usual and more opportunity for differences to emerge. For example, Mount Crawford seems to have been considerably cleaner than other prisons and 'lockups' (remand cells in police stations). Lawry remembered the lockup at Christchurch as 'absolutely filthy, and the blankets issued to us bore very considerable indications from both ends of the spectrum … the walls carried a number of interesting observations, many from minds as filthy as the matter deposited, matter not totally cleared away by chucking a bucket of water at it'.[16]

Whereas Mount Crawford appears to have been a remarkably peaceful institution, Hamilton remembered that 'violence was always in the offing'[17] at Mount Eden, possibly because there were more serious offenders housed there. Equally, it would appear that warders were generally more distant and reserved at other institutions. Handyside, for example, complained that while a warder 'should carry out the exercise of his authority accompanied by good temper and humanity … practically all their conversation was limited to orders, requests or explanations'.[18] Of course, it must be remembered that Handyside was a CO who chose to confront the authorities and continue his opposition to war, first at the detention camp to which he was sent and then in prison, culminating in his hunger strike at Mount Eden. The reaction of the warders was perhaps unsurprising, since he was challenging their authority as well as that of the government; Barrington, on the other hand, went out of his way to establish congenial relations with prison staff, which most reciprocated irrespective of their views on the war. The less peaceful inmate–staff relations at other institutions are also a likely explanation for the lack of references to the sort of illicit working arrangements found at Mt Crawford.

Overall, then, despite some important differences between the respective penal institutions, the conditions of confinement at Mount Crawford were typical of the time: a mixture of inadequate and primitive hygiene; inefficient, often pointless work; rags for uniforms; and ample, if drearily monotonous, food servings.[19] To a certain extent the nineteenth-century 'less eligibility' principle[20] – that people in prison ought to endure worse conditions than those of the lowest free people outside – still dictated prison arrangements.

It helps to explain the under-investment and decrepit futility of much of what took place.

That said, prison arrangements were also more complex than mere insistence on the appropriate level of deprivation that was thus demanded. The regular meals of meat, potatoes and vegetables were a reflection of the New Zealand norm, made possible by an almost wholly agricultural economy. The authorities saw no reason to provide less. This is perhaps another pointer to the relatively short social distances then in existence between prisoners and the rest of the community. At the time there was no political climate demanding that prisoners should suffer much more than a loss of liberty; the relaxed attitude to escaping prisoners is another indication of this.

Mount Crawford was also characterised by the largely peaceful co-existence between staff and inmates. There was nothing like the high levels of disorder, tension and excitement that subsequently became features of the 'underlife of the prison' studies generated in the US from around this time.[21]

Lost in the past

In many respects this type of prison life has disappeared. The closure of Mount Crawford in 2012 is symptomatic of the line that has been drawn between that era of prison administration and the present. In the former, prisoners might come into contact with prison officers' families and exchange pleasantries with them; well-known civil servants and academics would come to the prison to give lectures to inmates; senior government ministers would rush to a prison to investigate on hearing that an assault had occurred. Work outside the prison was a routine part of its operation: the meths drinkers, men with one arm or one eye, fantasists and the like who were then predominant in the prison population, were sent out to the gardens or the farm to potter around as best they could.

It was an era when prisoner classification was merely on the basis of age and type of offence. Since then, security classifications have been vastly expanded and become much more restricted – there were six separate categories for both internal and external risk assessment in 2012. As a consequence, employment opportunities beyond the prison have mostly disappeared. Rather than escapes being viewed as an inevitable part of life as they were then, any security breach or problematic incident is now likely to bring further restrictions that affect the whole of the prison population rather than the single recalcitrant.[22] For the few who do satisfy the security criteria, work outside is accompanied by thorough strip searches (involving significantly more than the lackadaisical pat-downs Barrington experienced) each time they enter and leave the institution.

This overwhelming emphasis on security has imposed new humiliations and debasements on prisoners. While they are now likely to be clothed in tracksuits rather than rags, the opportunity to briefly throw off their prisoner identity and put on their own clothes during Visits, available in 1941, has gone. Instead, they are strip searched before the visit, must don a red Guantanamo Bay-style jumpsuit that makes them stand out to the watching officers, and are strip searched afterwards.

Similarly, the strong links that existed between the community at large and New Zealand prisons, marked by events such as Christmas and New Year concerts given by local charities and dignitaries, have long since disappeared. Barrington had found no evidence of them, but whether these were real or fictional at that time is beside the point. Not only do they no longer exist; there is no *possibility* of their existence. The hours of 'association' following the evening meal, which used to be available for these occasions, have mostly disappeared. Instead, prisoners are likely to be locked down for 15-hour periods without respite, and often share a cell that may have been built for just one person. During lockdown, in-cell television has become a regular form of pacification.[23] There are still prison visits from groups such as Alcoholics Anonymous, but these have to be packaged into rehabilitative 'programmes' and attendances are monitored and noted. Such activities are considered to contribute to the managerial performance of each prison, rather than being benevolent expressions of goodwill with inmates free to attend as they wish. Gratuitous concerts and the like do not fit the 'throughputs' and 'outputs' columns of the key performance indicators (KPIs) that have come to be regarded as measures of a prison's success or failure.

Visits by well-known personalities, possible in Mount Crawford in 1941, have also become unthinkable because they would be too costly, would necessitate extra staff on duty and would interfere with the lockdown; besides, there would be too much risk involved in their attendance, the result of the far greater social distance that has come to exist between prisoners and non-prisoners. For the same reason, any such visits might now be detrimental to the reputation of those making them. Since the 1980s, when law and order came to feature more prominently in New Zealand public discourse,[24] politicians have regularly tried to make capital of this distance by further extending it, rather than rushing to the prison to investigate any kind of prisoner mistreatment that comes to their attention. In response to high levels of public outrage at prisoners winning redress for mistreatment while in prison, the Prisoners and Victims Claims Act (2005) effectively nullifies any further legal proceedings that prisoners might take against the Department of Corrections for ill-treatment since, if successful, they will not be allowed to receive any compensation under the terms of this legislation.[25]

As this has happened, the autonomy of prison authorities has also been undermined. The politicisation of crime and punishment, enthusiastically driven by the media and the Sensible Sentencing Trust, means that the authorities are under far greater public scrutiny.[26] They are no longer able to decide that rehabilitation should not be jeopardised by security demands, nor are they able to brush aside escapes as inconsequential matters. In recent times the *Department of Corrections Annual Report* stated that its 'vision' (itself another indicator of the break with the past) was to 'have the New Zealand public's understanding and confidence'.[27]

Some aspects of the conditions of confinement have, undeniably, continued along the steady course of amelioration that began in the late nineteenth century. Catering reflects the greater diversity of food preparation and eating habits that now exist beyond the prison: there are vegetarian and vegan options, Hindi, Kosher and Halal food preparation, and special diets for pregnant prisoners and those with allergies. Some of the more obvious signs of degradation and humiliation associated with imprisonment at the time of Barrington's diary have gone. The chamber pots have all but disappeared, replaced with in-cell sanitation, and most prisoners are now able to take daily showers. Formally, at least, there is a more ostentatious demonstration of 'respect' shown by officers to inmates in the aftermath of the highly influential work of Alison Liebling.[28] There are programmes that enable Māori prisoners to recover and embrace their cultural identity. And although prisoner–prisoner and staff–prisoner violence became a more regular feature of prison life in the post-Barrington era[29] and continues to be so, formally it is tolerated less.[30] Violent incidents look bad on the KPIs, even though, because of overcrowding and staff reductions, stress levels are probably more conducive to aggression.

However, there also seems no doubt that the prison experience has simultaneously become much more intense and more difficult to endure.[31] The changing nature of the prison population itself has contributed to this. In 2003 (the most recent data available), adult male prisoners serving three months or less constituted just 6.7% of the prison population of 7500; those serving between three and six months made up 3.8%. In contrast, those serving determinate sentences of more than five years (so few in 1941), constituted 16%. Indefinite sentences of life imprisonment or preventive detention were being served by 9.2%. The preponderance of short-sentence prisoners seen in 1941 has given way to inmates serving much longer terms, usually for violent and/or sexual offences: in 2012, 40% of the daily average prison population of 8700 had violence as their most serious offence and 22% had sexual offences.

Further, between 1941 and 2012 the prison population became younger: in 2012, 24% of New Zealand prisoners were aged under 24. Most are now likely to have drug as well as alcohol dependency issues and psychiatric problems. There are also more distinctive ethnic divisions within the prison population. Barrington mentioned two or three Māori prisoners (but no Pacific Islanders); the overwhelming majority of inmates were European. Now, 50% of prisoners are Māori and 17% are Islanders. Many of these inmates – and some of the Pākehā – also have gang affiliations.

Such a population ensures that the experience of imprisonment is volatile and unpredictable, as has been regularly noted since the 1950s;[32] it makes the survival of newcomers to prison, particularly those whose offence or publicity outside brings them to the attention of other prisoners, much more problematic. David Bain, for example, was assaulted several times during the 13 years he spent in prison from 1995 to 2008.[33] Like Bain, Barrington, Burton and Carman were all well known before their imprisonment, yet Burton merely complained of feeling 'lonely' before his companions joined him.[34] He experienced none of the unwanted and very threatening attention that another 'celebrity' prisoner, Jeffrey Archer, later complained of.[35] Barrington and Carman reported no threats at all to their personal safety.

Furthermore, Barrington's diary indicates that the sex offenders in 1941 served their sentences without any special protection or unwanted attention. By the 1960s, however, this had changed. Priestly[36] provides examples from English prisoner biographies of that period, which show that assaults on sex offenders, often with the collusion of prison officers, had become a standard occurrence. Given the similarities between New Zealand and British prisons,[37] it is likely the same developments took place here.

Improvements to some prison conditions have been offset by a decline in others. Barrington appreciated the quiet of the prison at night. Since then, the availability of powerful in-cell 'sound systems', the absence of the consideration that Barrington displayed in ensuring that the noise of his personal radio did not intrude on the comfort of others, and more unremitting use of lockdowns so that there can be no escape from the noise on the wing, has turned imprisonment into a babel-like experience in New Zealand and similar societies. In the United States George Jackson wrote, 'the early hours of morning are the only time of day that one can find any respite from the pandemonium caused by the most uncultured San Quentin inmates ... in the evenings ... it rises to maddening intensity'.[38] Newbold complained that 'the considerable noise made by other inmates was a constant source of friction ... almost every night some moron would start singing or rattling his bars just as everybody else was trying to get some sleep'.[39] Archer, who described the disturbance caused by 'window warriors' (prisoners standing by their cell window during the night, trying to engage all and sundry to talk to them), referred also to 'prisoners shouting from cell to cell, and loud rap music coming from every corner of the block'.[40]

Some of the improvements have anyway proved illusory: the prison experience has become more, rather than less, difficult to endure. While prisoners no longer experience the indignities of using a chamber pot followed by slopping-out procedures, the introduction of in-cell sanitation has meant that most have to 'sleep in their toilets' (and a shared toilet at that, in many cases). In addition, from the 1980s, most opportunities for work *within* the New Zealand prisons disappeared, largely because of a new economic rationalism in prison policy: its industries had to be cost effective. The manufacture of toys to give to children's hospitals, for example, which up to that point had become something of a cottage industry, was stopped. This meant that a large number of prisoners simply became idle for most, if not all, of their sentence.

The prison experience has also changed dramatically for those employed in the institutions. It is inconceivable that anything like the systemic black economy that existed at Mount Crawford in 1941 would now be able to flourish. Deviant practices still occur between individual officers and inmates, of course, but as Crewe has written of Wellingborough Prison in England, 'staff ... consistently stated that they would inform management without hesitation if they were to discover staff corruption'.[41] In New Zealand as well, the conduct of each officer can now affect the achievement or non-achievement of KPIs, on which bonuses are likely to be dependent or penalties forthcoming.

In Barrington's time rudimentary strip searches were undertaken on a rota basis, or avoided altogether where trust was established between an inmate and officers. A daily search of all inmates would have necessitated a complete reorganisation of the prison routine and a reduction of prisoner working hours. Now there are no exceptions: strip searches are invariably performed by two or more officers, thereby ensuring the scrutiny over and awareness of each by all. The maintenance and enforcement of security at all possible breach points has become the central feature of prison life. Working hours must be tailored to suit security, rather than the reverse; prison escapes now point to a failure of what has become the most fundamental requisite of prison life – 'the protection of society from those sentenced to it'.[42]

Meanwhile, prison superintendents have become 'managers', indicative of the changing role and responsibilities of their position. Their once supervisory role is now focused on governance, leadership and organisational responsibility, and includes ensuring, through the KPIs, that the institution adheres to the departmental 'mission statement'. As a result of the preoccupation with local policy development and implementation, these managers have next to none of the visibility within the prison that the superintendent had in Barrington's time, when the two met frequently. In contrast, Archer, imprisoned from 2001–05, 'never got to see the governor of Wayland prison'.[43] As Crewe suggests, this transition from superintendent to manager is symptomatic of the way 'the system [now] appear[s] faceless, and its decisions (about home leave, for example, or a prisoner's right to personal property) [are] almost impossible to challenge through interpersonal negotiation or direct appeals to humanity'.[44]

Barrington's prison experiences are indeed relics of the past: a past where each prison was administered as a semi-autonomous entity with its own informal codes and culture within a central system; a past where standards of hygiene were deplorably low; a past where the prison for the most part acted as a receptacle, not for dangerous or uncontrollable offenders, but for the relatively harmless casualties of society. It made no great demands on the shambling mass of humanity received; nor was any commitment to rehabilitation expected from them.

But it was also a past where prisoners were not completely shut out of society; a past where there were no self-styled representatives of 'public opinion' demanding that prisons should be run according to their own uninformed and harsh specifications; where the high levels of homogeneity running through New Zealand as a whole helped to bring about the regular expressions of trust and informality that shortened the social distance between prisoners and the rest of society, and which were reflected in much of Barrington's experience of prison life and, to a degree, softened it for him.

Continuity between past and present

Barrington's diary also allows us to perceive a strong sense of continuity between prisons of the past and present: the ubiquity of regulations that strip prisoners of autonomy; the difficulty of recruiting suitably qualified prison officers; the narrowness of the prison experience that imbues any event that interrupts it – visits and letters, for example – with a significance far greater than it would outside the institution. Nelson Mandela wrote that on Robben Island, 'when letters did arrive, they were cherished. A letter was like the summer rain that could make even the desert bloom.'[45] Discussions about food – about ice cream and chocolate cake and so on – retain their ability to temporarily transport inmates to a world beyond the prison. Five illustrations of this continuity stand out in particular.

The monotony of prison

The unchanging rhythms and regularity of the prison so vividly portrayed in Barrington's diary cross jurisdictions and time. Reflecting on the pre-war British prison experience, Stanley wrote, 'Life in prison consists of the same monotonous routine, day in, day out.'[46] This is echoed by Goodall, a British CO imprisoned during World War II: 'Day after day the same things happened at exactly the same time. Always the same routine, always the same wasting of time.'[47] The Irish political prisoner Gusty Spence, imprisoned between 1971 and 1974, wrote that 'prison equals frustration, frustration and more frustration. The roof leaks and the rats are rampant and the food mostly cold and uneatable. There are no educational facilities, no relaxation or recreations provided. You have nothing except your own initiative.'[48]
Mandela noted,

Prison life is about routine: each day is like the one before; each week like the one before it, so that the months and years blend into each other. Anything that departs from this pattern upsets the authorities, for routine is the sign of a well-run prison. Routine is also comforting for the prisoners which is why it can be a trap. Routine can be a pleasant mistress whom it is hard to resist, for routine makes the time go faster.[49]

Any departure from this routine is the cue for excitement and anxiety from both inmates and officers. Barrington described this at Mount Crawford after the assault on Parsons. Several decades later Newbold wrote, 'any mood change or long term alteration in behaviour is soon noted and commented upon by other prisoners. It is impossible to keep any sentiment or feeling secret for long. Somebody always notices it.'[50]

The weekends continue to be the time when this monotony is most painful. Burton wrote, 'for most men the weekend tedium sets in about 11.00 am on Saturday and continues until the unlocking for labour on Monday morning.'[51] The British COs reported that 'from Saturday midday until Monday morning there were only two exercise periods, two slopping-outs, chapel and your locked cell.'[52] Sixty or 70 years later, little has changed. Archer noted, 'Weekends are deadly in prison.'[53]

Restrictions on personal space and freedom of movement add to the unvarying routine. The 'association' opportunities given to inmates are still likely to be spent in 'the yards', an enduring feature of prison architecture and design. Burton wrote that 'men walk round and round the yard … The prison authorities supply nothing and do nothing.'[54] For Lawry the exercise period at Paparua prison in the 1940s took place in 'a high walled cage with a grass square in the middle that had a sign "keep off the grass".'[55] Newbold wrote of the exercise yard at Mount Eden in the 1970s: 'the square compound was 20 x 20 metres, surrounded by a concrete block inner wall. Three or four dilapidated benches lie around the yard and these provide the only seating … [there was] an open flush toilet, totally lacking in privacy and fully visible from all parts of the yard.'[56] Crewe's British research describes how, in the exercise yard at Wellingborough, 'many prisoners walked around in ethnically uniform groups or pairings. Most talked quietly with their heads down. Some sat around the edges of the yard, leaning on wing buildings or the fence. One or two prisoners walked or jogged alone.'[57]

The ethnic divisions within the prison population that Crewe refers to are a new phenomenon. This apart, the images of inmates in the early twenty-first century aimlessly trying to kill time is strikingly similar to Barrington's description of time hanging so heavily in the yards. In these respects, prison is not simply a 'timeout' experience.[58] Time, the most valuable commodity there is outside prison and which prisoners have forfeited to the state, is worthless and seems to stand still during their sentence.

Everything has a value in prison

In this monochromatic world where the prison takes all from those who enter and gives so little in return, everything comes to have value. No matter what level of deprivation is placed on prisoners, human ingenuity will find ways of subverting this. The scavenging practices exhibited by Barrington and his colleagues are hardly unique. One contemporaneous British account, provided by Phelan, demonstrates the inventiveness of Maidstone prisoners in their attempts to improve and bring variety to their living conditions: 'Few archaeologists can have had such expert vision as the men who marched the yards and paths, slowly and with downcast eyes, apparently repenting their crimes and not missing the shape or colour of a single stone on the ground.'[59] He records how prisoners made 'telescopes, fountain pens, jail-briar pipes (a great luxury), rabbit-skin slippers, tools for carving bone, tiny sets of chessmen, belts and braces, brushes and bits of canvas for painting, pocket-knives (worth their weight in tobacco) and little note books'.

Newbold[60] referred to the manufacture of drugs and home-brewed alcohol. For Mandela the seashore where he worked towards the end of his time on Robben Island provided an illicit but fruitful harvest: 'we ate extremely well there. Each morning when we went to the shore, we would take a large drum of fresh water ... to make a kind of Robben Island sea food stew. For our stew we would pick up clams and mussels. We also caught crayfish which hid in the crevices of the rocks. Abalone ... were my favourite.'[61] Crewe noted that at Wellingborough Prison,

> ... illicit activity was built into the everyday fabric of prison life. Most jobs carried benefits of some kinds, and many prisoners specifically sought out positions that allowed them to supplement their income or enhance their everyday comforts ... makeshift boiling devices could be made by fitting wires into the lead-holes of stereo cords and placing them in cups of water. Television aerials could be fashioned out of coat hangers, and tattoo guns out of motors from tape recorders, biro pens and sterilised needles smuggled from the health care centre.[62]

The black economy

Although inmates are never allowed to possess 'real' money, illicit prison currencies of one form or another have always facilitated trading between prisoners. In Barrington's era the units were matches and cigarettes, supplemented by bartering. In the early twenty-first century, mobile phones, phonecards, cigarettes and cigarette lighters (because of the ban on smoking in prisons) have become the most valued items. If this owes much, again, to the inventiveness and resourcefulness of inmates, it is also a reflection of the way the prison experience itself encourages such activities, whether out of necessity, or to feed addictions, or simply to break the monotony. Of course, the more security is intensified to prevent access to such commodities, the higher their value and purchase price become. The accumulation of very large debts with attendant threats and violence resulting from non-payment is often a product of this prison-created black economy.[63] In these ways, the very nature of imprisonment succeeds in generating new forms of deviance – the very thing it has been designed to eliminate.

The imagined world of the prison authorities

Prison bureaucracy protects itself from the futility of much of what takes place in its institutions by continuing to 'imagine'[64] a different reality in its accounts. We saw in Barrington's diary that little was done to enable a realisation of the rehabilitative aspirations of the period – no resources were supplied, and no strong central authority ensured changes were implemented. Inmates were being trained to become farm labourers, even though job opportunities in this area were rapidly diminishing. Belich observed, 'farming mechanised substantially during the war. Its paid workforce dropped by 22 per cent between 1936 and 1945; tractors doubled and electric motors increased 50 per cent.'[65] The world outside the prison had moved on, yet the authorities insisted on perpetuating their own values and aspirations that ran contrary to it.

In the eyes of the prison authorities, however, the difficulties in implementing change resulted from the type of offenders being sent to prison – the flotsam and jetsam of New Zealand society rather than those who might be amenable to the rehabilitation they claimed to be offering (even if, in reality, there was none); or they were forced to recruit the wrong type of officer to implement their imaginary schemes (even though the low pay and status of this occupation ensured that there was little prospect of more suitable recruitment). Seventy years later, there is nothing new in the gulf between the success stories of prison life, now measured in terms of KPI scores (reductions in escapes, suicides, violence; increases in enrolment in programmes and so on), and the additional constraints and greater intensity of imprisonment that inmates now report.[66]

Imprisonment can sustain the beliefs of prisoners of conscience/political prisoners

Imprisonment often provides opportunities for solidarity among prisoners of conscience or political prisoners, sustaining rather than suppressing their beliefs. Many such inmates have been determined that incarceration would not strip them of their pre-prison identity. The Christian pacifists at Mount Crawford were prime examples, resolved to live by their values rather than have these subsumed beneath the weight of prison culture. Solidarity was facilitated by the authorities' decision to house the group together. The separation of such groups from the rest of the prison population seems to have been the most usual – but perhaps not the wisest – course of action that prison authorities took. As Mandela wrote, 'It is very hard, if not impossible for one man alone to resist ... the authorities' greatest mistake was to keep us together, for together, our determination was reinforced.'[67]

At Mount Crawford this separation also enabled Barrington and Burton, with their strong personalities and lengthy commitment to the cause, to play the role of informal leaders of the pacifist group. Following their example, the others tried to make the most productive use of their incarceration in ways that strengthened or affirmed their beliefs. In particular, they used art and literature to give expression to their experiences of confinement, as well as developing their political education in the broadest sense of this expression. They studied the Bible, held religious services, drew, wrote and read widely. According to Jim Doherty,

> ... we spent long hours together in the yard. We established an organised lifestyle which included much time for small talk. Ormond and Barry, both very widely read, provided a fund of topical material, but there was plenty of light-hearted comment.[68]

Mandela and his colleagues referred to Robben Island as 'the university'; the republican prisoners of Northern Ireland developed 'their own informal system of education, particularly in relation to the Irish language.'[69] Both groups of Irish political prisoners in the 1970s organised themselves in paramilitary fashion, just as they did outside the prison. The strength of their beliefs and commitment to their cause, reinforced by their shared experiences within the prison, offset any sense of shame or culpability for the crimes they were judged to have committed.

The modes of resistance and opposition to the prison authorities also reflected the values and beliefs these groups held before their incarceration.

While all practised what Crewe refers to as 'wheeling in'[70] – seeking out weaknesses in individual officers (such as openness to corruption) and then exploiting these once they had them 'hooked' – the pacifists tried to use the regulations themselves to their own advantage, as did Mandela: 'it was always valuable to be familiar with the regulations, because the warders were often ignorant of them and could be intimidated by one's own superior knowledge'.[71] Barrington's 'wheeling in' of Mount Crawford officers seems to have been conducted simply as an extension of Christian fellowship in the hope that this would be able to break down the prison's internal barriers and suspicions. Mandela took a similar approach: 'Prison officials responded much better to private overtures … hostility to warders is usually self-defeating.'[72]

The high levels of support from outside the prison, both from their families and the broader community, also helped to sustain these prisoners of conscience. These links ensured that the values of the outside world permeated the prison walls and remained with them during their sentence. Barrington's family supported him throughout his sentence, and also received considerable community support themselves, especially from immediate neighbours and professional acquaintances, in the form of food, help in the house and garden and donations of money, often made anonymously. Whatever hostility there might have been to the pacifists and other dissenters at government level and from powerful groups and organisations, individuals were prepared to help. In so doing, they demonstrated their respect both for Barrington and for what he was trying to achieve. Knowing him personally, rather than relying on the media for knowledge, no doubt made it more difficult to demonise him.

The position was much the same for the Northern Ireland prisoners, except that local community support was more systemic, co-ordinated and extensive: 'For the families of politically motivated prisoners, much of the basic assistance such as transport to prison or babysitting was organized through the paramilitary welfare organizations.'[73] Subsequent discharge has been relatively unproblematic for these groups of prisoners: like Barrington, they returned to communities in which they were held in high esteem, and where they continue to play a significant role in the causes that led to their imprisonment in the first place.

What do these contrasts tell us about the nature of prison in a society such as New Zealand? On the one hand we see a prison system that now exists only in the past: that system had appalling facilities for personal hygiene, rather than today's in-cell sanitation; it insisted on prisoners performing unremitting hard labour rather than remaining idle as many now do; and it had a prison population largely made up of society's derelicts rather than the more youthful and violent inmates of today. It was also a system not overtly troubled or regimented by security concerns, which provided more than ample quantities (at least) of food for its inmates and where there was no unbridgeable barrier, as now, between community and prison.

On the other hand, we can read Barrington's diary and think that little has changed between prison in 1941 and prison today: the attempts to kill time, especially when it hangs so heavily at the weekends or on public holidays, for example; the inevitable black economy of prison; the impossibility of having any secrets within such an institution; and the way in which prison authorities maintain their rhetoric on how purposeful and productive these institutions are.

Chapter 7

Dissent, Intolerance and the Dark Side of Paradise

Let us return to the issue of what made the diary possible in the first place. Why were Barrington and all the other dissenters imprisoned or sent to defaulters' camps? Why was New Zealand so intolerant of them?

At the end of World War II millions of people in Europe began the task of rebuilding their lives. The *Dominion* reported that in Britain, almost immediately after VE day, 'the release of all persons detained under defence regulations had been authorised'.[1] In New Zealand, however, the struggle against internal dissent continued. Remarkable though it may now seem, rather than celebrating what the overseas troops had achieved, at its annual conference the Returned Services' Association (RSA) was reported to be 'in a grim mood'. It remained preoccupied with the dangers of pacifist sentiments and unanimously passed a motion that 'defaulters should be deprived of civil rights for ten years and not released until twelve months after all the men from overseas have returned'.[2]

This continuing intolerance seems all the stranger because it stood in such contrast, throughout the war, to British policy. In February 1941 the RSA journal *Review* described Churchill as 'the Man of the Hour', one who was 'typical of the British nation'. However, his proscriptions against 'man-hunting' were manifestly ignored here. Nor was it the case that New Zealanders simply did not know how repressive their own country was by comparison. The *Otago Daily Times* reported, 'BBC lifts ban on pacifists in the aftermath of Churchill's pronouncements'.[3] Yet when sentencing Barrington and others for public dissent, Chief Judge Sir Michael Myers stated:

> [T]he court was not concerned with what might be said or published in other jurisdictions. The state cannot stand by complacently and permit this. This is a time of war – a war in which the very liberties to which Christian pacifists appeal as sanction for their conduct are at stake. To advocate peace at this time is to advocate surrender, and the loss of all the rights and liberties of democracy. For its own protection, democracy has assented to a reasonable limitation of its right until the war is won.[4]

A number of explanations have been put forward for this intolerance. Grant[5] suggests it was the product of the personality of Prime Minister Peter Fraser – a combination of rigid authoritarianism and loyalty to Britain. Oestreicher[6] proposed that because the Labour government was particularly vulnerable to public pressure (four of its ministers had their own histories of opposition to conscription in World War I and imprisonment) its punitive stance against World War II dissenters was intended to head off the criticism that their past made them unfit to be wartime leaders. A third view suggests it was the product of the assiduous Director of National Service, J.S. Hunter, who took the view that 'shirking on a large scale could interfere with government plans if precautions are not taken'.[7]

What I want to argue, however, is that rather than this policy being seen as an aberration, it should be understood as one episode in a long history of intolerance and repression in this country: one that had deep structural causes, which the war and attendant issues now brought to the surface. 'Man of the Hour' Churchill, in his position as home secretary three decades earlier, had declared, 'The mood and temper of the public in regard to the treatment of crime and criminals is one of the most unfailing tests of the civilisation of any country.'[8] The fact that it was thought necessary to detain opponents of the war, the conditions of their detention and the continuing hostility shown to many of them following their release, speaks of much more than the personalities and politics of the time. It speaks of the nature of New Zealand society itself.

This is not to deny those more benign characteristics – of informality, helpfulness and hospitality – with which New Zealand is usually associated. Rather it is to argue that these contrasts are in fact *complementary* characteristics, products of New Zealand's colonial past. As Michael King has explained, 'the positive effect of conformity – a society in which there was widespread agreement about what was right and what was wrong ... gave pre-war New Zealand considerable social cohesion. The negative effect was that people who did not conform in their views or behaviour were either harshly treated or lived in fear of disclosure and retribution.'[9]

New Zealand as a 'better Britain'

New Zealand has always advertised itself as a physical paradise. Michener referred to it as 'probably the most beautiful country on earth'.[10] In addition, its social arrangements have also seemed to possess paradisical qualities.

From the mid-nineteenth century it had been advertised as a country with everything Britain had to offer but with none of the social problems or other undesirable aspects; there was no rigid class structure to hold back the deserving lower-middle and respectable working classes. Those who fell on hard times through no fault of their own were not confronted with the workhouse here. Instead, from the late nineteenth century the New Zealand state's social reforms earned an international reputation for fairness and justice. These reforms, Pember Reeves wrote, were the product of

> ... a young democratic society, still almost free from extremes of wealth and poverty ... and which supplies an unequalled field for safe and rational experiment in the hope of preventing and shutting out some of the worst social evils and miseries which afflict great nations alike in the old world and the new.[11]

Some of Barrington's 1930s contemporaries agreed. Harrop claimed, 'there is an absence of class distinction in its extreme forms in New Zealand';[12] according to Cowie, 'New Zealand boasts not a single millionaire nor any who are starving.'[13] Visitors observed workplace relations that would have been unthinkable in class-conscious Britain: '[I]n my first New Zealand office I was flabbergasted to discover the office boy perched on the manager's desk discussing Saturday football with that high functionary as if he had known him all his life.'[14] In *New Zealand: Land of my choice*, Roberts noted that 'New Zealand has scarcely known poverty, even in the period of world depression. There has been no starvation and want, although everyone has felt the pinch of added taxation and salary cuts. At the same time, people are still living happy and contented lives.'[15]

The state played a large role as the guarantor of these qualities. The commitment to utilitarian social reform reached new heights when the Labour government passed the 1938 Social Security Act that 'gave the country a virtually free health system, a means-tested old age pension at 60 and universal superannuation at 65'.[16] At the same time, the state's role in providing a modern infrastructure continued to expand. Cowie observed,

> [T]he Government of New Zealand today has its share in every second economic enterprise from usury to dentistry. These paternal rulers look after the railways of the country, make sure that other means of transport do not expand too rapidly and provide an organisation to attract tours from overseas. On the West Coast of the South Island they have a state coal line and in every centre they have state coal offices. To provide

against emergencies they have a state Fire Insurance Office; they have a
share in a general insurance organisation ... the rulers of New Zealand
have a forestry department which controls large scale conservation,
regeneration and afforestation; a health department which invades every
branch of medicine; a Public Works Department which, in a country
where private contractors cannot afford to operate on a large scale, builds
most of the railways, bridges, roads and hydro-electric schemes.[17]

Of course, these extensive state guarantees came at a price. Cowie continued, 'New Zealanders now pay more taxation per head than Englishmen, whose fiscal burden is usually regarded as the highest in the world.'[18] The high taxes needed to support a rapidly growing central state seemed a burden worth bearing, however. New Zealand had never promoted itself as a country where unparalleled riches were to be made. Instead, by cutting the country's economic cake into progressively smaller slices, it was guaranteed that there would be servings for all. Extensive state regulation and acquiescence to it had become an accepted, unremarkable feature of everyday life.[19]

There was also a strong populist tradition, one that favoured 'big government', but one where, in accordance with 'fair go' traditions, the opinions of 'ordinary people' were just as important, if not more so, as those of the authorities. As Jackson and Harré described it, 'The preference for the opinion of the ordinary man over that of the expert is but one aspect of the uncompromising assertion of the principle of equality which is a national fetish.'[20] The highest echelons of government could seem directly accessible, 'because [government ministers] are the men with influence in cabinet and caucus, yet like MPs, regarded essentially as ordinary mortals, they constitute a prime target for those wishing to influence policies.'[21]

New Zealanders themselves were actively involved in local government and community affairs – often to a remarkable degree. This was another demonstration of the egalitarian nature of New Zealand society, one where involvement in service to the community became an expectation. As Hall pointed out, 'New Zealanders must indeed be regarded as inveterate "joiners", and the smaller the place, the greater the pressure to conform.'[22]

By 1941 then, if New Zealand was not an ostentatiously wealthy society, it was friendly and egalitarian and had a strong communitarian ethos. There were high levels of trust in personal relationships, reflected in the handshakes proffered to one and all and a readiness to initiate conversations with complete strangers. Newspaper advertisements of this period spoke to these same values and expectations. Products were often endorsed by 'ordinary' (and thereby trustworthy) citizens. The manufacturers of De Witt's pills, for example, told readers, 'Mrs E.W. has a hopeful, encouraging message for all who suffer from backache and kidney trouble'. Similarly, 'Mr H.H.' assured readers that although 'kidney trouble laid me up for six months', after taking the pills he was 'a different man'.[23]

The dark side of paradise

Yet by this time, Barrington, Burton and others had been imprisoned and any signs of dissent were being vigilantly hunted down. In effect, the same emphasis on conformity, homogeneity, communitarianism and respect for state authority also led to high levels of informal and formal suppression of difference. This was evident throughout popular culture. Herz claimed, 'this evident disdain of culture finds expression in the clothes of people. They are neither elegant nor fashionable. The suit of the man is rough and substantial. He is far too fond of his soft shirt with its limp collar and loose tie.'[24] Historian F.M.L. Wood reflected that 'New Zealanders have somehow lost the art of meeting in public places other than beaches and football matches. There are few cafes or restaurants in European style ... the characteristic of New Zealand life is lived, with friends and frequent guests, in small family homes ... Conventionality of design, of course, heavily predominates.'[25] Indeed, it seemed that in no sphere of life was there any desire to step outside the norms of utility and functionality: '[I]f the proprietors of cafes, some of whom have come from notable traditions in the use of food, are asked why they make no attempt to introduce a little more variety, they declare that customers will not touch the unfamiliar, and are quite happy with braised sausages and a dab of mashed potato.'[26]

The point is, of course, that in a society where utility was a necessary virtue, where egalitarianism had largely replaced class distinction and where practical capabilities had a higher value than aestheticism, one would be judged not on appearances but on capabilities – the extent to which one 'fitted in' and demonstrated conformity rather than difference. As Siegfried observed, this had brought about 'a strange narrowness which seems anchored to the very depths of the New Zealand soul'.[27]

The very nature of the qualities most sought after in prospective immigrants during the nineteenth and into the twentieth century had ensured, as Fairburn noted, that there would be no incipient intelligentsia: 'conventional education was no use for getting ahead and … attitudes towards it [were] somewhat negative or indifferent'.[28] As a consequence, in the society where trust and acceptance were so readily and enthusiastically displayed, Duff wrote,

> … *mistrust of intellectuals is not a new phenomenon. It runs right throughout our political history … it is doubtful if it could ever be said of any nation that it has been collectively intellectual, but it has never been possible to say it [of New Zealand]. We follow our instincts, trust our emotions, mistrust theory. So we mistrust, and even fear, men who march to strange music.*[29]

The qualities of friendliness, informality and openness for which New Zealand became so renowned also made critical debate and intellectual argument difficult and awkward: the society that was open and transparent was, ironically, also closed and opaque. Holcroft observed,

> *[V]isitors from overseas, and especially from England, have noticed the wide use of pen-names in newspaper correspondence. It is still not easy for men to be outspoken over their own signatures when they could meet the person affected by their criticism when they next walk through the streets.*[30]

The limited nature of news broadcasting also contributed to this 'narrowness'. According to Siegfried,

> … *almost all the news comes from London. As in the leading articles, England takes first place … It is apparent from reading these papers, as from a thousand other signs, that it is London which is the capital for New Zealanders … next come bulletins from the colonies … lastly, a few telegrams inform the reader, as a rule very imperfectly, of events on the continent of Europe.*[31]

By the 1940s, the advent of radio had done little to change the nature of the mainstream media: '[It] provides news and entertainment but not yet, in New Zealand, ideas.'[32]

It was not simply that news from Britain had priority because of the strength of colonial ties, however. In this society, where standardisation was so entrenched, there was little to report that was newsworthy. The very qualities that had brought stability and social cohesion had also caused an intense conformity, enforced by the fear of appearing different, of not belonging and of being rejected by this tightly drawn homogeneous community. Summarising contemporary reports of the muted celebrations at the end of World War II, Phillips commented that these 'showed how far New Zealanders had become not only respectful of public authority, but also to a considerable extent self-controlled and mindful of public decorum.'[33] New Zealand had become a society with a wide regard for common sense, and one where anything that suggested free thinking or intellectualism immediately raised suspicions.

Nontheless, New Zealand's famed friendliness was denied those who fell outside its narrow parameters of acceptability. Some of the earliest examples of this dark side of paradise were reflected in its immigration policies. New Zealand was never intended to be a haven for all-comers: only specific groups that could be accommodated within its homogeneous domains would be welcome. Immigration came to be regarded not as a vital source of diversity of both people and capital, but at best as an unwelcome necessity requiring extensive controls because of its likely disruption to homogeneity and uniformity:

> [I]mmigration policy discriminated positively in favour of Britons; it discriminated negatively against most other groups. Restrictive legislation began in 1881 and progressively tightened to the late 1920s. From 1897, prospective immigrants other than British and Irish were made to pass a language test, which from 1908 could be manipulated by officials to exclude almost anyone. The system remained largely intact at least until the 1950s and arguably until 1974.[34]

The dark side was also reflected in penal policy. In the first half of the twentieth century New Zealand had a significantly higher imprisonment rate than corresponding societies. Laing, de la Mare and Baughan wrote, 'New Zealand has on the whole very little serious crime. Its prisons, nonetheless, are always full to overflowing and there is daily on an average, a prison population more than three times as great, in proportion to the general population, as that of England and Wales.'[35] In 1933 the Howard League stated:

> [O]n a general population basis, New Zealand should have had in the year 1931–2, compared with Queensland less than 450 daily prisoners; compared with South Australia less than 1000; and compared with New

*South Wales and Victoria, less than 1200; while the number that she
actually did have was over 1600.*[36]

Intolerance of difference (along with an unctuous loyalty to Britain)
was similarly manifested in New Zealand's rigorous policy towards COs
and others in opposition to conscription in World War I. Prime Minister
William Massey had determined that there was 'not the slightest possibility
of the shirker escaping'.[37] As Grant wrote,

*only a handful of fundamentalist Christians ... were exempted from
active service, and that was conditional on their performing non-
combatant duties in New Zealand. Other objectors – socialist, religious,
humanitarian, Irish or Maori – were not considered genuine and were
imprisoned as military defaulters for up to two years' hard labour, being
reimprisoned on release if they still refused to enlist ... in December
1918, 2,600 of them were released from jail, lost their voting rights
for ten years, and were barred from working for government or local
bodies.*[38]

Intolerance and the suppression of dissent during World War II

The treatment of pacifists, COs and other dissenters during World War
II was another episode of intolerance. This was most evident during
1940–42 when it was directed against expressions of public dissent, and
again in 1945–46, when the continued detention and anticipated release of
defaulters came under public scrutiny.

1940–42

New Zealand's isolation and distance from the fighting seemed to provoke
anxiety rather than security. In 1940 Prime Minister Fraser announced,

*[P]eople who malign the Allies will be stopped. The leaflets which have
been flooding the Dominion have not done much harm, but the people
and the Government are in no mood to stand any more of it, and we
will put a stop to it. Anyone who stands in the way will be swept aside.*[39]

Nonetheless, fears of subversion and its corrosive effects proliferated
in this 'insular community'.[40] For example, the *Observer* warned that 'there

has grown up in this country a large underground organisation, devoted not only to anti-war doctrines but also to spreading the perilous thesis that it is noble and glorious to repudiate absolutely the duties accepted by the patriotic men'.[41]

In reality, there was no need for such concerns. In 1940 the *Dominion* reported:

Remarkable evidence of the refusal by an overwhelming majority of New Zealanders to tolerate any discordant note in the demand for vigorous leadership and action in the present crisis was seen at Wanganui today at a great public meeting in the Opera House, convened by the Wanganui Branch of the [RSA].[42]

The involvement of the RSA in this event is particularly significant. The government was keen to align itself with this organisation to popularise the Allied cause and enhance recruitment. Formed during World War I to provide support and comfort for service men and women and their families, the RSA had initiated a day of remembrance to honour those whose lives were lost in the Gallipoli Campaign, commemorated on 25 April as Anzac Day. This was marked throughout the country by columns of veterans marching in procession. The RSA's central involvement in this day gave it unquestionable authority.

By 1920 the RSA had 50,000 members and was already a powerful extra-parliamentary force: 'the men viewed themselves as an elite group, with the right to speak on many issues, by virtue of having served their country'.[43] During the inter-war period it promoted the need to remember and care for former soldiers while arguing that a strong military presence was needed to safeguard the defence of the Empire. It firmly rejected any attempts to tone down the idea of 'glorious suffering' on which Anzac Day had been founded. Instead, the march of the former soldiers began to take on a more uniformed, military appearance.[44]

Although membership of the organisation declined as World War I experiences receded, it then increased with the growing certainty of further conflict, and by 1943 stood at 43,000.[45] As an indicator of the organisation's importance, the governor-general regularly opened its AGM with an address. In 1943, for example, he hoped the RSA would exercise 'a stabilising and beneficial influence on the country – its members were citizens who understood the meaning of loyalty and discipline, courage and endurance'.[46] Furthermore, the Wellington RSA head, Bill Perry, was recruited to the

Advisory War Council in June 1940 and in 1943 became a member of the Cabinet (although not an MP), when made minister for armed forces and war co-ordination. As MP William Downie Stewart had earlier stated in parliament, '[The RSA] is undoubtedly a well enough organised body and a powerful enough body to make it almost impossible for any government to resist its demands if it sought to exploit the situation.'[47]

Campaigning forcefully for compulsory military service, the RSA had become an important ally of the Labour government, despite the very different antecedents of their respective leaders.[48] At the outbreak of war there was swift consultation and collaboration between the RSA and Prime Minister Fraser; following an 'ultimatum' from the RSA in May 1940, Fraser agreed to 'compulsory, universal, national service – civil, military and financial'.[49] This reflected the RSA's insistence that involvement in the war necessitated equality of service in line with egalitarian and communitarian expectations: those who were not conscripted should receive the same payment as those who were. Those who were imprisoned or sent to the camps because of their opposition to the war should not be released before the last soldiers had returned home at the end of the conflict.

Although the emergency regulations and the equality of service that these prescribed demanded a high level of state regulation, this would be considered entirely acceptable in a society where state intervention – including punishing and supressing difference – had an established history. The Man-power Office was established in 1942 and had the authority to direct labour to wherever it was needed. By this time, the defaulters' detention camps were functioning as a new tier of incarceration.

However, while the RSA was very close to the government, particularly in the critical early years of the war, it simultaneously kept a distance from it, maintaining its populist credentials as an organisation that spoke for the people rather than the authorities. On occasion it publicly criticised the government, as when it expressed 'dissatisfaction with the way in which enemy alien problems were being dealt with by the government'.[50]

The RSA's forthright and often alarmist views – particularly about the corrupting influence of internal dissent – also ensured that it received a high level of coverage in the New Zealand press, providing the newspapers with gifts to brighten their otherwise drab wartime pages. The *Otago Daily Times* reported that the RSA was very suspicious of what it considered 'the extensive spread of communist propaganda throughout the universities, schools and public libraries of the Dominion'.[51] *Truth*, in particular, was attracted to the RSA and its sensational revelations of subversion, with reports such as: 'RSA's strong protest. Shirkers. Allegedly using farms to dodge military service. Speakers cited a variety of cases in which they said men not entitled to consideration have had their appeals upheld … in one district people were burning with indignation.'[52] In New Zealand it was much more difficult than in the other Allied countries to convince the authorities that one's objection to the war was genuine and sincere.

The newspapers added to the framework of intolerance by filling their pages with extensive reports on the prosecution of dissenters. Appeal Board hearings were reproduced in full, as if these proceedings illustrated and confirmed the differences that existed between these objectors and 'normal' people. The *Evening Post* trumpeted:

Man breaks down. Brother abuses board. Apology follows.
The appellant, in great excitement said, 'I will not go to war. No matter what happens, I will never go to war. Even if you send for me I will not go. You cannot send me.' He then broke down and wept loudly, kneeling on the floor with arms across the witness table. Assisted by members of the audience … the appellant's brother then led him away. At the door leading from the room offensive remarks were hurled at the members of the board.[53]

The *Observer* ran a series of articles belittling dissenters as unpatriotic cowards, in stark contrast to the valiant expectations of New Zealand manhood:

There is a remarkable absence of heroism among them. They are a poor type. Those who are not of poor physique (spectacles are tediously common among them) are dull mentally and vice versa. Mens sana in corpore sane is not a characteristic of the 'conchie'.[54]

Curious consciences
Most of the young men appear to be exceedingly well-dressed and to offer exceedingly little evidence of monastic habits. I have nothing but respect for the man who follows conscience to the bitter end. But I have nothing but contempt for the man who, at the first taste of bitterness, sidetracks it.[55]

Dissenters were presented as effete dilettantes – the antithesis of all those who, mostly through hard physical work, had made New Zealand a 'better

Britain' and were now working just as hard to defend it. The *Dominion*, under the headline 'No place for objectors', insisted,

> *Questions as to the so-called rights of men who are attempting to refuse service to New Zealand, questions as to the fine shades of meaning in their various utterances, or the previous character of the sacrifice which may be demanded of them – these things are out of place and out of date. There is work to be done and service to be rendered on the home front. It is wholly intolerable that hundreds of our young men should shirk this work and service, whatever their views.*[56]

There was also suspicion that university intellectuals might be subverting the war effort:

> *[T]he presence of subversive influences in unexpected quarters has become rather commonplace … While the university authorities angrily demand proof of such matters as 'communist influence' in the minds of university teachers, the public at large could hardly fail to know that the difficulty or impossibility of obtaining 'proof' satisfactory to the authorities may be quite consistent with the truth of the allegations.*[57]

There was particular outrage at anything that appeared to be an organised attempt to undermine the war effort – as when it became public knowledge that COs were receiving advice from leading pacifists on how to present their cases to the conscription boards. These would-be objectors were being manipulated by sinister 'older men', it was reported: '[I]n past months, a disturbing feature of many appeals on allegedly conscience grounds has been the apparent adhesion of groups of able bodied young men of military age to formulae obviously prepared by older persons having some influence over them.'[58] Barrington himself had been seen taking notes for these purposes at the Wellington board. When asked what authority he had to do so, the *Evening Post* reported, 'he replied, "I did not think any authority was required. I am simply a member of the public." Later the writer explained that he was A.C. Barrington. He represented the Peace Pledge Union and the CPS [Christian Pacifist Society], and he was watching the proceedings on behalf of COs.'[59]

The 'Letters to the Editor' columns of these papers – then an important valve of public opinion – also fuelled the widespread public antagonism towards dissent. In the first eight months of 1941 the *Otago Daily Times* carried 80 such letters on this subject: 55 of them were hostile to dissenters,

25 broadly sympathetic. In line with conventions, these were usually signed by a *nom de plume* that very clearly signalled the views of the writer, such as 'One Who Has Served', 'Home Guard' and 'Fight for your Freedom'. 'Reservist' insisted:

> [T]here is no such person as a CO. The man who refuses to fight for his country has no vestige of conscience. The school teacher who will not salute our flag and all it stands for, has no conscience either and should not be allowed to teach our children. I sometimes think, sir, in these critical days, that in a land like New Zealand, there is a lot to be said in favour of a military dictatorship. I know what would happen then to these so-called COs.[60]

There were even moves to penalise and exclude the families of objectors. The *Evening Star* supported Auckland City Council's resolution to dispense with the services of women employees whose husbands were not serving with the armed forces:

> [C]ouncil has always given preference of employment to returned soldiers. Departmental heads will now have instructions – which should not be necessary – to avoid engaging any person known to have expressed subversive opinions. If any employee uses his position to express anti-war views, 'Out', very properly, will be the word.[61]

Such sentiments were not universal, of course. Barrington and his family received considerable sympathy and support. By this juncture, however, dissenting views had been driven underground, only occasionally to be brought to public prominence by eager journalists. The *Observer* reported on

> Woodkraft, [a] workshop founded on co-op lines [and] staffed almost exclusively by COs and prospective military defaulters. Michael Young, a 25-year-old printer, who was recently sentenced to two years imprisonment by the Chief Justice, is the recognised leader of the intractable objectors … in a country fighting for its life, he is a dangerous character, and many will share the regret of the Chief Justice that he could not be imprisoned for the duration of the war, and subsequently deprived of his civil rights for a lengthy period.[62]

1945–46

By 1945 the government was caught in a dilemma of its own making: how to release the defaulters and close this episode without running into conflict and confrontation with those forces – the RSA in particular – that had not only campaigned so vociferously for their detention, but wanted to continue the struggle against the internal enemy. As the *Otago Daily Times* put the matter, 'If ever the Government has been hoist with its own petard, it is in subjecting itself to angry and indignant criticism for its treatment of defaulters from military service.'[63] Public interest in maintaining vigilance against dissent was also greatly reduced. In the first six months of 1945, the *Otago Daily Times* printed only 12 letters to the editor on this topic: five were hostile to the defaulters and seven sympathetic to them.

Pressure to release the defaulters from the camps had been building. In 1943 the government was warned by its civil servants that prolonged, indefinite detention might lead to their 'mental deterioration', but not in the direction of 'weakening their resolve to resist the regulations'.[64] A petition urging their release, signed by 'many prominent citizens including leaders of the churches, trade unionists and many university teachers',[65] was in itself an indication that those who claimed to speak for the public – such as the RSA – did not have unanimous support. Meanwhile, the extent of the differences between the New Zealand and British approaches to dissent were becoming increasingly difficult to justify. As Justice Minister Rex Mason acknowledged,

> *The position is illogical in the extreme. Few would [now] be sent to the front to fight if willing, as many are unfit. To keep the men in detention for the whole war for not doing what we do not want them to do offends common sense ... further, I notice a return of over a quarter million pounds spent on those camps. This emphasises the question of the justification of so many men being retained in them.*[66]

By the end of the war, the drive to suppress dissent began to falter. Some sections of the press became critical of government policy. The *Southland Times* declared,

> *[I]t is difficult to compare the scrupulous regard for principles in Britain with the harshness shown in New Zealand without feeling a sense of humiliation. The propaganda that has emanated from one or two sources and has received most publicity is noteworthy for its low intellectual and moral standard. The utterances of some, including MPs, have been marked by their misrepresentations and disregard for the truth.*[67]

There was growing international criticism of this country's policy on dissent. Sixteen US bishops had written to the Ministry of Internal Affairs in 1944 arguing for clemency for Burton following his two-and-a-half-year reformative detention sentence in 1942. During his visit to Britain in 1944 Prime Minister Fraser was approached by British COs and parliamentarians who deplored the indefinite detention of defaulters.[68] A letter asking the government to reconsider its policy, written by various British notables including Vera Brittain, Laurence Housman, Bertrand Russell and Dame Sybil Thorndike, was published in the *New Zealand Herald*.[69]

The approach of victory brought increased militancy among the defaulters, in recognition that there was no longer any logic to their detention. Walter Lawry recalled, '[W]e agreed that those who decided to make a protest of some kind should do so from 22 January 1945, and that we would try to get word out to other prisons and detention camps about our intentions.'[70] Those who had been sent to Mount Eden orchestrated noisy disturbances there and began the hunger strikes that were to bring some of them close to death.[71] In a parliamentary debate on 28 June 1945 the Labour government acknowledged its policy had been over-zealous. Nash conceded that some of the defaulters were 'very fine people'.[72] Labour MP D.G. Sullivan acknowledged that 'The right of appeal of decisions from local courts runs through our judicial system, but in this country it has not been granted and genuine COs have been denied a right that the country intended that they should have.'[73] Prime Minister Fraser at last agreed, 'It was necessary to see New Zealand conditions in the light of those in other British countries.'[74] Even the controller-general of prisons, Dallard, admitted that imprisoning dissenters and defaulters had been a mistake, leading to unforeseen difficulties for his administration:

At the end of [1945] there were 48 military defaulters in prison. With the passing of time one is constrained to conclude that the transfer of military defaulters to criminal prisons has not been an altogether satisfactory or happy arrangement, for the reason that many of these prisoners have constantly laboured under a sense of grievance and injustice – in many cases for so long a period that it has become obsessional ... in some cases offenders have flagrantly persisted in refractory conduct, apparently in a desire to seek notoriety or to bask in the sunshine of martyrdom, in the result that controlling officers have been obliged to have recourse to Justices and punishment to maintain discipline among the general body of prisoners'.[75]

In late 1944 the government decided the dissenters' cases would be reheard by a one-man tribunal. On release, all would be required to assent to Man-power direction (that is, to work as and where directed by government) and not participate in any activities prejudicial to the war effort.[76] But it was May 1946 before all were finally released, and not until June that year that they ceased to be subject to the Man-power provisions.

Why was there no speedier resolution? The government clearly tried to appease the RSA and its press allies, both of which had a vested interest in continuing the war against internal dissent: the RSA, to maintain its role as the outraged conscience of the New Zealand public; and the press, to continue to feed on the excitement it generated by dividing society into normal citizens who served the country, and shirkers who spent their time lounging in camps.

As their release got under way, the *Observer* reported:

Alleged release of defaulters. Ex-soldiers up in arms.
Auckland RSA quoted the case of a defaulter being out on parole and being employed in an industry to which he had been directed by the man-power authorities … such a position was intolerable, for it not only caused dissension in industry but it caused uneasiness among a large section of the community.[77]

In contrast to the way that civil rights came to provide the foundations for the development of Western democracy in the post-war period, the RSA demanded that such rights be stripped from the defaulters for 10 years, as at the end of World War I:

[I]t is significant that a member of the War Council and a 'Digger' who lost an arm in the last war, recently spoke for the RSA in demanding that the same penalty be inflicted again. Here again, the Government is totally out of touch with public opinion.[78]

In such ways, newspapers orchestrated 'public opinion', and then invoked it in support of their own causes. And while the RSA spokesmen protested about the procedure for the release of the defaulters – 'one-man tribunals which were to be heard in private' – they were more likely concerned about being starved of the oxygen that gave them power and prominence. There would no longer be any outlet for the organisation's members to express their indignation at such injustices: '[N]either the press nor any other person can be present, and the press can only publish any report that may be authorised by the revision authority.'[79]

By this juncture the wartime pact between the government and the RSA had outlived its usefulness. There seem to have been no qualms on either side about it breaking down. The *Observer* reported:

V-Day for Shirkers. Plain speaking likely at RSA conference.
The government's policy, announced last week, after five and a half
years of war, in regard to defaulters, was characterised by the Dominion
President [of the RSA] as 'spineless action' that will certainly arouse the
disgust and indignation of former fighting men.[80]

At its annual conference the RSA even voted to march on parliament and 'stated in plain and definite language its complete opposition to the release of military defaulters'.[81] As the *Otago Daily Times* asked,

Is it not strange that the thought of some imagined injustice to any of
these defaulters should have so closely followed upon the victory in
Europe? ... What are the general public going to do about it? If [they]
do their part, the RSA will have the backing it merits in its determined
attitude towards betrayal by the Government of all law-abiding citizens.[82]

Acting Prime Minister Nash told the conference delegates that 'he had never yet heard of a right thinking returned soldier who did not respect an [honestly held] objector conscience'.[83] The RSA president replied that there had been no need for him to express his attitude on the subject of early release: 'my first reaction was more than disappointment – it was one of disgust'.[84] However, Nash outflanked bids by the RSA to challenge the authority of parliament by, first, refusing to summon its leaders, as they demanded, to appear before the Bar of the House of Representatives to give their views on the release of the defaulters; and, second, arranging to be out of Wellington at the time of the RSA's intended march on parliament, which deflated its purpose. The march did not proceed.

Government authority was still not strong enough to allow the immediate release of the defaulters, however. Only after trade unionists threatened industrial action in January 1946[85] did it finally agree that all would be released by the end of April. The RSA continued its opposition to the end, ironically deriding the government for giving in to outside pressure groups:

Blueprint for Bedlam ... to even suggest that such men [defaulters] should
be allowed to steal a march on those who have poured out their blood
and sweat on the world's battlefields is a negation of the elementary
principles of justice ... the RSA will not deviate one inch from its policy

that military defaulters should be held in detention until all servicemen
have been satisfactorily rehabilitated, that they should be deprived of
the civil rights they refused to defend, and that they should be debarred
from employment in any position for which the salary is paid from funds
provided by taxpayers.[86]

Could it happen again?

The release of the last defaulters and termination of the manpower regulations formally concluded the suppression of wartime dissent, notwithstanding the further disqualifications that were placed on many as they tried to make their way back into New Zealand society. Barrington himself, of course, with his indomitable personality and unswerving self-belief, remained unwavering in his anti-war activities while helping to build the alternative community, Riverside, near Motueka.

His eloquent and evocative diary has helped us to reconstruct this neglected area of New Zealand's history and sparked our analysis of how this degree of intolerance and suspicion could ever have existed here. But in undertaking historical enquiry, our purpose is not simply to uncover the past but also to understand the present. Could what happened to Barrington and others in 1941 – the suspicion, mistrust, outraged media headlines, extra-parliamentary forces angrily demanding that the government should act as they insisted – ever happen again? Reflecting in 1958 on the prosecution of dissent during the war, Wood suggested that it would not: what had occurred was the product of 1940s New Zealand society, a community 'not greatly experienced in dealing with groups who departed widely from the average'.[87]

New Zealand is no longer anything like the country Wood was describing. Certainly, until the 1970s immigration continued to be almost exclusively from Britain; state power continued to grow along with attendant levels of taxation. As Jackson and Harre noted, '[T]he maximum rate of 68 cents in the dollar is reached in New Zealand on a taxable income of $7200. Equivalent tax in the United Kingdom is paid on incomes of $19,000; in Australia on $25,600; in the United States on $29,000; and in Canada on $82,000.'[88] After 1984, however, successive Labour and National governments undertook a massive economic and social restructuring programme. Neo-liberal reforms changed the economic constitution of New Zealand society and ensured that, almost overnight, it moved from being one of the most regulated to one of the most deregulated Western democracies.

Instead of living standards being restricted to an egalitarian norm by state regulation, individuals were exhorted to take responsibility for this themselves – the harder they worked, the more they would achieve, and the more they would be able to enjoy the fruits of their successes and distance themselves from non-achievers. In the aftermath of this reorganisation of New Zealand society, the *Lonely Planet* guide reported, 'There is … a growing cultural life with some great nightlife, live theatre, dancing and arty cafes. Arts and crafts are popular and many … cities have fine art galleries.'[89] At the same time, the growth of immigration ensured that New Zealand has become a much more pluralistic society. This greater heterogeneity, along with the realisation that New Zealand's identity lies in the Pacific region, has weakened colonial ties to Britain.

It might be thought that such radical departures from the New Zealand on which Wood was reflecting now mean that opportunities for the dark side of paradise to re-emerge have disappeared. Nonetheless, the answer to the question 'could it happen again?' is that it *has* been happening again. While the economic and social reforms of the 1980s did indeed bring about greater individual choice, this necessarily meant that the state divested itself of much of its previous authority and sovereignty: it was to be a more open, fluid society with much wider horizons than before.

However, for many in this society, where the state had had an enlarged and accepted role and where economic and social policies had restricted differences rather than widening them, this only heightened the innate sense of anxiety and insecurity associated with a small, isolated society. Indeed, in the aftermath of Britain joining the European Common Market in 1973 New Zealand seemed more vulnerable than ever to global forces. A new identity was also needed because that event simultaneously sounded the death knell for any lingering colonial ties. Following the 1980s restructuring, King wrote, 'the price for plurality in so many sectors of national life might prove to be a permanent degree of disjunction and social divergence.'[90] The post-1980s social and economic changes had made New Zealand even more vulnerable to these further bouts of intolerance, and more vulnerable to anti-establishment populism.

During the 1990s and the first decade of this century these possibilities were manifested around crime and punishment issues. Why here, when crime rates, as in most other Western societies, were beginning to fall significantly?[91] This is because levels of punishment are not simply determined by the particular level of crime in a society. Following the dramatic decline in trust in mainstream political parties following the reforms of the 1980s and early 1990s, governments of both left and right began to invest heavily – politically, economically and symbolically – in punishment, irrespective of falling crime, in an attempt to bring about cohesion and order and thereby win back credibility from disenchanted electorates. Because of the inability of other sectors of New Zealand society to perform cohesive functions in the aftermath of restructuring, punishment would have to perform this role.

Extra-parliamentary populist forces once again have been able to act as prominent 'players' and opinion-formers in engineering this. The 1999 'law and order' referendum (supported by 91.75 per cent of voters) ignored the realities of crime trends and posed the following question, written by the then leader of the Christian Heritage Party (later sentenced to nine years' imprisonment for sexual offences against minors): 'Should there be a reform of our criminal justice system, placing greater emphasis on the needs of victims, providing restitution and compensation for them and imposing minimum sentences and hard labour for all serious offenders?'

Despite its obvious inconsistencies and contradictions, the referendum was allowed to frame public debate on crime and punishment for most of the following decade. Here, too, it seems likely that Labour did not wish to be 'outbid' on law and order by National, just as in World War II it was fearful that any vacillation shown to dissenters would be conceived by its political opponents as a weakness and exploited. Once again, governments made alliances with these extra-parliamentary populist forces – this time with the Sensible Sentencing Trust (SST), formed in 2002. Senior ministers spoke at SST conferences and received their representatives in parliament while simultaneously shunning or denouncing those members of the criminal justice establishment who criticised their policies. Once again, we have a populist organisation that allies itself with government but, in order to maintain its extra-parliamentary posture, distances itself from it. Once again, much of the media has built its reporting of these issues around rumour, suspicion and mistrust rather than scientific knowledge and objectivity.[92]

And once again, there has been a series of unintended, unforeseen consequences as new, more punitive policies were introduced. Scandals have emerged regarding prison overcrowding brought about by the new policies and public concerns about 'holiday camp' prisons. Just as in Barrington's day, however, the real scandal has been the lack of resources and adequate training for the rehabilitation of inmates. In these respects, Barrington's diary still captures much of the flavour of imprisonment – its monotony, futility and the way, self-defeatingly, it actually creates more crime and deviance, rather than reforming those sentenced to it.

And then, once again, a Labour government, realising the damage its policies had caused to the fabric of New Zealand society, recanted. It launched its 'Effective Interventions Strategy' in 2006, designed to bring about reductions to the prison population it had done so much to enlarge from 1999 to 2005. As Workman has since pointed out,

> [W]e are not in the Western European [Imprisonment] League Table [at all]. At the present time, Germany [has a rate of] 83 [per 100,000 of population], France has 102, Australia has 130, Scotland has 151, and England has 154 (the top of the Western European league). Over the last 20 years we have moved out of that league into a different league. Last year New Zealand was in the Eastern European league – joining the former Soviet bloc countries. We were sandwiched between Moldavia at 183, and Slovakia at 203. The recent decline from 197 to 194 per 100,000 now puts us in the African bloc, between Gabon and Namibia.

Once more, a New Zealand government had been hoist by its own petard. As the *Dominion Post* stated in an editorial, 'New Zealand has proved itself very good at locking up criminals. It is what is happening after the prison door slams that is an unacceptable failure.'[94] Once again, extra-parliamentary populist forces had no wish to bring this latest episode of intolerance to an end. Intolerance gave the SST prominence and power and allowed the media to make capital out of the government's perceived weakness. Rather than bringing unity and cohesion, the punitive policies have been divisive and New Zealand's reputation as a 'fair go' society has been questioned.

As this has occurred, however, the other side of New Zealand's identity – the friendliness and informality, the handshakes and hospitality, that other much more pleasing side of paradise – has endured. The *Lonely Planet* guide states that 'for the visitor, perhaps the most immediately obvious trait of all the New Zealanders is their friendliness'.[95] Michael King concludes his bestselling history of New Zealand by referring to his fellow citizens as 'good hearted' and 'tolerant'.[96] Immigration consultants IMMagine describe 'the uniqueness of the people. Warm, welcoming and friendly, [they] have a wonderful laid-back attitude to life.'[97]

Such qualities help to make this country a magnet for visitors and immigrants. They are the same qualities that helped Barrington and his family endure his prison sentence largely unscathed and brought to an end the continued detention of the defaulters after the war. His diary captures this side of New Zealand life, while at the same time demonstrating the less hospitable, suspicious and distrustful side that was the very reason why he found himself writing a diary in prison in 1941. So, too, the recent emphasis on penal saturation, the product of similar intolerance, suspicion and deep-seated antipathies, demonstrates the ability of the dark side of paradise to come to the surface.

Notes

Introduction

1. *Evening Post*, 26 March 1941.
2. Grant, David, 1986, *Out in the Cold: Pacifists and conscientious objectors in New Zealand during World War II*, Auckland: Reed Methuen, 45–46.
3. Browne, Samuel, 1941, 'Detective Samuel Browne to Chief Detective 27 March, 1941', Papers held by the Security Intelligence Service on A.C. Barrington, MS-Papers-6139-2, Alexander Turnbull Library, Wellington, NZ.
4. Ibid.
5. Taylor, Nancy, 1986, *The New Zealand People at War: The home front*, vol. 1. Wellington, NZ: Historical Publications Department, Department of Internal Affairs, Government Printer, 246.
6. Dingwall, Evalyn & Elizabeth A. Heard, 1937, *Pennsylvania 1681–1756: The state without an army*, London: C.W. Daniel.
7. Warburton, Frank L., 1931, *Jesus of Galilee*, London: Nicholson & Watson.
8. In 3 March 2009 an article on Frank Flipp, then in a Masterton resthome, appeared in the *Cook Strait News*. When I telephoned him he told me he could not recall my father or the diary but was 'not surprised as I often did good turns for people at the prison'. This was borne out by a diary entry that recorded him smuggling cream buns in for my father!
9. Grant, *Out in the Cold*, 45–46; Grant, David, 2004, *A Question of Faith: A history of the New Zealand Christian Pacifist Society*, Wellington: Philip Garside.
10. Newbold, Greg, 1982, *The Big Huey: An inmate's candid account of five years inside New Zealand's prisons*, Auckland: Collins.
11. Taylor, *The New Zealand People at War*, 63.
12. Markwell, Carol, 2000, 'Barrington, Archibald Charles 1906–1986', in *Dictionary of New Zealand Biography*, New Zealand Department of Internal Affairs (ed.), vol. 5, 36–37, Auckland: Auckland University Press.
13. Grant, David, 2000, 'Burton, Ormond Edward, 1893–1944', in *Dictionary of New Zealand Biography*, New Zealand Department of Internal Affairs (ed.), vol. 5, 80–82, Auckland: Auckland University Press.
14. Nash, Walter, 1939, 'Walter Nash to A.C. Barrington, 17 October 1939', MS-Papers 0439-5, Alexander Turnbull Library, Wellington, NZ.
15. Barrington, Archibald C., 1970, *Trials of a Pacifist: Being two broadcast talks over New Zealand YC stations*, Christchurch, NZ: Christian Pacifist Society, 15. See also the report of a public meeting on admitting refugees in which he urged the government to adopt a liberal immigration policy (*Evening Post*, 25 February 1939).
16. Barrington, Archibald C., 1929–71, Barrington, Archibald Charles, 1906–1986: Papers. MS-Papers-0439, Alexander Turnbull Library, Wellington, NZ.
17. Grant, *Out in the Cold*, 48.
18. Burton, Ormond E., n.d., *A Rich Old Man*, MS-Papers 0438-059, MS-Copy-Micro-0144, Alexander Turnbull Library, Wellington, NZ, n.p.
19. *Evening Post*, 20 April 1954.
20. Davies, Sonja, 1984, *Bread and Roses: Sonja Davies, her story*, Auckland: Fraser Books, 26.
21. Grant, *A Question of Faith*, 33.
22. Burton, Ormond E, 1945, *In Prison*, Wellington: A.H. & A.W. Reed, 11.

23. Ibid., 57.
24. Barrington, Archibald C., n.d., Unpublished MS, Ref: 86-062-10, Alexander Turnbull Library, Wellington, NZ, 7.
25. Ibid., 8.
26. Barrington, *Trials of a Pacifist*, 11.
27. Dominion Council of the Wellington Workers' Education Association (WWEA), 1941, 'Minutes', *Minute Books, Financial Statements and Annual Reports (1915–1991)*. Reference Number 93-132-4, Alexander Turnbull Library, Wellington, NZ.
28. Barrington, *Trials of a Pacifist*, 11.
29. Wellington Workers' Education Association (WWEA), 1942, 1943, 'Summary of the 28th and 29th Annual Reports for the years ending 31 December 1942, 1943', *Annual Reports, Annual General Meetings, Summer Schools Files and Cash Ledgers (1928–1991)*, Ref. No. 93-132-5, Alexander Turnbull Library, Wellington, NZ.
30. Taylor, *The New Zealand People at War*, 64.
31. Grant, *A Question of Faith*, 33.
32. Benjamin Barrington, pers. comm.
33. Parr, Alison, 2010, *Home: Civilian New Zealanders remember the Second World War*, Auckland: Penguin.
34. Taylor, *The New Zealand People at War*.
35. Grant, 'Carman, Arthur Herbert 1902–1982', 88.
36. Taylor, *The New Zealand People at War*, 218.
37. Burton, *A Rich Old Man*.
38. Burton, *In Prison*, 86.
39. Mayson, Rev. William (Bob), 1994, 'The trials of a parson', in *No Other Option: Experiences of New Zealand Conscientious objectors and supporters during World War II*, New Zealand Christian Pacifist Society, 4–5, Christchurch: Christian Pacifist Society.
40. Grant, *A Question of Faith*, 50.
41. Parr, *Home*, 31.
42. Barrington, *Trials of a Pacifist*, 12.
43. *Christian Pacifist Society Bulletin*, 1938, Further Papers, AC Barrington, Ref: 86-062-08/07B, Alexander Turnbull Library, Wellington, NZ.
44. Barrington, Unpublished MS, 11.
45. Barrington, *Trials of a Pacifist*, 19–20.
46. *Standard*, 19 November 1943.
47. Barrington, Unpublished MS, 15.
48. Rain, Lynn, 1991, *Community: The story of Riverside 1941–1991*, Lower Moutere, NZ: Riverside Community Trust Board.
49. Ibid.
50. Brittain, Vera, 1933, *Testament of Youth: An autobiographical study of the years 1900–1925*, London: Gollancz.
51. Brittain, Vera, 1951, *Search After Sunrise*, London: Macmillan.

Chapter 1. Dissent, Imprisonment and the Barrington Diary

1. *Evening Post*, 5 June 1941, 7.
2. Efford, Lincoln, 1945, *Penalties on Conscience: An examination of the defaulters' detention system in New Zealand*, Christchurch: Caxton Press, 5.
3. Ibid., 28.
4. Ibid., 10.
5. Grant, David, 1986, *Out in the Cold: Pacifists and conscientious objectors in New Zealand during World War II*, Auckland: Reed Methuen, 49.
6. *New Zealand Herald*, 15 November 1941, 6.

7. Hansard [UK], HC Deb, vol. 370, 20 March 1941, 284.
8. Hansard [UK], HL Deb, vol. 118, 3 April 1941, 1007–08.
9. Barker, Rachel, 1982, *Conscience, Government and War: Conscientious objection in Great Britain, 1939-45*, London: Routledge & Kegan Paul, 62.
10. Grant, *Out in the Cold*, 47.
11. Cited in Efford, *Penalties on Conscience*, 4.
12. Barker, *Conscience, Government and War*.
13. Hansard [Aus], HoR Deb, vol. 161, 7 September 1939, 164–65.
14. Parr, Alison, 2010, *Home: Civilian New Zealanders remember the Second World War*, Auckland: Penguin, 31.
15. Brock, Peter & Thomas P. Socknat, 1999, *Challenge to Mars: Essays on pacifism from 1918 to 1945*, Toronto: University of Toronto Press.
16. Grant, *Out in the Cold*, 84.
17. Efford, *Penalties on Conscience*, 40.
18. *Dominion*, 12 February 1940, 4.
19. Dunstall, Graeme, 1999, *A Policeman's Paradise? Policing a stable society 1918-1945*, Palmerston North: Dunmore Press, 309.
20. Belich, James, 2001, *Paradise Reforged: A history of the New Zealanders from the 1880s to the year 2000*, Auckland, NZ: Allen Lane, 287.
21. Orange, Claudia, 2001, 'An exercise in Maori autonomy: The rise and demise of the Maori war effort organization', in *The Shaping of History: Essays from the New Zealand Journal of History, 1967-1999*, Judith Binney (ed.), 62–77, Wellington: Bridget Williams Books, 67.
22. Baxter, Archibald, 1939, *We Will Not Cease: The autobiography of a conscientious objector*, London: Victor Gollancz.
23. Cited in Dunstall, *A Policeman's Paradise?*, 309.
24. Grant, David, 1998, 'Carman, Arthur Herbert 1902–1982', in *Dictionary of New Zealand Biography*, New Zealand Department of Internal Affairs (ed.). Vol. 4, 87–88, Auckland: Auckland University Press.
25. Grant, *Out in the Cold*, 244.
26. Ibid., 141.
27. Burton, Ormond E, 1945, *In Prison*, Wellington: A.H. & A.W. Reed.
28. Crane, Ernest, 1986, *I Can Do No Other: A Biography of the Reverend Ormond Burton*, Auckland: Hodder & Stoughton.
29. Hamilton, Ian, 1984, *Till Human Voices Wake Us*, Auckland: Auckland University Press.
30. Lawry, Walter, 1994, *We Said 'No!' to War*, Dunedin: Wordspinners Unlimited.
31. Young, William, 1995, *Time to Tell of New Zealand's World War II Concentration Camps*, Tauranga: Limited Edition Publications.
32. Handyside, Allan, 2005, *Indeterminate Sentence*, Wellington: Philip Garside.
33. Grant, David, 2000, 'Burton, Ormond Edward, 1893-1944', in *Dictionary of New Zealand Biography*, New Zealand Department of Internal Affairs (ed.), Vol. 5, 80–82, Auckland: Auckland University Press.
34. See Pratt's *Punishment in a Perfect Society* (1992) for an account of that earlier period.
35. Ministry of Justice, 1910, *Scheme for the Reorganization of the Prison System of New Zealand*, Wellington: Government Printer, AJHR, H.20B.
36. Findlay, John, 'Criminal reform', *Otago Daily Times*, 20 March 1909, 5.
37. Ibid.
38. *A Penal Policy for New Zealand* (Department of Justice 1954) was the next formal review of penal and prison policy at government level.
39. There is no ethnographic research from this period to provide any contrasting view in New Zealand or in similar societies. The first in this tradition, from the US, was Donald Clemmer's *The Prison Community* (Boston: Christopher Publishing, 1940).

40. *Report on the Prisons Department for the Year 1928–29*, 1929, Wellington, NZ: Government Printer. AJHR, H.20, 7.
41. *Report on the Prisons Department for the Year 1927–28*, 1928, Wellington, NZ: Government Printer. AJHR, H.20, 5.
42. *Report on the Prisons Department for the Year 1932–33*, 1933, Wellington, NZ: Government Printer. AJHR, H.20, 5.
43. Ibid., 16.
44. Ibid., 11.
45. *Report on the Prisons Department for the Year 1933–34*, 1934, Wellington, NZ: Government Printer. AJHR, H.20, 8.
46. *Report on the Prisons Department 1927–28*, 13.
47. *Report on the Prisons Department for the Year 1926–27*, 1927, Wellington, NZ: Government Printer. AJHR, H.20, 9.
48. *Report on Prisons for the Year 1920–21*, 1921, Wellington, NZ: Government Printer. AJHR, H.20, 9.
49. Ibid.
50. *Report on the Prisons Department 1933–34*, 10; 12.
51. *Report on the Prisons Department 1928–29*, 5–6.
52. *Report on the Prisons Department 1926–27*, 12.
53. *Report on the Prisons Department for the Year 1935–36*, 1936, Wellington, NZ: Government Printer. AJHR, H.20, 4.
54. *Report on the Prisons Department for the Year 1934–35*, 1935, Wellington, NZ: Government Printer. AJHR, H.20, 7.
55. *Report on the Prisons Department for the Year 1929–30*, 1930, Wellington, NZ: Government Printer. AJHR, H.20, 19.
56. *Report on the Prisons Department 1935–36*, 5.
57. *Report on Prisons for the Year 1936–37*, 1937, Wellington, NZ: Government Printer. AJHR, H.20, 15.
58. *Report on the Prisons Department 1928–29*, 7.
59. *Report on Prisons for the Year 1919–20*, 1920, Wellington, NZ: Government Printer. AJHR, H.20, 9.
60. *Report on Prisons for the Year 1920–21*, 1921, Wellington, NZ: Government Printer. AJHR, H.20, 10.
61. *Report on Prisons for the Year 1938–39*, 1939, Wellington, NZ: Government Printer. AJHR, H.20, 4.
62. George Wilder escaped from prison three times between 1962 and 1964, leaving apologies and thank you notes to further victims of his crimes as he burgled houses to sustain himself during his periods of freedom. Rather than creating panic and fear, however, he became an escaper who 'caught the heart of a nation' (*Dominion Post*, 18 May 2013). The Howard Morrison Quartet even recorded a song about him – 'George the Wilder Colonial Boy'.
63. Belich, *Paradise Reforged*.
64. *Report on the Prisons Department 1926–27*, 17.
65. *Report on the Prisons Department 1928–29*, 16.
66. *Report on Prisons 1919–20*, 8.
67. Grew, Benjamin, 1958, *Prison Governor*, London: Herbert Jenkins.
68. *Report on Prisons 1931–32*, 3.
69. *Report on the Prisons Department 1932–33*, 3.
70. Phelan, Jim, 1940, *Jail Journey*, London: Secker & Warburg, 31.
71. Archer, Jeffrey, 2004, *A Prison Diary: From hell to heaven*, London: Macmillan.
72. Newbold, Greg, 1982, *The Big Huey: An inmate's candid account of five years inside New Zealand's prisons*, Auckland: Collins.
73. Ibid., 8.

74. Ibid., 164.
75. Ibid.
76. Sands, Bobby, 1981, *The Writings of Bobby Sands: A collection of prison writings*, Dublin: Sinn Fein POW Dept.
77. Denning, Ray, 1982, *The Ray Denning Diary*, Haymarket: Ray Denning Publications.
78. From the UK, see Sparks, Richard, Anthony E. Bottoms & Will Hay, 1996, *Prisons and the Problem of Order*, Oxford: Clarendon Press; and Crewe, Ben, 2009, *The Prisoner Society: Power, Adaptation, and social life in an English prison*, Oxford: Oxford University Press.
79. Sykes, Gresham M., 1958, *The Society of Captives: A study of a maximum security prison*, Princeton, NJ: Princeton University Press.
80. His work is all the more remarkable since this was occurring during and immediately after the highly publicised Nagle inquiry into brutality and corruption elsewhere in the New South Wales prison system (Nagle, John F., 1976–78, *Report of the Royal Commission into New South Wales Prisons [The Nagle Report]*, Sydney: Government Printing Office).
81. *Report on the Prisons Department 1935–36*, 8.
82. Newbold, *The Big Huey*, 8.
83. Archer, *A Prison Diary*, 1053.
84. Harrop, Angus J., 1935, *Touring in New Zealand*, London: Allen & Unwin.
85. Duff, Oliver, 1941, *New Zealand Now*, Wellington: Department of Internal Affairs, 82.

Chapter 2. Mount Crawford Prison, 1941

1. Ormond Burton was allowed to keep a typewriter to enable him to finish a book manuscript.
2. The origins of the use of this word are not clear but it was the equivalent of the British term 'chokey'. See Benney, 1948, *Gaol Delivery: For the Howard League for Penal Reform*, London: Longmans, Green.
3. Ian Hamilton spent 90 days in solitary confinement during his 16 months in prison, mostly at Mount Eden.
4. Carman confirms, 'We played many games of chess, OEB and ACB [Barrington] both good players' (Carman, 1994, 'The prison diary 1941', in *A Full Life: Three score years and ten: One man's life (Collected from the papers of Arthur H. Carman, 1902–1982)*, Ray Carman (ed.), 58–72, Chapel Hill, QLD: Ray Carman, 6).
5. *Evening Post*, 19 November 1943, 4.
6. Ken Baxter was a prominent trade unionist. He was elected national secretary of the Federation of Labour in 1944 and held the position until his retirement in 1960.
7. Cedric Firth's interest in providing good low-income housing led him to join the newly formed Department of Housing Construction in 1939. His expertise continued to be recognised both nationally and internationally.
8. Dr William Sutch was an economist and public servant with broad national and international experience; he was appointed secretary of the Department of Industries and Commerce.
9. Barrington may not be correct in his reference to Beech, an otherwise unknown architect whom he notes won the prize for the design for the Auckland memorial to Michael Joseph Savage, who had died in 1940. The Ministry for Culture and Heritage (2010) records that the prize was awarded to the architects Tibor Donner and Anthony Bartlett: www.mch.govt.nz/nz-identity-heritage/national-monuments-and-war-graves/savage-memorial
10. Harold Innes was then a senior civil servant and later managing director of Waikato Breweries, which his family owned. At the outbreak of war his knowledge of the

dairy industry led to him being appointed liaison officer between the Minister of Marketing, Walter Nash, and the producer boards. In 1945 he was appointed director of the milk marketing division of the marketing department.

11. The Reverend Colin Scrimgeour, although never actually ordained as a minister, was involved in high-profile social work and social action for the Methodist Church in the inter-war period. He also became a well-known but controversial broadcaster through his politicised 'Man in the Street' reports. He was appointed controller of the National Broadcasting Service in 1936 by Michael Joseph Savage. In 1943, however, he was removed from his position by Peter Fraser who was implacably opposed to him. Prior to this, his right to broadcast had been suspended several times during the war (Davidson, 2014, 'Colin Graham Scrimgeour', from the Dictionary of New Zealand Biography: www.teara.govt.nz/en/biographies/4s16/scrimgeour-colin-graham

12. H.C. McQueen was employed in 1941 by the New Zealand Council for Educational Research as research assistant to the director Arnold Campbell. He became a prominent figure in the area of vocational guidance.

13. Ben Roberts MP was a lifelong Methodist. He was elected to parliament in 1935 and appointed minister of agriculture and marketing in 1943, a position he held until 1946.

14. Goffman, E., 1961, *Asylums: Essays on the social situation of mental patients and other inmates*, Garden City, NY: Anchor Books.

15. For Burton, the medical examination took the following format: '"Anything the matter with you?", asked the doctor. As there was nothing, I was then passed fit for hard labour. "Salute the doctor." This was a typical medical examination' (Burton, Ormond E., 1945, *In Prison*, Wellington: A.H. & A.W. Reed, 45).

Chapter 3. Life in Mount Crawford Prison

1. According to Burton, 'the radio was just one more punishment they sent to try us' (Burton, Ormond E., 1945, *In Prison*, Wellington: A.H. & A.W. Reed, 98).

2. A reference to a popular 1940s radio programme *Fred and Maggie Everybody*.

3. The generosity of these servings is all the more apparent when compared to the British prison diet. The frugal servings had been a regular concern in the late nineteenth century (see Priestley 1989 and Pratt 2002). By the 1930s, the standard menu consisted only of porridge, bread and tea (breakfast); a meat pie for 'dinner' (lunch); and bread, half an ounce (14 g) of margarine, cheese and cocoa (supper) (Benney, Mark, 1948, *Gaol Delivery: For the Howard League for Penal Reform*, London: Longmans, Green).

4. In Britain a typical ration for an adult for one week during the war was '50 gr of butter; 540 gr of meat; 1 fresh egg per week; 225 gr of sugar; 50 gr of cheese; 50 gr of tea; 1800 ml of milk'. Fresh vegetables and fruit were not rationed but supplies were greatly limited; nor was bread rationed, but its quality was greatly reduced: www. bbc.co.uk/history/topics/rationing_in_ww2

Chapter 4. Prison Staff and Officials

1. Burton, Ormond E., 1945, *In Prison*, Wellington: A.H. & A.W. Reed, 142.

2. Ibid., 146.

3. Thomas, James E., 1972, *The English Prison Officer since 1850: A study in conflict*, London: Routledge & Kegan Paul.

4. See the continued resistance of defaulters Handyside and Hamilton, both of whom ultimately spent time in Mount Eden Prison, Auckland, on hunger strike. (See

Hamilton, 1984, *Till Human Voices Wake Us*, Auckland: Auckland University Press; Handyside, 2005, *Indeterminate Sentence*, Wellington: Philip Garside.)

5. Burton had witnessed another such incident in 1940 that provoked a widespread disturbance in the prison (Burton, *In Prison*, 106–07).

6. See Cookson, John E., 1983, 'Illiberal New Zealand: The formation of government policy on conscientious objection, 1940–41', *New Zealand Journal of History* 17: 138.

Chapter 5. The Inmates

1. Newbold, however, reports extravagant and extensive farewells then taking place between inmates – although the men he writes about were serving quite lengthy sentences that had allowed much deeper bonds and personal relationships to be built up between them (Newbold, 1982, *The Big Huey: An inmate's candid account of five years inside New Zealand's prisons*, Auckland: Collins). In contrast, those in Mount Crawford in 1941 were nearly all serving very short sentences and were likely to be in and out of prison anyway.

2. Burton, Ormond E., 1945, *In Prison*, Wellington: A.H. & A.W. Reed, 69.

3. Basil Dowling seems to have been the most accomplished of those who turned their hand to poetry. Barrington (27 July 1941) noted that his 'prison communion poem has appeared in this week's *Methodist Times*'. Jack Hamerton was another aspiring poet whose work included the following, written while he was waiting for the outcome of his appeal against conviction in the cells of the Supreme Court. Barrington copied it into his diary (11 June 1941):

> *We sit like silent actors in some farce or comedy*
> *While Callan cracks his quips & Blair shows mirth*
> *And Parry labours through his 27 cases & Kennedy*
> *Sits back & smiles as if he owned the earth*
> *Then Weston takes the field: he's in fine fettle*
> *And cites a case or two in trenchant tongue*
> *But Callan knocks him over like a skittle*
> *About some bloke who dared to forge a cheque*
> *Northcroft appears to sleep – yet he emerged*
> *To add a contribution to the fun*
> *To Weston he suggests with knowing gestures*
> *You lead us down the garden path my son!*

4. Crewe, Ben, 2009, *The Prisoner Society: Power, adaptation, and social life in an English prison*, Oxford: Oxford University Press.

5. Archer, Jeffrey, 2004, *A Prison Diary: From hell to heaven*, London: Macmillan.

6. Ugelvik, Thomas, 2011, 'The hidden food: Mealtime resistance and identity work in a Norwegian prison', *Punishment and Society* 13: 48.

7. *An Innocent Man* (1989), Peter Yates (director), Touchstone Pictures.

Chapter 6. Prison Past and Present

1. Burton, Ormond E., 1945, *In Prison*, Wellington: A.H. & A.W. Reed, 92.

2. Ibid., 64.

3. Ibid., 60.

4. Ibid., 111.

5. Carman, Arthur, 1994, 'The prison diary 1941', in *A Full Life: Three score years and ten: One man's life (Collected from the papers of Arthur H. Carman, 1902–1982)*, Ray Carman (ed.), 58–72, Chapel Hill: Ray Carman, 6.

6.   Ibid., 16.
7.   Handyside, Allan, 2005, *Indeterminate Sentence*, Wellington: Philip Garside, 19.
8.   Hamilton, Ian, 1984, *Till Human Voices Wake Us*, Auckland: Auckland University Press, 271.
9.   Lawry, Walter, 1994, *We Said 'No!' to War*, Dunedin: Wordspinners Unlimited, 36.
10. Young, William, 1995, *Time to Tell of New Zealand's World War II Concentration Camps*, Tauranga: Limited Edition Publications, 66.
11. Lawry, *We Said 'No!' to War*, 37.
12. Hamilton, *Till Human Voices Wake Us*, 71.
13. Ibid., 155.
14. Ibid., 126.
15. Lawry, *We Said 'No!' to War*, 36.
16. Ibid., 46.
17. Hamilton, *Till Human Voices Wake Us*, 155.
18. Handyside, *Indeterminate Sentence*, 21.
19. See Priestly, Philip, 1989, *Jail Journeys: The English prison experience since 1918*, London: Routledge; and Pratt, John, 2002, *Punishment and Civilization: Penal tolerance and intolerance in modern society*, London: Sage.
20. This principle was first set out in the report of the (British) Poor Law Commissioners: when relief was given to the poor, '[their] situation ... shall not be made really or apparently so eligible as the situation of an independent labourer of the lowest class' (Poor Law Commission, 1835, *First Annual Report of the Poor Law Commissioners for England and Wales*, London: Government Printer. Command No. 500, 167). This rule still dominates welfare and prison policy in Britain, Australia and New Zealand.
21. The first of these studies was by Clemmer (Clemmer, Donald, 1940, *The Prison Community*, Boston: Christopher Publishing).
22. Following the escape in November 2014 of Philip Smith, who had been involved in a Mount Eden release-to-work programme, the Corrections Department banned all other such release-to-work opportunities for the entire inmate population of New Zealand (www.stuff.co.nz/national/65098150/phillip-smiths-escape-affects-killers-privileges).
23. Crewe, Ben, 2009, *The Prisoner Society: Power, adaptation, and social life in an English prison*, Oxford: Oxford University Press.
24. Pratt, John & Phillip Treacher, 1988, 'Law and order and the 1987 New Zealand election', *Australian and New Zealand Journal of Criminology* 21: 253–68.
25. The Prisoners and Victims Claims Act 2005 provides that any windfall that the prisoners receive should go to the victims of their claims during the course of their sentence and their first year of release. Furthermore, should they successfully sue any government officials for mistreatment while in prison, any damages they are awarded will also be made available for their victims to claim.
26. Pratt, John, 2008, 'When penal populism stops. Legitimacy, scandal and the power to punish in New Zealand', *Australian and New Zealand Journal of Criminology* 41: 364–83.
27. *Department of Corrections Annual Report*, 1996, Wellington: Government Printer, Appendices to the Journal of the House of Representatives [AJHR], E.61, 11.
28. See Liebling, Alison, 2004, *Prisons and their Moral Performance: A study of values, quality and prison life*, Oxford: Oxford University Press. In British prisons at least, 'staff are being marked down in assessments if they can't prove they have treated inmates decently' (*Daily Telegraph*, 30 September 2008).
29. See Newbold, Greg, 1982, *The Big Huey: An inmate's candid account of five years inside New Zealand's prisons*, Auckland: Collins.
30. See www.rethinking.org.nz/assets/GeneralPDF/Prison_safety_Review.pdf

31. Sim, Joe, 2009, *Punishment and Prisons: Power and the carceral state*, London: Sage; Crewe, Ben, 2009, *The Prisoner Society: Power, adaptation, and social life in an English prison*, Oxford: Oxford University Press.

32. See, for example, Sykes, Gresham M., 1958, *The Society of Captives: A study of a maximum security prison*, Princeton, NJ: Princeton University Press; Newbold, *The Big Huey*; Archer, Jeffrey, 2004, *A Prison Diary: From hell to heaven*, London: Macmillan; Crewe, *The Prisoner Society*.

33. David Bain, wrongfully imprisoned from 1995 to 2007 for murdering five members of his family and subsequently found not guilty at a retrial, remembered that 'shortly after being imprisoned in the east wing of Christchurch Men's Prison, I was assaulted by another prisoner and left with two teeth smashed in and a bruised and cut face' (www.nzherald.co.nz/nz/news/article.cfm?c_id=1&objectid=10854521).

34. Burton, after being joined by Barrington and others in prison, wrote to Reverend Arthur Liversedge that 'this time is quite different to the first lonely month I spent here. Now there is the joy of fellowship of so many others' (cited in Crane, Ernest, 1986, *I Can Do No Other: A biography of the Reverend Ormond Burton*, Auckland: Hodder & Stoughton, 141–42).

35. Archer, *A Prison Diary*.

36. Priestly, Philip, 1989, *Jail Journeys: The English prison experience since 1918*, London: Routledge, 50–52.

37. Pratt, John, 1992, *Punishment in a Perfect Society: The New Zealand penal system 1840–1939*, Wellington: Victoria University Press.

38. Jackson, George, 1971, *Soledad Brother: The prison letters of George Jackson*, Harmondsworth: Penguin Books, 64.

39. Newbold, *The Big Huey*, 48.

40. Archer, *A Prison Diary*, 58.

41. Crewe, *The Prisoner Society*, 391.

42. *Report of the Department of Justice*, 1991, Wellington, NZ: Government Printer. AJHR, E.5, 67.

43. Archer, *A Prison Diary*, 359.

44. Crewe, *The Prisoner Society*, 111.

45. Mandela, Nelson, 1994, *A Long Walk to Freedom: The autobiography of Nelson Mandela*, Boston: Little, Brown, 475.

46. Stanley, Frank, 1938, *A Happy Fortnight*, London: P. Davis, 273.

47. Cited in Goodall, Felicity, 1997, *A Question of Conscience: Conscientious objection in the two world wars*, Stroud: Sutton, 185.

48. Cited in Garland, Roy, 2001, *Gusty Spence*, Belfast: Blackstaff Press, 158.

49. Mandela, *A Long Walk to Freedom*, 462.

50. Newbold, *The Big Huey*, 65–66.

51. Burton, Ormond E., 1945, *In Prison*, Wellington: A.H. & A.W. Reed, 147.

52. Goodall, *A Question of Conscience*, 196.

53. Archer, *A Prison Diary*, 360.

54. Burton, *In Prison*, 69.

55. Lawry, *We Said 'No!' to War*, 41.

56. Newbold, *The Big Huey*, 29.

57. Crewe, *The Prisoner Society*, 420.

58. Cohen, Stanley & Laurie Taylor, 1972, *Psychological Survival: The experience of long-term imprisonment*, New York: Vintage Books.

59. Phelan, Jim, 1940, *Jail Journey*, London: Secker & Warburg, 62.

60. Newbold, *The Big Huey*.

61. Mandela, *A Long Walk to Freedom*, 554.

62. Crewe, *The Prisoner Society*, 388.

63. Archer, *A Prison Diary*; Crewe, *The Prisoner Society*.
64. Carlen, Pat, 2008, 'Imagine', in *Imaginary Penalities*, Pat Carlen (ed.), xii–xv, Cullompton, UK: Willan Publishing.
65. Belich, James, 2001, *Paradise Reforged: A history of the New Zealanders from the 1880s to the year 2000*, Auckland, NZ: Allen Lane, 292–93.
66. Crewe, *The Prisoner Society*.
67. Mandela, *A Long Walk to Freedom*, 463.
68. Doherty, Jim, n.d., Unpublished Papers, MS-Papers-0536, Alexander Turnbull Library, Wellington, NZ, 6.
69. McKeown, Laurence, 2001, *Out of Time: Irish republican prisoners, Long Kesh, 1972–2000*, Belfast: Beyond the Pale, 68.
70. Crewe, *The Prisoner Society*.
71. Mandela, *A Long Walk to Freedom*, 469.
72. Ibid., 496.
73. McEvoy, Kieran, 2001, *Paramilitary Imprisonment in Northern Ireland: Resistance, management, and release*, Oxford: Oxford University Press, 302.

Chapter 7. Dissent, Intolerance and the Dark Side of Paradise

1. *Dominion*, 5 June 1945, 3.
2. *Observer*, 27 June 1945, 3.
3. *Otago Daily Times*, 25 March 1941, 8.
4. *Dominion*, 8 May 1941, 8.
5. Grant, David, 1986, *Out in the Cold: Pacifists and conscientious objectors in New Zealand during World War II*, Auckland: Reed Methuen.
6. Oestreicher, Paul, 1955, 'They would not fight: Being a survey of the position of conscientious objectors and military defaulters during World War II', Master's Thesis, Victoria University of Wellington, NZ.
7. Cited in Cookson, John E., 1983, 'Illiberal New Zealand: The formation of government policy on conscientious objection, 1940–41', *New Zealand Journal of History* 17: 125.
8. Hansard [UK], HC Deb, vol. 19, 20 July 1910, 1354.
9. King, Michael, 2003, *The Penguin History of New Zealand*, Auckland: Penguin, 298.
10. Michener, James, 1951, *Return to Paradise*, New York: Random House, 243.
11. Pember Reeves, William, 1898, *The Long White Cloud*, London: Marshal, 323.
12. Harrop, Angus J., 1935, *Touring in New Zealand*, London: Allen & Unwin, 270.
13. Cowie, Donald, 1937, *New Zealand from Within*, London: George Routledge & Sons, 187.
14. Ibid., 38.
15. Roberts, Ellen, 1935, *New Zealand: Land of my choice*, London: George Allen & Unwin, 166.
16. King, *The Penguin History of New Zealand*, 358.
17. Cowie, *New Zealand from Within*, 166.
18. Ibid., 192.
19. Hursthouse had written that 'in old-world lotteries of life, there is one gigantic prize to innumerable blanks; in new-world lotteries of life there may be no gigantic prize, but there are innumerable goodly prizes and scarcely any blanks' (Hursthouse, Charles, 1857, *New Zealand, or, Zealandia, the Britain of the South*, London: Edwin Stafford, 109).
20. Jackson, Keith & John Harré, 1969, *New Zealand*, London: Thames and Hudson, 71.
21. Ibid., 69.
22. Hall, David, 1966, *Portrait of New Zealand*, Wellington: A.H. & A.W. Reed, 191.
23. *Dominion*, 20 August 1941, 7.

24. Herz, Max, 1912, *New Zealand, the Country and the People*, London: T. Werner Laurie, 351–52.
25. Wood, Frederick L.W., 1958a, *This New Zealand*, London: Hammond, Hammond & Co., 172.
26. Holcroft, M.H., 1968, *New Zealand*, Wellington: A.H. & A.W. Reed, 40.
27. Siegfried, André, 1914, *Democracy in New Zealand*, London: Bell, 56.
28. Fairburn, Miles, 1989, *The Ideal Society and its Enemies: The foundations of modern New Zealand society, 1850–1900*, Auckland: Auckland University Press, 55.
29. Duff, Oliver, 1941, *New Zealand Now*, Wellington: Department of Internal Affairs, 32.
30. Holcroft, *New Zealand*, 90.
31. Siegfried, *Democracy in New Zealand*, 327–28.
32. Duff, *New Zealand Now*, 32.
33. Phillips, J., 2000, 'New Zealand celebrates victory', in *Kia Kaha: New Zealand in the Second World War*, John Crawford (ed.), 302–16, Auckland: Oxford University Press, 308.
34. Belich, James, 2001, *Paradise Reforged: A history of the New Zealanders from the 1880s to the year 2000*, Auckland, NZ: Allen Lane, 223–24.
35. Laing, R., F. de la Mare & B. Baughan, 1933, 'The penal system of New Zealand', *Howard Journal of Penology and Crime Prevention* 3: 48–54 (50).
36. Cited in Burdon, Randal, 1965, *The New Dominion: A social and political history of New Zealand, 1918–39*, Wellington: A.H. & A.W. Reed, 311.
37. Hansard [NZ], vol. 177, 21 July 1916, 331.
38. Grant, David, 1998, 'Carman, Arthur Herbert 1902–1982', in *Dictionary of New Zealand Biography*, New Zealand Department of Internal Affairs (ed.). vol. 4, 87–88, Auckland: Auckland University Press, 18.
39. *Evening Post*, 24 May 1940, 3.
40. Wood, Frederick L.W., 1958b, *The New Zealand People at War: Political and external affairs*, Wellington: Department of Internal Affairs.
41. *Observer*, 17 May 1942, 6. Advertising itself as 'an illustrative journal of interesting and amusing literature', the *Observer* ceased publication in 1954.
42. *Dominion*, 25 May 1940, 4.
43. Sharpe, Maureen, 1981, 'Anzac Day in New Zealand 1916–1939: Attitudes to peace and war', *New Zealand Journal of History* 15: 97–114 (102).
44. Ibid.
45. Belich, *Paradise Reforged*.
46. New Zealand Returned Services' Association, 1943, 'Diggers parliament in session: 1943 Dominion Council', *Review: The official R.S.A. journal* 19, July: 4.
47. Hansard [NZ], vol. 226, 20 October 1930, 901.
48. The RSA's leaders had fought with distinction in World War I, with some being wounded in action, in contrast to some of the leading members of the government who had been steadfastly opposed to the war and imprisoned for their beliefs.
49. Cooke, Peter, 2008, *All Formed Up: A history of Wellington's Returned & Services' Association, 1916–2007*, Wellington: Ngaio Press, 78.
50. *Truth*, 21 May 1941, 23. *Truth* was first published in 1887 and reached the high point of its popularity in the 1950s and 1960s as 'the voice of the ordinary New Zealander'. Despite espousing left-wing causes in the 1920s, it had become markedly right wing in its politics. From the 1980s, its circulation began to decline and it folded in 2013.
51. *Otago Daily Times*, 13 March 1941, 8.
52. *Truth*, 28 May 1941, 25.
53. *Evening Post*, 5 March 1941, 6.
54. *Observer*, 2 April 1941, 7.

55. *Observer*, 26 July 1941, 8.
56. *Dominion*, 12 December 1941, 8.
57. *Dominion*, 6 February 1941, 6.
58. *Otago Daily Times*, 20 June 1941, 6.
59. *Evening Post*, 28 January 1941, 8.
60. *Otago Daily Times*, 2 August 1941, 2.
61. *Evening Star*, 8 December 1942, 3.
62. *Observer*, 17 May 1942, 4.
63. *Otago Daily Times*, 30 June 1945, 6.
64. Oestreicher, 'They would not fight', 138.
65. Ibid., 148–49.
66. Mason, Rex, 1944, 'Minister of Justice to War Cabinet, 1 May 1944', ACIE 8798 EA1/460 83/10/1, Archives New Zealand, 2.
67. *Southland Times*, 27 June 1945, 4.
68. Oestreicher, 'They would not fight', 148.
69. *New Zealand Herald*, 3 May 1945, 3.
70. Lawry, Walter, 1994, *We Said 'No!' to War*, Dunedin: Wordspinners Unlimited, 163.
71. Grant, *Out in the Cold*, 218.
72. Hansard [NZ], vol. 268, 28 June 1945, 14.
73. Ibid., 19.
74. Ibid., 24.
75. *Report on Prisons for the Year 1944–45*, 1945, Wellington, NZ: Government Printer. AJHR, H.20, 2.
76. Oestreicher, 'They would not fight', 157.
77. *Observer*, 21 March 1945, 7.
78. *Observer*, 4 March 1945, 5.
79. *Otago Daily Times*, 8 June 1945, 4.
80. *Observer*, 13 June 1945, 12.
81. *Observer*, 27 June 1945, 3.
82. *Otago Daily Times*, 26 June 1945, 4.
83. *Otago Daily Times*, 20 June 1945, 4.
84. Ibid.
85. *Dominion*, 17 January 1946.
86. New Zealand Returned Services' Association, 1946, 'Editorial', *Review: The official R.S.A. journal* 22: 1.
87. Wood, *The New Zealand People at War*, 155.
88. Jackson & Harré, *New Zealand*, 71.
89. Williams, Jeff, Christine Niven & Peter Turner, 2000, *New Zealand*, London: Lonely Planet Publications, 13.
90. King, *The Penguin History of New Zealand*, 505.
91. From 1980 to 2013, the number of crimes reported in New Zealand increased from 327,612 to 360,411. However, the crime rate per 100,000 of population shows a significant decline (reflecting the increase in the New Zealand population from 3.2 million to 4.5 over the same period), from 10,420 to 8053. In the United States, where reported crimes actually declined from 13,295,400 in 1980 to 10,1189,900 in 2012, the crime rate declined from 5900 per 100,000 of population to 3246. The reasons for these declines are complex but it is highly likely that fewer young men in the population aged between 15 and 24 (the most criminogenic group in any modern society) in conjunction with the development of security technology that has now become commonplace in cars, homes etc, has played a major role in this. In England and Wales, the fall in crime began rather later, but a fall is now well underway there as well. Reported crime reached a level of 4,543,611 offences in

1990, with a crime rate of 8987 per 100,000 of population. By 2012, crime levels had fallen to 3,700,349 and the crime rate to 6541 per 100,000.

92. Pratt, John, 2007, *Penal Populism*, London: Routledge; Pratt, John, 2008, 'When penal populism stops. Legitimacy, scandal and the power to punish in New Zealand', *Australian and New Zealand Journal of Criminology* 41: 364–83.

93. Workman, Kim, 22 February 2012, 'Justice matters', Speech delivered at a public meeting sponsored by the Third Space Trust, Normanby Hotel, Mt Eden, Auckland, 2.

94. *Dominion Post*, 28 August 2006, 4.

95. Williams et al., *New Zealand*, 32.

96. King, *The Penguin History of New Zealand*, 505.

97. IMMagine, 2005, 'IMMagine New Zealand': www.immigration.co.nz/immagine-nz/

Bibliography

Archer, Jeffrey, 2004, *A Prison Diary: From hell to heaven*, London: Macmillan.

Barker, Rachel, 1982, *Conscience, Government and War: Conscientious objection in Great Britain, 1939–45*, London: Routledge & Kegan Paul.

Barrington, Archibald C., n.d., Unpublished MS, Ref: 86-062-10, Alexander Turnbull Library, Wellington, NZ.

Barrington, Archibald C., 1929–71, Barrington, Archibald Charles, 1906–1986: Papers. MS-Papers-0439, Alexander Turnbull Library, Wellington, NZ.

Barrington, Archibald C. [c. 1941] 1962, Scrapbook of Communications from A.C. Barrington, MS-Papers-5312, Alexander Turnbull Library, Wellington, NZ.

Barrington, Archibald C., 1970, *Trials of a Pacifist: Being two broadcast talks over New Zealand YC stations*, Christchurch, NZ: Christian Pacifist Society.

Barrington, Janet, 1941, *Diaries of Janet Elizabeth Barrington*, MS-Group-0073, Alexander Turnbull Library, Wellington, NZ.

Baxter, Archibald, 1939, *We Will Not Cease: The autobiography of a conscientious objector*, London: Victor Gollancz.

Belich, James, 2001, *Paradise Reforged: A history of the New Zealanders from the 1880s to the year 2000*, Auckland, NZ: Allen Lane.

Benney, Mark, 1948, *Gaol Delivery: For the Howard League for Penal Reform*, London: Longmans, Green.

Brittain, Vera, 1933, *Testament of Youth: An autobiographical study of the years 1900–1925*, London: Gollancz.

Brittain, Vera, 1951, *Search After Sunrise*, London: Macmillan.

Brock, Peter & Thomas P. Socknat, 1999, *Challenge to Mars: Essays on pacifism from 1918 to 1945*, Toronto: University of Toronto Press.

Browne, Samuel, 1941, 'Detective Samuel Browne to Chief Detective 27 March, 1941', Papers held by the Security Intelligence Service on A.C. Barrington, MS-Papers-6139-2, Alexander Turnbull Library, Wellington, NZ.

Burdon, Randal, 1965, *The New Dominion: A social and political history of New Zealand, 1918–39*, Wellington: A.H. & A.W. Reed.

Burton, Ormond E., n.d., *A Rich Old Man*, MS-Papers 0438-059, MS-Copy-Micro-0144, Alexander Turnbull Library, Wellington, NZ.

Burton, Ormond E., 1935, *The Silent Division: New Zealanders at the front, 1914–1919*, Sydney: Angus & Robertson.

Burton, Ormond E., 1945, *In Prison*, Wellington: A.H. & A.W. Reed.

Carlen, Pat, 2008, 'Imagine', in *Imaginary Penalities*, Pat Carlen (ed.), xii–xv, Cullompton, UK: Willan Publishing.

Carman, Arthur, 1994, 'The prison diary 1941', in *A Full Life: Three score years and ten: One man's life (Collected from the papers of Arthur H. Carman, 1902–1982)*, Ray Carman (ed.), 58–72, Chapel Hill: Ray Carman.

Christian Pacifist Society Bulletin, 1938, Further Papers, AC Barrington, Ref: 86-062-08/07B, Alexander Turnbull Library, Wellington, NZ.

Clemmer, Donald, 1940, *The Prison Community*, Boston: Christopher Publishing.

Cohen, Stanley & Laurie Taylor, 1972, *Psychological Survival: The experience of long-term imprisonment*, New York: Vintage Books.

Cooke, Peter, 2008, *All Formed Up: A history of Wellington's Returned & Services' Association, 1916–2007*, Wellington: Ngaio Press.

Cookson, John E., 1983, 'Illiberal New Zealand: The formation of government policy on conscientious objection, 1940–41', *New Zealand Journal of History* 17: 120–43.

Cowie, Donald, 1937, *New Zealand from Within*, London: George Routledge & Sons.

Crane, Ernest, 1986, *I Can Do No Other: A biography of the Reverend Ormond Burton*, Auckland: Hodder & Stoughton.

Crewe, Ben, 2009, *The Prisoner Society: Power, adaptation, and social life in an English prison*, Oxford: Oxford University Press.

Daily Worker, 1930–66, London: Workers Press.

Davidson, Allan, 2014, 'Colin Graham Scrimgeour', from the Dictionary of New Zealand Biography: www.teara.govt.nz/en/biographies/4s16/scrimgeour-colin-graham

Davies, Sonja, 1984, *Bread and Roses: Sonja Davies, her story*, Auckland: Fraser Books.

Denning, Ray, 1982, *The Ray Denning Diary*, Haymarket, NSW: Ray Denning Publications.

Department of Corrections Annual Report, 1996, Wellington: Government Printer, Appendices to the Journal of the House of Representatives [AJHR], E.61.

Department of Justice, 1954, *A Penal Policy for New Zealand*, Wellington: Government Printer.

Dingwall, Evalyn & Elizabeth A. Heard, 1937, *Pennsylvania 1681–1756: The state without an army*, London: C.W. Daniel.

Doherty, Jim, n.d., Unpublished Papers, MS-Papers-0536, Alexander Turnbull Library, Wellington, NZ.

Dominion Council of the Wellington Workers' Education Association (WWEA), 1941, 'Minutes', *Minute Books, Financial Statements and Annual Reports (1915–1991)*. Reference Number 93-132-4, Alexander Turnbull Library, Wellington, NZ.

Dunstall, Graeme, 1999, *A Policeman's Paradise? Policing a stable society 1918–1945*, Palmerston North: Dunmore Press.

Duff, Oliver, 1941, *New Zealand Now*, Wellington: Department of Internal Affairs.

Efford, Lincoln, 1945, *Penalties on Conscience: An examination of the defaulters' detention system in New Zealand*, Christchurch: Caxton Press.

Fairburn, Miles, 1989, *The Ideal Society and its Enemies: The foundations of modern New Zealand society, 1850–1900*, Auckland: Auckland University Press.

Findlay, John, 1909, 'Criminal reform', *Otago Daily Times*, 20 March 1909, 5.

Garland, Roy, 2001, *Gusty Spence*, Belfast: Blackstaff Press.

Goffman, Erving, 1961, *Asylums: Essays on the social situation of mental patients and other inmates*, Garden City, NY: Anchor Books.

Goodall, Felicity, 1997, *A Question of Conscience: Conscientious objection in the two world wars*, Stroud: Sutton.

Grant, David, 1986, *Out in the Cold: Pacifists and conscientious objectors in New Zealand during World War II*, Auckland: Reed Methuen.

Grant, David, 1998, 'Carman, Arthur Herbert 1902–1982', in *Dictionary of New Zealand Biography*, New Zealand Department of Internal Affairs (ed.). vol. 4, 87–88, Auckland: Auckland University Press.

Grant, David, 2000, 'Burton, Ormond Edward, 1893–1944', in *Dictionary of New Zealand Biography*, New Zealand Department of Internal Affairs (ed.), vol. 5, 80–82, Auckland: Auckland University Press.

Grant, David, 2004, *A Question of Faith: A history of the New Zealand Christian Pacifist Society*, Wellington: Philip Garside.

Grew, Benjamin, 1958, *Prison Governor*, London: Herbert Jenkins.

Hall, David, 1966, *Portrait of New Zealand*, Wellington: A.H. & A.W. Reed.

Hamilton, Ian, 1984, *Till Human Voices Wake Us*, Auckland: Auckland University Press.

Handyside, Allan, 2005, *Indeterminate Sentence*, Wellington: Philip Garside.
Hansard [Aus], HoR Deb, vol. 161, 7 September 1939.
Hansard [NZ], vol. 177, 21 July 1916.
Hansard [NZ], vol. 226, 20 October 1930.
Hansard [NZ], vol. 268, 28 June 1945.
Hansard [UK], HC Deb, vol. 19, 20 July 1910.
Hansard [UK], HC Deb, vol. 370, 20 March 1941.
Hansard [UK], HL Deb, vol. 118, 3 April 1941.
Harrop, Angus J., 1935, *Touring in New Zealand*, London: Allen & Unwin.
Herz, Max, 1912, *New Zealand, the Country and the People*, London: T. Werner Laurie.
Holcroft, M.H., 1968, *New Zealand*, Wellington: A.H. & A.W. Reed.
Hursthouse, Charles, 1857, *New Zealand, or, Zealandia, the Britain of the South*, London: Edwin Stafford.
IMMagine, 2005, 'IMMagine New Zealand': www.immigration.co.nz/immagine-nz/
Jackson, George, 1971, *Soledad Brother: The prison letters of George Jackson*, Harmondsworth: Penguin Books.
Jackson, Keith & John Harré, 1969, *New Zealand*, London: Thames and Hudson.
King, Michael, 2003, *The Penguin History of New Zealand*, Auckland: Penguin.
Laing, R., F. de la Mare & B. Baughan, 1933, 'The penal system of New Zealand', *Howard Journal of Penology and Crime Prevention* 3: 48–54.
Lawry, Walter, 1994, *We Said 'No!' to War*, Dunedin: Wordspinners Unlimited.
Lewis, F. Warburton, 1931, *Jesus of Galilee*, London: Nicholson & Watson.
Liebling, Alison, 2004, *Prisons and their Moral Performance: A study of values, quality and prison life*, Oxford: Oxford University Press.
Mandela, Nelson, 1994, *A Long Walk to Freedom: The autobiography of Nelson Mandela*, Boston: Little, Brown.
Markwell, Carol, 2000, 'Barrington, Archibald Charles 1906–1986', in *Dictionary of New Zealand Biography*, New Zealand Department of Internal Affairs (ed.), vol. 5, 36–37, Auckland: Auckland University Press.
Mason, Rex, 1944, 'Minister of Justice to War Cabinet, 1 May 1944', ACIE 8798 EA1/460 83/10/1, Archives New Zealand.
Mayson, Rev. William (Bob), 1994, 'The trials of a parson', in *No Other Option: Experiences of New Zealand conscientious objectors and supporters during World War II*, New Zealand Christian Pacifist Society, 4–5, Christchurch: Christian Pacifist Society.
McEvoy, Kieran, 2001, *Paramilitary Imprisonment in Northern Ireland: Resistance, management, and release*, Oxford: Oxford University Press.
McKeown, Laurence, 2001, *Out of Time: Irish republican prisoners, Long Kesh, 1972–2000*, Belfast: Beyond the Pale.
Michener, James, 1951, *Return to Paradise*, New York: Random House.
Ministry for Culture and Heritage, 2010, 'Savage memorial': www.mch.govt.nz/nz-identity-heritage/national-monuments-and-war-graves/savage-memorial
Ministry of Justice, 1910, *Scheme for the Reorganization of the Prison System of New Zealand*, Wellington: Government Printer, AJHR, H.20B
Nagle, John F., 1976–78, *Report of the Royal Commission into New South Wales Prisons [The Nagle Report]*, Sydney: Government Printing Office.
Nash, Walter, 1939, 'Walter Nash to A.C. Barrington, 17 October 1939', MS-Papers 0439-5, Alexander Turnbull Library, Wellington, NZ.
New Zealand Returned Services' Association, 1943, 'Diggers parliament in session: 1943 Dominion Council', *Review: The official R.S.A. journal* 19, July: 4.
New Zealand Returned Services' Association, 1946, 'Editorial', *Review: The official R.S.A. journal* 22: 1.
Newbold, Greg, 1982, *The Big Huey: An inmate's candid account of five years inside New Zealand's prisons*, Auckland: Collins.

Oestreicher, Paul, 1955, 'They would not fight: Being a survey of the position of conscientious objectors and military defaulters during World War II', Master's Thesis, Victoria University of Wellington, NZ.

Orange, Claudia, 2001, 'An exercise in Maori autonomy: The rise and demise of the Maori war effort organization', in *The Shaping of History: Essays from the New Zealand Journal of History, 1967-1999*, Judith Binney (ed.), 62-77, Wellington: Bridget Williams Books.

Parr, Alison, 2010, *Home: Civilian New Zealanders remember the Second World War*, Auckland: Penguin.

Peacemaker, 1945-2002, Christchurch: New Zealand Christian Pacifist Society.

Peace News, 1936-present, London: Peace News Ltd.

Pember Reeves, William, 1898, *The Long White Cloud*, London: Marshal.

Phelan, Jim, 1940, *Jail Journey*, London: Secker & Warburg.

Phillips, J., 2000, 'New Zealand celebrates victory', in *Kia Kaha: New Zealand in the Second World War*, John Crawford (ed.), 302-16, Auckland: Oxford University Press.

Poor Law Commission, 1835, *First Annual Report of the Poor Law Commissioners for England and Wales*, London: Government Printer. Command No. 500

Pratt, John, 1992, *Punishment in a Perfect Society: The New Zealand penal system 1840-1939*, Wellington: Victoria University Press.

Pratt, John, 2002, *Punishment and Civilization: Penal tolerance and intolerance in modern society*, London: Sage.

Pratt, John, 2007, *Penal Populism*, London: Routledge.

Pratt, John, 2008, 'When penal populism stops. Legitimacy, scandal and the power to punish in New Zealand', *Australian and New Zealand Journal of Criminology* 41: 364-83.

Pratt, John & Phillip Treacher, 1988, 'Law and order and the 1987 New Zealand election', *Australian and New Zealand Journal of Criminology* 21: 253-68.

Priestly, Philip, 1989, *Jail Journeys: The English prison experience since 1918*, London: Routledge.

Rain, Lynn, 1991, *Community: The story of Riverside 1941-1991*, Lower Moutere, NZ: Riverside Community Trust Board.

Report of the Department of Justice, 1991, Wellington, NZ: Government Printer. AJHR, E.5.

Report on Prisons for the Year 1918-19, 1919, Wellington, NZ: Government Printer. AJHR, H.20.

Report on Prisons for the Year 1919-20, 1920, Wellington, NZ: Government Printer. AJHR, H.20.

Report on Prisons for the Year 1920-21, 1921, Wellington, NZ: Government Printer. AJHR, H.20.

Report on Prisons for the Year 1921-22, 1922, Wellington, NZ: Government Printer. AJHR, H.20.

Report on Prisons for the Year 1936-37, 1937, Wellington, NZ: Government Printer. AJHR, H.20.

Report on Prisons for the Year 1937-38, 1938, Wellington, NZ: Government Printer. AJHR, H.20.

Report on Prisons for the Year 1938-39, 1939, Wellington, NZ: Government Printer. AJHR, H.20.

Report on Prisons for the Year 1944-45, 1945, Wellington, NZ: Government Printer. AJHR, H.20.

Report on the Prisons Department for the Year 1926-27, 1927, Wellington, NZ: Government Printer. AJHR, H.20.

Report on the Prisons Department for the Year 1927-28, 1928, Wellington, NZ: Government Printer. AJHR, H.20.

Report on the Prisons Department for the Year 1928–29, 1929, Wellington, NZ: Government Printer. AJHR, H.20.

Report on the Prisons Department for the Year 1929–30, 1930, Wellington, NZ: Government Printer. AJHR, H.20.

Report on the Prisons Department for the Year 1931–32, 1932, Wellington, NZ: Government Printer. AJHR, H.20.

Report on the Prisons Department for the Year 1932–33, 1933, Wellington, NZ: Government Printer. AJHR, H.20.

Report on the Prisons Department for the Year 1933–34, 1934, Wellington, NZ: Government Printer. AJHR, H.20.

Report on the Prisons Department for the Year 1934–35, 1935, Wellington, NZ: Government Printer. AJHR, H.20.

Report on the Prisons Department for the Year 1935–36, 1936, Wellington, NZ: Government Printer. AJHR, H.20.

Roberts, Ellen, 1935, *New Zealand: Land of my choice*, London: George Allen & Unwin.

Sands, Bobby, 1981, *The Writings of Bobby Sands: A collection of prison writings*, Dublin: Sinn Fein POW Dept.

Sharpe, Maureen, 1981, 'Anzac Day in New Zealand 1916–1939: Attitudes to peace and war', *New Zealand Journal of History* 15: 97–114.

Siegfried, André, 1914, *Democracy in New Zealand*, London: Bell.

Sim, Joe, 2009, *Punishment and Prisons: Power and the carceral state*, London: Sage.

Solzhenitsyn, Aleksandr, 1963, *One Day in the Life of Ivan Denisovitch*, New York: New American Library.

Sparks, Richard, Anthony E. Bottoms & Will Hay, 1996, *Prisons and the Problem of Order*, Oxford: Clarendon Press.

Stanley, Frank, 1938, *A Happy Fortnight*, London: P. Davis.

Stone, Irving, 1934, *Lust for Life*, New York: Longmans, Green.

Sykes, Gresham M., 1958, *The Society of Captives: A study of a maximum security prison*, Princeton, NJ: Princeton University Press.

Taylor, Nancy, 1986, *The New Zealand People at War: The home front*, vol. 1. Wellington, NZ: Historical Publications Department, Department of Internal Affairs, Government Printer.

The People's Voice, 1939–2002, Auckland: Communist Party of New Zealand.

Thomas, James E., 1972, *The English Prison Officer since 1850: A study in conflict*, London: Routledge & Kegan Paul.

Ugelvik, Thomas, 2011, 'The hidden food: Mealtime resistance and identity work in a Norwegian prison', *Punishment and Society* 13: 47–63.

Wellington Workers' Education Association (WWEA), 1942, 1943, 'Summary of the 28th and 29th Annual Reports for the years ending 31 December 1942, 1943', *Annual Reports, Annual General Meetings, Summer Schools Files and Cash Ledgers (1928–1991)*, Ref. No. 93-132-5, Alexander Turnbull Library, Wellington, NZ.

Williams, Jeff, Christine Niven & Peter Turner, 2000, *New Zealand*, London: Lonely Planet Publications.

Wood, Frederick L.W., 1958a, *This New Zealand*, London: Hammond, Hammond & Co.

Wood, Frederick L.W., 1958b, *The New Zealand People at War: Political and external affairs*, Wellington: Department of Internal Affairs.

Workman, Kim, 22 February 2012, 'Justice matters', Speech delivered at a public meeting sponsored by the Third Space Trust, Normanby Hotel, Mt Eden, Auckland.

Young, William, 1995, *Time to Tell of New Zealand's World War II Concentration Camps*, Tauranga: Limited Edition Publications.

Index